PREPARING FOR THE
New Jersey HSPA
GRADE 11

David J. Glatzer
Supervisor of Mathematics
West Orange Public Schools
West Orange, New Jersey

Joyce Glatzer
Mathematics Consultant

AMSCO

AMSCO SCHOOL PUBLICATIONS, INC.
315 Hudson Street, New York, N. Y. 10013

David J. Glatzer is Supervisor of Mathematics for the West Orange Public Schools, West Orange, New Jersey. He has served as President of the Association of Mathematics Teachers of New Jersey (AMTNJ), member of the Board of Directors of the National Council of Teachers of Mathematics (NCTM), and Northeast Director of the National Council of Supervisors of Mathematics (NCSM). He is a frequent speaker at professional conferences and has written numerous articles in professional journals including the *Arithmetic Teacher* and the *New Jersey Mathematics Teacher*. He has made contributions to NCTM yearbooks and to the NCTM *Algebra for Everyone* project. In 1993, he was the recipient of the Max Sobel Outstanding Mathematics Educator Award presented by the AMTNJ. In addition, he served as co-chair of the Mathematics Panel for New Jersey Core Course Proficiencies (New Jersey State Department of Education).

Joyce Glatzer is a Mathematics Consultant and former Coordinator of Mathematics (K-9) for the Summit Public Schools, Summit, New Jersey. She has served as President of the Association of Mathematics Teachers of New Jersey (AMTNJ) and is an active member of the NCTM. She was the 1999 recipient of the Max Sobel Outstanding Mathematics Educator Award presented by the AMTNJ. She is a frequent speaker and workshop leader at professional conferences and staff development programs. She has written numerous articles in professional journals including the *New Jersey Mathematics Teacher* and the *Arithmetic Teacher*. In speaking and conducting workshops, her interests include problem solving, questioning techniques, communications, active learning with manipulatives and use of calculators.

Reviewers

Sandra McKay Bussey
   Mathematics Supervisor (K-12), Trenton Public Schools
   Trenton, New Jersey

Katherine G. Ilardi
   Mathematics Educator
   Oak Ridge, New Jersey

Deborah D. Johnson
   Supervisor of Mathematics, Camden City Public Schools
   Camden City, New Jersey

Cover design by Howard S. Leiderman
Composition by Monotype Composition Company

Some questions in the Sample Tests are reprinted courtesy of the New Jersey State Department of Education

Please visit our Web site at: **www.amscopub.com**

When ordering this book, please specify: either **R 714 W** or PREPARING FOR THE NEW JERSEY HSPA MATHEMATICS.

ISBN 1-56765-544-0

Copyright © 2001 by Amsco School Publications, Inc.

5 6 7 8 9   05 04

CONTENTS

CLUSTER 3   Data Analysis, Probability, Statistics, and Discrete Mathematics   103

A. ABOUT THIS TEST

1. What is the HSPA?

The High School Proficiency Assessment (HSPA) is a graduation test required of all New Jersey public school students. It includes mathematics from the four content clusters of the New Jersey Core Curriculum Content Standards. The HSPA has been developed to show whether or not you have a satisfactory level of achievement in the specified areas. The HSPA in Mathematics is not a minimum competency or basic skills test; it is a test of your ability to do higher order thinking and to integrate topics in mathematics.

2. When do you take the HSPA?

The first time you take the HSPA is April of your junior year.

3. What math topics are included in the HSPA?

There are four math clusters in the HSPA.

1. **Number Sense, Concepts, and Applications**
2. **Spatial Sense and Geometry**
3. **Data Analysis, Probability, Statistics, and Discrete Mathematics**
4. **Patterns, Functions, and Algebra**

Several points need to be noted.

Problem-solving and measurement situations exist in each cluster; as a result, there is no separate problem-solving or measurement cluster.

Isolated computation questions do not appear on the HSPA.

Many of the mathematics questions involve a considerable amount of reading.

4. What kinds of math questions appear on the HSPA?

There are two kinds of math questions.

1. multiple-choice items
2. open-ended items

Although the multiple-choice questions on the test assess high levels of mathematical thinking, some abilities are difficult to assess with this format. Also, the format does not allow for multiple responses or for partial credit. To overcome these limitations, the test includes open-ended (free response) questions.

Open-ended questions require you to construct your own written or graphical responses and explain these responses. The responses can be scored for different levels of mathematical understanding as well as for partial credit. More about scoring and open-ended questions follows in Section C.

5. Do you need to memorize formulas?

No. *A Mathematics Reference Sheet* is distributed to each student along with the test. This reference sheet contains any formulas you may need on the mathematics questions. The reference sheet may also contain materials such as a ruler or figures to be cut out and used in the process of solving specific questions. Refer to page xiv for a sample of a *Mathematics Reference Sheet*.

6. Are calculators allowed on the HSPA?

Yes. You are allowed to use a calculator when you take the mathematics section of the HSPA. A more detailed discussion of types of calculators allowed follows in Section B.

7. How is the HSPA scored?

Multiple-choice items are one point each and open-ended responses are three points each. Refer to page xiii for more information on the scoring of open-ended questions.

8. What is the Grade Eight Proficiency Assessment?

The Grade Eight Proficiency Assessment (GEPA) is given to all eighth graders in order to provide students, teachers, guidance counselors, parents, and others with some idea of a student's potential for passing the HSPA. The GEPA covers the same math clusters as HSPA. The types of questions used on the HSPA (multiple-choice and open-ended) are also used on GEPA. Calculators may be used on GEPA.

9. How can you find out more about the HSPA?

For additional information about the HSPA, ask your math teacher or guidance counselor.

B. ABOUT USING A CALCULATOR

You will be allowed to use a calculator on the HSPA. The following information will help you make the most effective use of the calculator on the test.

1. On which questions should you use the calculator?

The calculator will not be needed for every question on the test. With respect to calculator use, questions will fall into three categories: calculator–active, calculator–neutral, or calculator–irrelevant.

Calculator-active questions contain data that can usefully be explored and manipulated using a calculator. These questions may deal with explorations of patterns, problem solving involving guess and check, problems involving calculations with real data, or problems involving messy computation.

Calculator-neutral questions could be completed using a calculator. They may be more efficiently answered, however; by using mental math skills or simple paper-and-pencil computation. For example, the average of $-6, -7, -8, 5, 6, 7, 8, 2, 3, 0$ can be more quickly found mentally by recognizing that the set contains three pairs of opposites that add up to zero. By the time you have put all the data into the calculator, you could have solved the problem mentally.

With calculator-irrelevant questions, a calculator is of no help because the solution involves no computation. For example, if you were asked to find the probability of selecting a red marble from a jar containing 2 red and 3 blue marbles, the calculator will not help you answer the question.

Determining which questions to answer with the calculator is an important skill for you to develop. Be sure that you do not waste your time on the test trying to use the calculator when it is not appropriate.

2. What calculator can you use?

The State Department of Education has indicated that you will be allowed to use a calculator that has at least the following functions:

a. algebraic logic (follows order of operations)
b. exponent key to do powers and roots of any degree
c. at least one memory
d. a reset button, or some other simple, straightforward way to clear all of the memory and programs

For the eleventh grade mathematics assessment, use of a graphing calculator is strongly recommended. However, calculators with QWERTY (i.e. typewriter) keyboards are not acceptable under the current guidelines.

3. What features of the calculator are you likely to need for the test?

In addition to the basic operation keys and number keys, be sure you can use these keys:

CE/C ON/AC	clear
M+ M− MR STO	memory
( )	parentheses
+/− (−)	sign change
%	percent
√	square root
x^2 y^x	powers
x!	factorial

4. What else should you consider when using the calculator on the test?

The most important thing is to be comfortable with the calculator you will be using on the test. Be sure you are familiar with the keypad and the functions available on the calculator.

If you are using a calculator on an open-ended question, remember that it is important to show the work by writing out what you put into the calculator and the answer given.

Think before pushing the buttons. If you try to use the calculator for every question, you will waste too much time.

Be sure to estimate answers and check calculator answers for reasonableness of response.

Remember:

Questions on the test will not be coded to tell you when to use your calculator. You must make the decision.

C. ABOUT OPEN-ENDED QUESTIONS

In addition to multiple-choice questions, the HSPA contains open-ended questions that require some writing. This section will deal with the variety of open-ended questions and offer suggestions for writing complete solutions.

1. What is an open-ended question?

An open-ended question is one in which a situation is presented, and you are asked to communicate a response. In most cases, the questions have two or more parts, and require both numerical responses and explanations, or mathematical arguments.

2. What might be asked in open-ended questions?

The following outline covers examples of what might be asked in these questions.

1. **A task with a request to show a procedure**
   (possibly a combination of tasks).

Example: Find the area of the shaded region.
Explain your procedure.

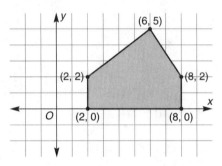

2. **A written explanation of why a result is valid or why an approach is incorrect.**

Example: The average test score in a class of 20 students was 80. The average test score in a class of 30 students was 70. Mich concluded that the average score for all 50 students was 75. He obtained the 75 by adding 80 and 70, and dividing by 2. Is his approach correct? Explain.

3. **A list to meet certain conditions.**
   You might be asked to list numbers, dimensions, expressions, equations, etc.

Example: By looking, you should be able to tell that the average (mean) for 79, 80, 81 is 80. List three other sets of three scores that would also have an average of 80.

4. **A diagram to fit specific conditions.**

Example: On the grid, draw three figures (a triangle, a rectangle, a parallelogram) each with an area of 12 square units.

5. **A description and/or extension of a pattern.**

Example: Suppose this pattern were continued.

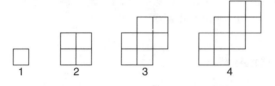

    a. Explain how the pattern is produced.

    b. How many small squares would be in the 100th diagram?

6. **An indication of what will happen when a change is made in an existing situation.**

Example: A rectangular prism (box) has dimensions of 8 cm × 4 cm × 2 cm. If you double each of the three dimensions, tell what happens to the volume of the box.

7. **A diagram to enhance an explanation.**

Example: Use a diagram to show that:

$$2\frac{1}{2} \times 2\frac{1}{2} = 6\frac{1}{4}$$

8. **A process involving measurement with a follow-up task.**

Example: Use a ruler to determine the lengths of the sides of the accompanying figure. Label the sides with the measurements you find. Use these measurements to find the perimeter and the area of the figure. Show all work clearly.

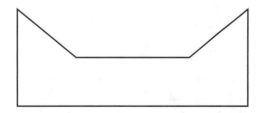

3. How are open-ended questions scored?

At the present time, the open ended questions on the HSPA are each worth three points. (The multiple-choice items are each worth one point). Partial credit is possible on the open-ended questions. You might receive a score of 3, 2, 1, or 0. [An analytic approach is used based on the requirements of each problem.] In multi-part questions, for example, the three points a response could earn are distributed among the parts. The following examples show how the scoring could take place on different open-ended questions.

A copy of the generic rubric used as a guide to develop specific scoring guides or rubrics for each of the Open-Ended items which appear on the HSPA is contained on page xiii.

Example 1: The bottom left corner is the origin of the coordinate grid in your Answer Folder. Suppose the coordinates of point *A* are (3, 1), the coordinates of point *B* are (10, 7), and the coordinates of point *C* are (3, 7). Sketch triangle *ABC*. Classify the triangle according to sides. Explain how you arrived at the classification.

Scoring:

You would most likely earn one point for correctly locating the points.

You would most likely earn one point for correctly classifying the figure. (scalene)

You would most likely earn one point for an acceptable explanation of the classification. (i.e., use of ruler, properties of right triangle)

Example 2: Karin knows that the average test score in her class of 20 students is 80. If each student in the class receives an additional 5 points in extra credit, Karin believes the class average will be 85. Is Karin correct? Explain or prove your answer to someone who disagrees with you.

Scoring: You would most likely earn three points if you:

    a. State that Karin is correct.

    b. Support your response with an algebraic or arithmetic proof:

$$\frac{(20 \times 80) + (20 \times 5)}{20} = 85$$

    c. Generalize your response in words: The sum will increase 100 points. The number of students remains constant. Hence, the change in the average is the increase divided by the number of students, or $100 \div 20 = 5$.

You would most likely receive two points if you state that Karin is correct and support your response with an arithmetic example, but do not generalize.

You would most likely receive one point if you state that Karin is correct but offer no explanation.

You would most likely receive zero points if you provide an unsatisfactory response that answers the question inappropriately.

4. What are some general guidelines for answering open-ended questions?

In answering open-ended questions, you will find the following suggestions helpful.
1. Write complete sentences.
2. Be concise, not wordy.
3. Make sure to explore different cases.
4. Make sure to answer each part of the question.
5. Make sure you answer the question that is being asked.
6. Use a diagram to enhance an explanation.
7. Label diagrams with dimensions.
8. As appropriate, give a clearly worked-out example with some explanation.
9. In problems involving estimation/approximation, make sure you do precomputational rounding.
10. Provide generalizations as requested.
11. When using a grid, follow specific instructions for the location of the origin, axes, etc.

12. Avoid assumptions that have no basis, such as assuming that a triangle is isosceles.
13. Double-check any computation needed within the open-ended response.
14. Be aware that a question may have more than one answer.

Holistic Scoring Guide for Mathematics Open-Ended Items (Generic Rubric)

3-Point Response

The response shows complete understanding of the problem's essential mathematical concepts. The student executes procedures completely and gives relevant responses to all parts of the task. The response contains few minor errors, if any. The response contains a clear, effective explanation detailing how the problem was solved so that the reader does not need to infer how and why decisions were made.

2-Point Response

The response shows nearly complete understanding of the problem's essential mathematical concepts. The student executes nearly all procedures and gives relevant responses to most parts of the task. The response may have minor errors. The explanation detailing how the problem was solved may not be clear, causing the reader to make some inferences.

1-Point Response

The response shows limited understanding of the problem's essential mathematical concepts. The response and procedures may be incomplete and/or may contain major errors. An incomplete explanation of how the problem was solved may contribute to questions as to how and why decisions were made.

0-Point Response

The response shows insufficient understanding of the problem's essential mathematical concepts. The procedures, if any, contain major errors. There may be no explanation of the solution or the reader may not be able to understand the explanation. The reader may not be able to understand how and why decisions were made.

Reprinted courtesy of the New Jersey State Department of Education.

Mathematics Reference Sheet

Use the information below as needed to answer questions on the mathematics portion of the eleventh-grade HSPA.

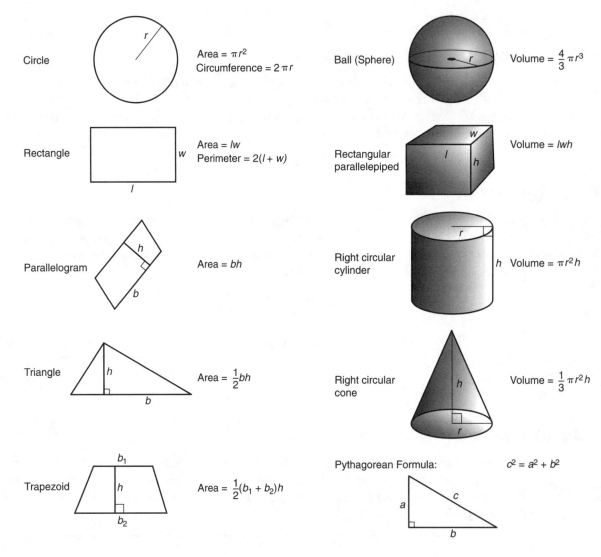

Circle — Area = πr^2
Circumference = $2\pi r$

Ball (Sphere) — Volume = $\frac{4}{3}\pi r^3$

Rectangle — Area = lw
Perimeter = $2(l + w)$

Rectangular parallelepiped — Volume = lwh

Parallelogram — Area = bh

Right circular cylinder — Volume = $\pi r^2 h$

Triangle — Area = $\frac{1}{2}bh$

Right circular cone — Volume = $\frac{1}{3}\pi r^2 h$

Trapezoid — Area = $\frac{1}{2}(b_1 + b_2)h$

Pythagorean Formula: $c^2 = a^2 + b^2$

Reprinted courtesy of the New Jersey State Department of Education.

Number Sense, Concepts, and Applications

Macro A

Understand types of numbers, our numeration system, and the ways they are used and applied in real-world situations.

1 A 1 Real Numbers

A *rational number* is any number that can be expressed as a ratio of two integers in the form $\frac{a}{b}$, with $b \neq 0$. This definition includes integers, fractions, and decimals.

In decimal form, a rational number is either a terminating decimal (such as 0.25; 0.165) or a repeating decimal (such as $0.3\overline{3}$; $4.\overline{31}$).

An *irrational number* in decimal form is neither a terminating decimal nor a repeating decimal. Examples of irrational numbers are 0.121221222 . . . ; $\sqrt{2} = 1.41421356. \ldots$ An irrational number cannot be written as a ratio of two integers.

The set of *real numbers* is formed by combining the set of rational numbers with the set of irrational numbers.

MODEL PROBLEMS

1. Which of the following is NOT equal to the other three?

A. $\dfrac{2}{10}$ B. $1.5 \div 7.5$ C. $1 \div \dfrac{1}{5}$ D. $\sqrt{\dfrac{1}{25}}$

Solution: Choice A: $\dfrac{2}{10} = \dfrac{1}{5}$

Choice B: $1.5 \div 7.5 = 0.2$ or $\dfrac{1}{5}$

Choice C: $1 \div \dfrac{1}{5} = 1 \times 5 = 5$

Choice D: $\sqrt{\dfrac{1}{25}} = \dfrac{1}{5}$

Answer: Choice C is not equivalent to the others.

2. Place the following rational numbers in order from LEAST to GREATEST:

$$-\dfrac{5}{2}, \dfrac{2}{5}, -3.2, 0.35$$

Solution: As you consider placement of rational numbers on a number line, numbers to the left are smaller than numbers to the right.

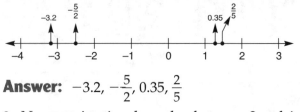

Answer: $-3.2, -\dfrac{5}{2}, 0.35, \dfrac{2}{5}$

3. Name an irrational number between 3 and 4.

Solution: There are an infinite number of irrational numbers between 3 and 4. To name one, it is necessary to write a decimal which is non-repeating and also non-terminating. Possible answers include $3.050050005 \ldots$; $\sqrt{13}$; $3.929929992 \ldots$; and π.

PRACTICE

1. Arrange the following numbers in order from LEAST to GREATEST:

$$\dfrac{1}{3}, \dfrac{2}{5}, 0.6, 0.125$$

A. $0.125, 0.6, \dfrac{1}{3}, \dfrac{2}{5}$ B. $0.125, \dfrac{1}{3}, \dfrac{2}{5}, 0.6$

C. $0.125, \dfrac{1}{3}, 0.6, \dfrac{2}{5}$ D. $\dfrac{1}{3}, \dfrac{2}{5}, 0.125, 0.6$

2. For a series of eight football plays, a team had the following results:

+4 yards, +3 yards, +9 yards, −4 yards, −5 yards, +10 yards, −5 yards, +8 yards

What is the average yardage for this series of plays?

A. 20   B. 6   C. 2.5   D. −2.5

3. Select the correct comparison between p and q.

$$p = \dfrac{1}{3} \times \dfrac{1}{5} \times \dfrac{2}{7} \text{ and } q = \dfrac{2}{3} \times \dfrac{1}{5} \times \dfrac{1}{7}$$

A. $p < q$
B. $p > q$
C. $p = q$
D. The comparison cannot be determined without more information.

4. Which point on the number line could represent the product of the numbers P, Q, and R?

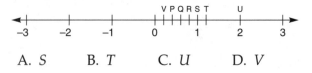

A. S B. T C. U D. V

5. A fraction is equal to $\frac{1}{2}$. If its numerator is increased by 1 and its denominator is increased by 5, the value of the resulting fraction is $\frac{4}{9}$. Find the original fraction.

   A. $\frac{6}{12}$ B. $\frac{7}{13}$ C. $\frac{9}{18}$ D. $\frac{11}{22}$

6. The number 0.67667667 . . . is between which pair of rational numbers?

   A. $\frac{1}{2}$ and $\frac{2}{3}$ B. $\frac{1}{3}$ and $\frac{4}{7}$

   C. $\frac{2}{3}$ and $\frac{3}{4}$ D. $\frac{4}{7}$ and $\frac{5}{8}$

7. Which of the following sets contain the numbers 0.33, $-\frac{5}{6}$, and $\sqrt{5}$?

   A. Real numbers   B. Rational numbers
   C. Irrational numbers   D. Integers

8. If you know that $\frac{1}{8} = 0.125$, how can you use that fact to find the value of $\frac{7}{8}$?

9. Explain why the decimal 0.33 is not exactly equivalent to the fraction $\frac{1}{3}$.

10. How many ratios of two whole numbers are equivalent to $\frac{7}{10}$ and have a two-digit denominator?

---

1 A 2 Powers, Roots, Exponents, and Scientific Notation

Exponents

An *exponent* tells how many times a base is used as a factor.

$$3^4 = 3 \cdot 3 \cdot 3 \cdot 3 = 81$$

where 4 is the exponent and 3 is the base.

Laws of Exponents ($x \neq 0$):	
Multiplication:	$x^a \cdot x^b = x^{a+b}$
Division:	$x^a \div x^b = x^{a-b}$
Powers:	$(x^a)^b = x^{ab}$
Zero Exponent:	$x^0 = 1$
Negative Exponent:	$x^{-a} = \dfrac{1}{x^a}$

MODEL PROBLEMS

1. In simplifying $\dfrac{5^5 \times 5^3}{5^6}$, Jessica is tempted to use her calculator to find 5^5, 5^3, and 5^6 individually prior to doing the multiplication and division. Explain how Jessica could use the laws of exponents to arrive at the result in a more efficient manner.

Solution: $5^5 \times 5^3 = 5^{5+3} = 5^8$
$$5^8 \div 5^6 = 5^{8-6} = 5^2 = 25$$

2. Which of these three expressions

$$\text{I. } 2^{12} \quad \text{II. } 4^6 \quad \text{III. } 2^3 \cdot 8^3$$

is equivalent to the expression 16^3?

A. I, II, and III
B. only I and II
C. only II and III
D. only I

Solution: Since 16 is equivalent to 2^4, then 16^3 is equivalent to $(2^4)^3$ or 2^{12}.
Thus, I is an equivalent expression.

Since 16 is equivalent to 4^2, then 16^3 is equivalent to $(4^2)^3$ or 4^6.
Thus, II is an equivalent expression.

$2^3 \cdot 8^3$ is equivalent to $(2 \cdot 8)^3$ or 16^3.
Thus, III is an equivalent expression.

Answer: A

3. Simplify: $(-4)^{-3}$

Solution: By definition, $(-4)^{-3} = \dfrac{1}{(-4)^3} = \dfrac{1}{-64} = \dfrac{-1}{64}$.

Roots

A *root* is the inverse of a power.

If $b^2 = a$, then b is a square root of a. $b = \sqrt{a}$
If $b^3 = a$, then b is a cube root of a. $b = \sqrt[3]{a}$
Examples: $5^2 = 25 \rightarrow 5$ is a square root of 25. $5 = \sqrt{25}$
$\qquad\qquad (-5)^2 = 25 \rightarrow -5$ is a square root of 25. $-5 = \sqrt{25}$
$\qquad\qquad 2^3 = 8 \rightarrow 2$ is a cube root of 8. $2 = \sqrt[3]{8}$
$\qquad\qquad 3^5 = 243 \rightarrow 3$ is a fifth root of 243. $3 = \sqrt[5]{243}$

MODEL PROBLEM

$x^4 = 16$, find two values of x so that the statement is true.

Solution: Since $2^4 = 16$ and $(-2)^4 = 16$, 2 and -2 are two values that satisfy the equation. Therefore, 2 and -2 are each fourth roots of 16.

Scientific Notation

A number in *scientific notation* is expressed as a product of two factors:

(first factor is between 1 and 10) × (second factor is an integral power of 10)

$$4,300,000 = 4.3 \times 10^6 \qquad 0.000043 = 4.3 \times 10^{-5}$$

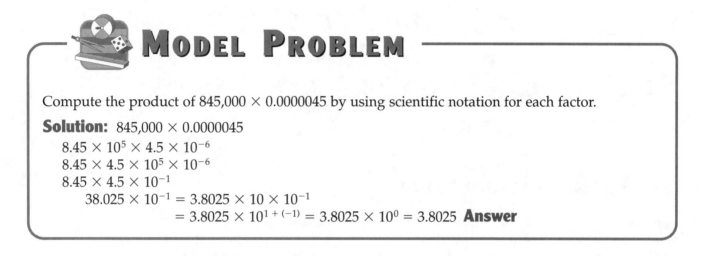

MODEL PROBLEM

Compute the product of 845,000 × 0.0000045 by using scientific notation for each factor.

Solution: 845,000 × 0.0000045

$8.45 \times 10^5 \times 4.5 \times 10^{-6}$

$8.45 \times 4.5 \times 10^5 \times 10^{-6}$

$8.45 \times 4.5 \times 10^{-1}$

$\qquad 38.025 \times 10^{-1} = 3.8025 \times 10 \times 10^{-1}$

$\qquad\qquad = 3.8025 \times 10^{1 + (-1)} = 3.8025 \times 10^0 = 3.8025$ **Answer**

PRACTICE

1. Choose the correct comparison for the following two quantities: $p = 4^8$ and $q = 2^{15}$

   A. $p < q$ B. $p > q$ C. $p = q$
   D. The comparison cannot be determined without additional information.

2. Choose the correct comparison for the following two quantities: $p = (0.9)^3$ and $q = (0.9)^5$

   A. $p < q$ B. $p > q$ C. $p = q$
   D. The comparison cannot be determined without additional information.

3. Which of the following statements are always TRUE?

   I. $6^a = 2 \times 3^a$ II. $(0.9)^4 > (0.9)^3$

   A. I and II   B. I only   C. II only
   D. Neither statement is always true.

4. If the volume of a cube is 512 cubic inches, which of the following represents the length of an edge of the cube?

   A. $512 \div 3$ B. $\sqrt{512}$
   C. 512^3 D. $\sqrt[3]{512}$

5. Which of the following is NOT correct?

   A. $3^8 = (3^4)^2$ B. $3^4 \times 3^4 = 3^{16}$
   C. $3^4 \times 3^4 = 3^8$ D. $3^{10} \div 3^5 = 3^5$

6. Which of the following relations could you write in the blank to produce a true statement?

   $$2.5 \times 10^{-4} \underline{\quad} 3.4 \times 10^{-3}$$

   A. $>$ B. $<$ C. $=$
   D. The comparison cannot be determined without more information.

7. Which of the following would NOT represent a large number?

   A. 5.9×10^{24} B. 3.92×10^{-6}

   C. 7.37×10^{22} D. 2.279×10^{8}

8. Which of the following is NOT equivalent to 5^{-2}?

   A. -25 B. $\dfrac{1}{25}$ C. 0.04 D. $\left(\dfrac{1}{5}\right)^{2}$

9. If $3^{\square} = 9^{4}$, what exponent goes in the box?

10. What is the missing exponent? $\dfrac{r^{12}}{r^{\square}} = r^{6}$

11. Explain the difference between $a^{3} \times a^{5}$ and $(a^{3})^{5}$.

12. Show how scientific notation can be used to simplify the amount of computation in the following problem:

$$52{,}000 \times 1{,}200{,}000$$

1 A 3 Absolute Value

The *absolute value* (symbol $|\ \ |$) of a nonzero number is always positive. The absolute value of zero is zero: $|0| = 0$.

We describe the absolute value of a nonzero number as a distance. Since the point representing $+3$ is a distance of 3 units from zero on a number line and the point representing -3 is also a distance of 3 units from zero, the absolute value of both $+3$ and -3 is 3.

In symbols:

$$|{+}3| = 3 \qquad |{-}3| = 3 \qquad |{+}3| = |{-}3| = 3$$

 **MODEL PROBLEMS**

1. Simplify: $|{-}7| + |8| - |{-}9|$

Solution: $|{-}7| = 7$
                 $|8| = 8$
             $|{-}9| = 9$
Therefore, $|{-}7| + |8| - |{-}9| = 7 + 8 - 9 = 6$

2. Solve for x: $|x| = 5$

Solution: Since $|x|$ is the distance x is from 0 on the number line, $x = 5$ or -5.

3. Solve for x: $|2x + 1| = 9$

Solution: If $|a| = 9$, then a must equal 9 or -9.
             Hence, $|2x + 1| = 9$ means

$$2x + 1 = 9 \quad \text{or} \quad 2x + 1 = -9$$
$$2x = 8 \qquad\qquad 2x = -10$$
$$x = 4 \qquad\qquad\; x = -5$$

1. Place the following in order from least to greatest:

$$-\frac{1}{2}, |-1|, -1.4, \left|-\frac{3}{8}\right|$$

A. $-1.4, -\frac{1}{2}, \left|-\frac{3}{8}\right|, |-1|$

B. $|-1|, \left|-\frac{3}{8}\right|, -\frac{1}{2}, -1.4$

C. $\left|-\frac{3}{8}\right|, -\frac{1}{2}, -1.4, |-1|$

D. $-1.4, \left|-\frac{3}{8}\right|, -\frac{1}{2}, |-1|$

2. If $|x - 4| = 3$, then x equals:

A. 7 only   B. 1 only   C. 7 or 1   D. 7 or −1

3. Which of the following would represent all of the real numbers at least 5 units away from 2 on the number line?

A. $|x| \geq 5$ B. $|x - 2| \geq 5$

C. $|x + 2| \geq 5$ D. $|x + 5| \geq 2$

4. Which of the following equations represents the situation: to qualify to be a member of the school's wrestling team, a student's weight (w) must be within 75 pounds of 180 pounds?

A. $w - 75 = 180$ B. $w - 180 < 75$

C. $|w - 75| < 180$ D. $|w - 180| < 75$

5. Simplify: $|12| - |-12|$

1 A 4 Properties of Arithmetic Operations and Equivalence Relations

Basic Properties of Operations		
	+	×
Commutative	$a + b = b + a$	$ab = ba$
Associative	$(a + b) + c = a + (b + c)$	$(ab)c = a(bc)$
Identity	$a + 0 = a$	$a \cdot 1 = a$
Inverse	$a + (-a) = 0$	$a \cdot \dfrac{1}{a} = 1, a \neq 0$
Distributive	$a(b + c) = ab + ac$	

Properties of Equivalence Relations	
Reflexive	$A \circledR A$
Symmetric	If $A \circledR B$, then $B \circledR A$.
Transitive	If $A \circledR B$ and $B \circledR C$, then $A \circledR C$.
Note: $\circledR$ represents any relation.	

MODEL PROBLEMS

1. Which property has been applied to allow the product of 15(98) to be computed mentally?

$$15(98) = 15(100 - 2) = 1500 - 30 = 1470$$

A. Associative multiplication
B. Distributive
C. Associative addition
D. Inverse for addition

Solution: 98 is rewritten as the equivalent expression $100 - 2$ and then the 15 is distributed over the 100 and the 2. The difference can easily be found. The key is to rewrite the problem using numbers that make mental computation simple.

Answer: D

2. Which property or properties does the given relationship have?

"is congruent to" (for geometric figures)

A. Reflexive only
B. Symmetric only
C. Transitive only
D. All of the above

Solution: Since every figure is congruent to itself, the relationship is reflexive. If figure #1 is congruent to figure #2, then figure #2 is congruent to figure #1—so the relationship is symmetric. If figure #1 is congruent to figure #2 and figure #2 is congruent to figure #3, then figure #1 is congruent to figure #3. Therefore, "congruent to" is transitive.

Answer: D

PRACTICE

1. Which of the following does NOT have the transitive property?

   A. "is greater than"
   B. "has the same slope as"
   C. "is perpendicular to"
   D. "is less than"

2. Which of the following would NOT be commutative?

   A. Addition ($p + q$ and $q + p$)
   B. Exponentiation (p^q and q^p)
   C. Multiplication (pq and qp)
   D. All of the above are commutative.

3. For the following relationship, which properties would be TRUE?

   "is perpendicular to" (for lines)

   A. Reflexive only
   B. Symmetric only
   C. Transitive only
   D. Reflexive, symmetric, and transitive

4. For which of the following could the distributive property be used to rewrite the expression?

   A. $a + (b - c)$
   B. $a(b - c)$
   C. $a - (b \div c)$
   D. $ab - c$

5. Which relation has all three equivalence properties?

  A. "has the same grandmother as"
  B. "is in the same time zone as"
  C. "has at least as many calories as"
  D. "lives across the street from"

6. Deanne bought 6 tee shirts at $8.95 each. She figured out her total purchase by using a shortcut: $6 \times \$9 - 6 \times \$0.05 = \$53.70$. Her shortcut is an illustration of which property?

1 A 5 Primes, Factors, and Multiples

Numbers can be classified as *prime* or *composite*.

A *prime number* is a whole number greater than 1 with exactly two factors, 1 and the number.

$$2, 3, 5, 7, 11, 13, \ldots$$

A *composite number* is a whole number greater than 1 with more than two factors.

$$4, 6, 8, 9, 10, 12, \ldots$$

One number is a *factor* of another number if it evenly divides that number.
Thus, 6 is a factor of 18, since $18 \div 6 = 3$.
But 8 is not a factor of 18, since $18 \div 8$ is not equal to a whole number.
Two or more numbers may share common factors.
The largest shared common factor is called the *greatest common factor* (*GCF*). The GCF of 18 and 48 is 6.
A *multiple* of a number is the product of that number and any other whole number.
Thus, 20 is a multiple of 5, since $4 \times 5 = 20$.
But 18 is not a multiple of 4, since no whole number times 4 equals 18.
Two or more numbers may share a common multiple.
The smallest shared common multiple is called the *least common multiple* (*LCM*). The LCM of 12 and 15 is 60.

 **MODEL PROBLEMS**

1. Mr. Smart likes to describe his age in the following way: "If you divide my age by 7, the remainder is 1. If you divide my age by 2, the remainder is 1. If you divide my age by 3, the remainder is 1. My age is not divisible by 5 and is less than 100. Now you know my age." How old is Mr. Smart?

Solution:

If Mr. Smart's age is divisible by 7, 2, and 3, his age would be $7 \cdot 3 \cdot 2 = 42$

To obtain a remainder of 1 on each division, his age must be $42 + 1$ or 43.
No other possible age fits the conditions.

Answer: 43

2. The members of the Decorating Committee for a school dance have 36 red carnations, 48 white carnations, and 60 pink carnations. They want to form identical centerpieces, using all of the carnations, so that each one has the same combination of colors as the other centerpieces. What is the largest number of centerpieces they can make?

Solution: Factor each number.

red: 36: (1, 2, 3, 4, 6, 9, 12, 18, 36)

white: 48: (1, 2, 3, 4, 6, 8, 12, 16, 24, 48)

pink: 60: (1, 2, 3, 4, 5, 6, 10, 12, 15, 20, 30, 60)

common factors: (1, 2, 3, 4, 6, 12)

Answer: GCF = 12

3. What is the least number of pencils that could be packaged evenly in groups of 8 pencils OR groups of 12 pencils?

Solution:

packages of 8 could hold: (8, 16, 24, 32, 40, 48, . . .)
packages of 12 could hold: (12, 24, 36, 48, 60, . . .)

Answer: Least number possible is 24.

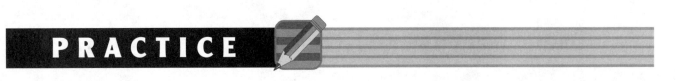 **PRACTICE**

1. Which of the numbers below has all the following characteristics?

   • It is a multiple of 12.
   • It is the least common multiple of two one-digit even numbers.
   • It is not a factor of 36.

   A. 12   B. 24   C. 36   D. 48

2. Which of the following is NOT a correct statement?

   A. If a is a multiple of b, then b is a factor of a.
   B. If b is a factor of a, then b is a multiple of a.
   C. Any two numbers can have a common multiple.
   D. If a is a multiple of b and b is a multiple of c, then a is a multiple of c.

3. 48 is NOT a multiple of 36 because

   A. 12 is the greatest common factor of 48 and 36.
   B. 9 is a factor of 36 but not a factor of 48.
   C. 48 is not a prime number.
   D. No whole number multiplied by 36 will give a product of 48.

4. 18 is NOT a factor of 84 because

   A. 84 is not prime.
   B. 18 is not prime.
   C. 6 is not a factor of 84.
   D. 9 is not a factor of 84.

5. What is the smallest three-digit number divisible by 3?

6. If 2, 3, and 5 are factors of a number, list three other factors of the number.

7. Lisa believes that a characteristic of a prime number is that prime numbers are odd. Explain why Lisa's generalization is incorrect.

8. If 2 is not a factor of a number, why can't 6 be a factor of the same number?

9. One rectangle has an area of 48 cm². Another rectangle has an area of 80 cm². The dimensions of each rectangle are whole numbers. If each rectangle is to have the same length, what is the greatest possible dimension, in centimeters, the length can be?

10. Jack believes that the larger a number is, the more factors the number has. Write an argument in support or contradiction of Jack's belief.

11. Chen believes that the LCM of two numbers is always greater than either number. Write an argument in support or contradiction of Chen's belief.

12. Stan and John begin a race at the same time. John runs a lap of the track in 8 minutes. Stan runs the same lap in 6 minutes. When is the first time that John and Stan will complete a lap together?

ASSESSMENT MACRO A

1. Which of the following sets contains the numbers $\frac{5}{8}$, π, 100, -4.75?

   A. Integers   B. Rational numbers
   C. Real numbers   D. Irrational numbers

2. Which properties would be true for the following relationship?

      "is parallel to" (for lines)

   A. Symmetric
   B. Transitive
   C. Symmetric and transitive
   D. None of these

3. The distance on the number line between a number x and -5 is 7 units. Find all possible values for x.

   A. $-12, 2$ B. $12, -2$ C. -12 D. -2

4. Two whole numbers are called *relatively prime* if their only common factor is 1. For example, 5 and 8 are relatively prime. How many of the following pairs represent numbers that are relatively prime?

   8 and 9, 18 and 21, 60 and 99, 51 and 200

   A. 1   B. 2   C. 3   D. 4

5. Which of the numbers below has all the following characteristics?

   - It is a multiple of 9.
   - It is a factor of 144.
   - It is a perfect square.

   A. 18   B. 36   C. 49   D. 72

6. Select the correct comparison between $(0.9)^2$ and $(0.9)^3$.

   A. $(0.9)^2 < (0.9)^3$
   B. $(0.9)^2 > (0.9)^3$
   C. $(0.9)^2 = (0.9)^3$
   D. The comparison cannot be determined without more information.

7. Select the correct comparison for the following: $(-1)^r$ and $(-1)^{r+2}$, where r is a positive integer

   A. $(-1)^r < (-1)^{r+2}$
   B. $(-1)^r > (-1)^{r+2}$
   C. $(-1)^r = (-1)^{r+2}$
   D. The comparison cannot be determined without more information.

8. For which of the following are the numbers NOT in correct order from SMALLEST to LARGEST?

   A. $-3.1, -\dfrac{7}{2}, 0, 0.7, \dfrac{3}{2}$

   B. $-2.3, -\dfrac{3}{2}, 0.1, \dfrac{1}{3}, 0.35$

   C. $-6.1, -\dfrac{16}{3}, -4, -\dfrac{1}{4}, 0$

   D. $-2.3, -\dfrac{3}{2}, -0.9, 0, 0.9$

9. Select the correct comparison between the following two quantities:

   $$p = \left(\frac{1}{2}\right)^a \text{ and } q = \left(\frac{1}{3}\right)^b$$

   A. $p < q$ B. $p > q$ C. $p = q$
   D. The comparison cannot be made without further information.

10. What must be added to $(-3)^3$ to produce a sum of 0?

    A. -27 B. 0   C. 9   D. 27

11. If $r = -2$ and $t = -5$, find the value of $r^4 + t$.

12. How many ratios of two whole numbers are equivalent to $\dfrac{3}{11}$ and have a two-digit denominator?

13. Calculate this quotient using scientific notation: $\dfrac{20{,}000 \times 300{,}000}{0.000005}$

    Express the answer in scientific notation. Show your procedure.

14. How many prime numbers are factors of 210?

15. How many two-digit numbers are multiples of 3 and also factors of 81?

16. A fraction is equivalent to $\dfrac{4}{5}$. The sum of the numerator and the denominator of the fraction is 36. What is the fraction?

17. If $2^{\square} = 8^3$, what exponent goes in the box?

18. Gerry knows that $2^4 = 4^2$. He concludes that $a^b = b^a$. Give an example to illustrate that this is NOT always true.

19. Write two different algebraic expressions to find the area of the given rectangle.

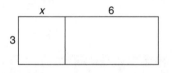

20. Explain why a multiple of 17, greater than 17, cannot be a prime number.

21. You are making up fruit baskets from 45 apples and 54 pears. Each basket must contain the same combination of apples and pears as all of the other baskets. What is the greatest number of baskets that you can make up using all the fruit? Explain how you arrived at your answer.

22. If a number is divisible by 8, is twice the number divisible by 8? Explain.

23. Given the four-digit number $84\triangle3$, can you find a value for $\triangle$ such that the number will be divisible by 5? Explain your response.

24. Two nearby lights are flashing, one every 7 seconds and the other every 5 seconds. How many seconds long are the intervals between simultaneous flashings? Explain how you arrived at your answer.

25. Plastic spoons come in packages of 20, plastic forks in packages of 15, and plastic knives in packages of 12. A place setting requires a knife, a spoon, and a fork. What is the least number of spoons, forks, and knives you can buy in order to get an equal number of each? Explain your work.

26. Find two sets of three numbers, each of which satisfies all these clues:

    • Each number is a two-digit number.
    • The greatest common factor for the three numbers is 6.
    • The largest number is twice the smallest number.

27. A palindrome is a number which reads the same from left-to-right and from right-to-left. For example, 737 and 8,228 are palindromes.

    a. How many palindromes are there between 2,000 and 5,000? Explain an efficient procedure for arriving at the answer.
    b. What fraction of these palindromes are multiples of 3?
    c. What is the first palindrome greater than 10,000 which also is a multiple of 3?

28.

$\frac{1}{2}$	$\frac{1}{3}$	$\frac{1}{4}$	$\frac{1}{5}$	$\frac{1}{6}$	$\frac{1}{7}$	$\frac{1}{8}$	$\frac{1}{9}$
$\frac{2}{3}$	$\frac{2}{5}$	$\frac{2}{7}$	$\frac{2}{8}$	$\frac{2}{9}$	$\frac{2}{10}$	$\frac{2}{11}$	$\frac{2}{12}$
$\frac{3}{4}$	$\frac{3}{5}$	$\frac{3}{6}$	$\frac{3}{7}$	$\frac{3}{8}$	$\frac{3}{9}$	$\frac{3}{10}$	$\frac{3}{11}$

Twenty-four fractions are shown above.

    • Eliminate all fractions which are not in simplest form.
    • Eliminate all fractions with values that are less than 0.4.

    a. How many fractions remain?
    b. Write the remaining fractions in order from least to greatest.
    c. How do you know that no two of the remaining fractions can be equivalent to one another?
    d. How do you know that no three of the remaining fractions could have a sum less than 1?

Macro B

Apply ratios, proportions, and percents to a variety of situations.

1 B 1 Ratio and Proportion

A *ratio* is a comparison of two numbers by division.
The ratio of two numbers a and b (where $b \neq 0$) can be expressed as:

$$a \text{ to } b \quad \text{or} \quad a : b \quad \text{or} \quad \frac{a}{b}$$

A ratio that compares two unlike quantities is called a *rate*.

To Find a Unit Rate:

1. Set up a ratio comparing the given units.
2. Divide to find the rate for one unit of the given quantity.

A *proportion* is a statement that two ratios are equal. In a proportion, the *cross products* are equal.

Example: $\dfrac{2}{3} = \dfrac{8}{12}$

$2 \times 12 = 3 \times 8$

MODEL PROBLEMS

1. Find the unit rate if you travel 150 miles in 2.5 hours.

Solution: $\dfrac{\text{miles} \rightarrow}{\text{hours} \rightarrow} \dfrac{150}{2.5} = \dfrac{1{,}500}{25} = \dfrac{60}{1}$

Answer: The rate is 60 mph.

2. A store has a 10-oz. package of oat cereal for $2.29 and a 15-oz. package of the same cereal for $2.89. Which is the better buy?

Solution:

$\dfrac{\text{price} \rightarrow}{\text{oz.} \rightarrow} \dfrac{2.29}{10} = \dfrac{0.229}{1} = 0.229$ cent/oz.

$\dfrac{\text{price} \rightarrow}{\text{oz.} \rightarrow} \dfrac{2.89}{15} = \dfrac{0.193}{1} = 0.193$ cent/oz.

Answer: The 15-oz. package is the better buy.

3. Solve: $\dfrac{1.2}{1.5} = \dfrac{x}{5}$

Solution: $(1.5)(x) = (1.2)(5)$

$1.5x = 6$

$x = \dfrac{6}{1.5}$

Answer: $x = 4$

4. In the scale on a map, 1 cm represents 250 km. What is the actual distance represented by a length of 1.75 cm?

Solution: $\dfrac{\text{cm} \rightarrow}{\text{km} \rightarrow} \dfrac{1}{250} = \dfrac{1.75}{x}$

$x = (1.75)(250)$

Answer: $x = 437.5$ km

PRACTICE

1. In a class of 25 students, there are 13 boys. What is the ratio of girls to boys?

A. 12 : 13 B. 12 : 25 C. 13 : 12 D. 13 : 25

2. John is paid at the rate of $8.50 an hour for the first 40 hours a week that he works. He is paid time and a half for any hours over 40. What would John's gross pay be for a week in which he worked 48 hours?

A. $340 B. $408 C. $442 D. $610

3. A basketball player makes 3 out of every 5 of her foul shots. At this rate, if she attempts 55 foul shots, how many will she miss?

A. 50 B. 40 C. 33 D. 22

4. If three students share $180 in the ratio of 1 : 2 : 3, how much is the largest share?

A. $30 B. $60 C. $90 D. $120

5. In a recipe, 4 eggs are used to make 36 muffins. How many eggs are needed to make 90 muffins?

A. 8 B. 9 C. 10 D. 12

6. If 30 cards can be printed in 40 minutes, how many hours will it take to print 540 cards at the same rate?

A. 6 hours B. 9 hours
C. 12 hours D. 15 hours

7. Which proportion does NOT represent the given question?

If 48 oz. cost $1.89, what will 72 oz. cost?

A. $\dfrac{48}{1.89} = \dfrac{72}{x}$ B. $\dfrac{48}{72} = \dfrac{1.89}{x}$

C. $\dfrac{1.89}{72} = \dfrac{x}{48}$ D. $\dfrac{1.89}{48} = \dfrac{x}{72}$

8. With which roll of film would the cost of a single exposure be less? By how much less would it be?

   a roll of 20-exposure film for $2.30
   a roll of 12-exposure film for $1.50

A. 20 exposures, $0.08
B. 20 exposures, $0.01
C. 12 exposures, $0.80
D. 12 exposures, $0.01

9. Which of the following is a better buy? Explain why.

   a 3-pack of blank videotapes for $8.85
   a 2-pack of blank videotapes for $5.95

10. Which of the following situations represents a better salary offer? Explain why.

   a salary of $504.50 per week
   $12.50 per hour for 40 hours

11. One car travels 468 miles on 18 gallons of gas. Will 40 gallons of gas be enough for the car to travel 1,200 miles? Explain.

12. Solve the given proportion. $\dfrac{28}{32} = \dfrac{x}{40}$

13. The scale on a map is $\dfrac{1}{2}$ inch = 55 miles. How far apart are two cities that are shown as being 5 inches apart on the map?

---

1 B 2 Percent

Percent means per hundred $\left(\% \text{ symbol} = \dfrac{1}{100}\right)$. A percent is a ratio that compares a number to 100.

  A percent can be written as a fraction or as a decimal.

$$25\% = 0.25 = \frac{1}{4}$$

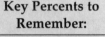

Key Percents to Remember:

100% is all.
50% is one-half.
25% is one-quarter.
10% is one-tenth.
1% is one-hundredth.
200% is double.

MODEL PROBLEM

Barry's restaurant check for dinner totaled $18 before the tip. He wanted to leave a 15% tip. Explain how Barry would be able to compute the tip mentally.

Solution: 15% = 10% + 5%

  10% of $18 = $1.80   5% of $18 = $\dfrac{1}{2}$ of 10% of $18 = $0.90

Answer: 15% of $18 = $2.70

In general, percent applications involve three terms:

percentage: part of the total   *rate:* percent   *base:* total amount

To solve percent problems, use the formula: *percentage = rate × base*

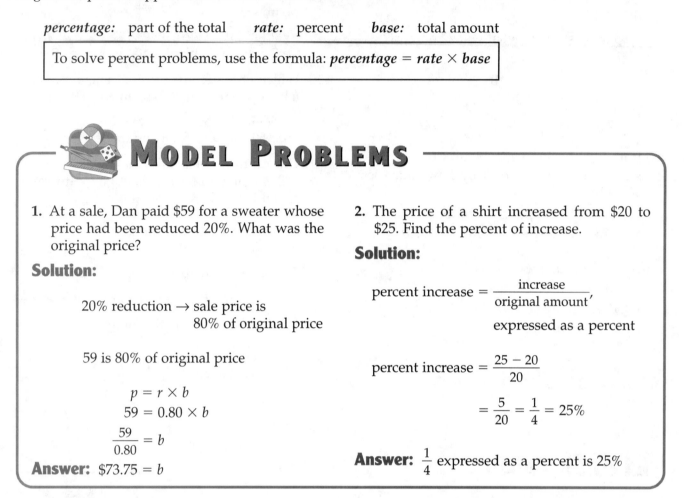

MODEL PROBLEMS

1. At a sale, Dan paid $59 for a sweater whose price had been reduced 20%. What was the original price?

Solution:

20% reduction → sale price is
80% of original price

59 is 80% of original price

$$p = r \times b$$
$$59 = 0.80 \times b$$
$$\frac{59}{0.80} = b$$

Answer: $73.75 = b$

2. The price of a shirt increased from $20 to $25. Find the percent of increase.

Solution:

$$\text{percent increase} = \frac{\text{increase}}{\text{original amount}},$$
expressed as a percent

$$\text{percent increase} = \frac{25 - 20}{20}$$

$$= \frac{5}{20} = \frac{1}{4} = 25\%$$

Answer: $\frac{1}{4}$ expressed as a percent is 25%

PRACTICE

1. The number of students in the senior class is 240. This figure is 112% of what it was the previous year. This means that:

A. 12 more students are in the senior class now.
B. The number of students in the senior class decreased from last year to this year.
C. The total population of the school increased.
D. The number of seniors increased from last year to this year.

2. Which of the following is NOT a correct statement?

A. 63% of 63 is less than 63.
B. 115% of 63 is more than 63.
C. $\frac{1}{3}\%$ of 63 is the same as $\frac{1}{3}$ of 63.
D. 100% of 63 is equal to 63.

3. On a math test of 25 questions, Mary scored 72%. How many questions did Mary get wrong?

A. 7   B. 9   C. 18   D. 20

4. Laura bought a softball glove at 40% off the original price. This discount saved her $14.40. What was the original price of the glove?

   A. $5.76   B. $20.16   C. $36   D. $50.40

5. The sale price of a chair is $510 after a 15% discount has been given. Find the original price.

   A. $76.50 B. $433.50 C. $586.50 D. $600

6. The regular price of an exercise bike is $125. If it is on sale for 40% off the regular price, what is the sale price?

   A. $90   B. $80   C. $75   D. $48

7. The Sound System Store is selling AM-FM radios for $\frac{1}{3}$ off the regular price of $63. Murphy's Discount Store is selling the same radios at 25% off the regular price of $60. What is the lower sale price for the radio?

   A. $35   B. $42   C. $45   D. $48

8. If a price is doubled, it is increased by ___%.

9. If you needed to compute $33\frac{1}{3}$% of $45 without a calculator, would it be better to represent $33\frac{1}{3}$% as a fraction or a decimal? Explain your response.

10. When the sales-tax rate decreased from 7% to 6%, how much less in sales tax did you pay in purchasing an item priced at $480?

11. To obtain a score of 75% on a test containing 40 questions, how many questions must Juan get correct?

12. On a 10 × 10 grid, 31 squares are shaded. How many squares would have to be shaded on a 5 × 10 grid in order to have the same percent of the total squares shaded?

13. The cost of a first-class stamp increased from 29¢ to 32¢. Find the percent of increase.

14. The enrollment in a school went from 750 students to 600 students over a 10-year period. Find the percent of decrease.

15. Using the simple interest formula, $I = PRT$, what is the interest on $400 borrowed at 6% for 2 years?

16. Norma received a commission of 5% on her sales. Her gross sales for November were $12,500. How much more would she receive if her commission were raised to 7%?

17. Is there a difference between buying an item at 50% off the regular price versus buying an item reduced by 30%, and then reduced by an additional 20%? Give examples to justify your answer.

ASSESSMENT MACRO B

1. Find the value of x:

   $$\frac{9}{x} = \frac{63}{112}$$

   A. 7   B. 9   C. 16   D. 58

2. Every 4 days, 180 cars come through the assembly line. At this rate, how many cars come through in 7 days?

   A. 45   B. 315   C. 720   D. 1,260

3. Which of the following is a correct representation for the ratio of 12 ounces to 2 pounds?

   A. 6 : 1   B. 3 : 8   C. 1 : 2   D. 8 : 3

4. A jacket was on sale at a 25% discount. This discount was worth a savings of $5.00. What was the original price of the jacket?

   A. $30   B. $25   C. $20   D. $12.50

5. Which of the following does NOT represent a 50% increase?

   A. $3   → $4.50
   B. $120   → $180
   C. $9   → $18
   D. $6.50 → $9.75

6. A box of machine parts contains 3 times as many good parts as defective parts. There were exactly 72 parts in the box. How many of the parts were defective?

   A. 18   B. 24   C. 48   D. 54

7. About 15 percent of the students are absent from school today. If 595 students are in school today, how many students are enrolled in the school?

   A. 89   B. 506   C. 700   D. 3,967

8. The school board projects a 2.5% increase in enrollment for next year. If the present enrollment is 8,657, what is the projected enrollment?

   A. 10,822   B. 8,874   C. 8,682   D. 8,660

9. A mail-order company sells wrapping paper for $3.75 a roll. Find the cost of an order of 8 rolls including tax and shipping. Tax is charged at the rate of 6% and is charged only on the purchase, not the shipping.

Shipping Costs	
Cost of Paper (with tax)	Add
less than $10.00	$0.55
$10.01–20.00	$1.00
$20.01–30.00	$1.75
over $30.00	$2.25

   A. $33.55   B. $33.66   C. $34.05   D. $36.46

10. Wally's Used Car Lot is selling a used van at 20% off the usual price of $4,770. Mr. L's Used Car Lot is selling the same van at $\frac{1}{3}$ off the usual price of $5,643. Which offers the lower price and by how much?

    A. Wally's by $54   B. Wally's by $927
    C. Mr. L's by $54   D. Mr. L's by $927

11. Frescesca is buying a computer system from a mail-order house. The sale price is $2,599. She must pay 6% sales tax and a 5.5% shipping and handling charge. (The shipping charge does not apply to the sales tax.) How much is her total cost for the computer with tax and shipping?

    A. $298.89   B. $2,741.95
    C. $2,754.94   D. $2,897.89

12. Melissa answered 15 questions correctly on a 45-question multiple-choice test. How many questions will she answer correctly on a 75-question multiple-choice test if she gets the same ratio of questions correct on it as she did on the shorter test?

    A. 15   B. 25   C. 45   D. 60

13. A picture has a ratio of length to width of 8 to 5. If the width is 35 cm, how many centimeters is the length of the picture?

14. For a holiday musical show, the ratio of adult tickets to student tickets to senior citizen tickets was $4:3:5$. If 420 seats were sold, how many of each type of ticket was sold?

15. Judy bought a computer printer for $410. If sales tax was 7%, what was the total purchase price?

16. If four individuals share $270 in the ratio of $1:1:2:5$, how much is the largest share?

17. The cost of a blank tape went from $3.50 to $3.85. Find the percent of increase.

18. Using the simple interest formula, $I = PRT$, what is the interest on $350 borrowed at 5% for 3 years?

19. The scale on a map is $\frac{1}{2}$ inch = 65 miles. How far apart are two cities that are $6\frac{1}{2}$ inches apart on the map? Explain your answer and approach.

OPEN-ENDED QUESTIONS

20. The price of a certain brand of cough drops was increased as follows:

    Before: 18 cough drops for $0.50
    After: 16 cough drops for $0.60

    Michael claims that the percent increase is 20%. He figured this out by taking the difference of $0.10 and determining that $0.10 is $\frac{1}{5}$ or 20% of the original $0.50. Wendy claims that Michael is wrong because he did not take into account the difference in the number of cough drops. Determine the correct percent increase. Explain your procedure.

21. A store offers successive discounts of 10%, 15%, and 20% on a purchase. These discounts can be applied in any order. If you were the customer, which would be the best order for the three discounts to be applied? Defend your response.

22. The formula for the volume of a rectangular solid is

    $$V = lwh$$

    a. What happens to the volume of a rectangular solid if the length is increased by 10%, the width is increased by 10%, and the height is also increased by 10%?

    b. Suppose you want the volume of a second rectangular solid to be double the volume of the original solid. If each dimension of the original solid is to be increased by the same percent, what does this percent (to the nearest tenth of a percent) have to be?

    c. In changing the dimensions of a rectangular solid, the length and width are each increased by 10%. The height is decreased by 20%. Marie says that the result is that the volume remains the same. Linda says the volume is decreased by a very slight percent. Who is correct? Explain.

ASSESSMENT CLUSTER 1

1. Which of the following types of numbers would solve the equation $x^2 = 45$?

   A. Whole numbers   B. Rational numbers
   C. Integers   D. Irrational numbers

2. Which of the following equations represents the following situation: to qualify to be a member of the school's math team, a student's cumulative points on a qualifying exam must be within 15 points of 275?

   A. $|x - 15| \leq 275$ B. $x - 275 \leq 15$
   C. $x - 15 \leq 275$ D. $|x - 275| \leq 15$

3. Which of the following represents a commutative operation?

A. $a * b = a^2 - b$ B. $a * b = 4(a + b)$
C. $a * b = a^b$ D. $a * b = a \div (3b)$

4. Which of the following is NOT equal to the other three?

A. 1.5×10^1 B. $\dfrac{15}{10}$ C. 150% D. $\sqrt{2.25}$

5. Which of the following numbers is between $\dfrac{1}{10,000}$ and $\dfrac{1}{100,000}$, and is also correctly expressed in scientific notation?

A. 4.5×10^{-3} B. 4.5×10^3
C. 4.5×10^{-4} D. 4.5×10^{-5}

6. A $32 sweater is reduced by 25% for a holiday sale. By what percent must the sale price of the sweater be multiplied to restore the price to the original price before the sale?

A. $133\frac{1}{3}\%$ B. 125%   C. 25%   D. 8%

7. The members of the Decorating Committee for a school dance have 24 red carnations, 32 white carnations, and 40 pink carnations. They want to form as many identical centerpieces as possible, using all of the carnations so that each centerpiece has the same combination of colors as all of the other centerpieces. How many pink carnations will each centerpiece have?

A. 4   B. 5   C. 8   D. 10

8. Which of the following is NOT a way to find 120% of a number?

A. Multiply the number by 1.20.
B. Divide the number by 5 and add the result to the number.
C. Divide the number by 5 and multiply the result by 6.
D. Multiply the number by 0.20 and multiply the result by 5.

9. On some days, a bakery packages cupcakes 4 to a package. On other days, cupcakes are packaged in packages of 6 or 8. On a given day, all of the cupcakes baked were packaged and there was one cupcake left over. Which of the following could NOT be the number of cupcakes baked on that day?

A. 22   B. 25   C. 49   D. 97

10. There are three times as many girls as boys in the Spanish Club of Central High School. If there are 36 members in the club, how many of them are boys?

A. 9   B. 12   C. 15   D. 27

11. Light travels at a speed of about 186,281.7 miles per second. How far would light travel in 365 days?

A. 5.87×10^{12} miles   B. 6.79×10^7 miles
C. 7.05×10^{13} miles   D. 9.7×10^{10} miles

12. Mr. Kim, a salesperson, is paid $300 a week plus commission. His commission is 5% of his weekly sales. In the month of January, his weekly sales totals were:

Week 1	Week 2	Week 3	Week 4
$8,576	$9,500	$7,362	$10,567

What is his average weekly commission?

A. $429   B. $450   C. $528   D. $1,800

13. Knowing that $2^3 = 2 \times 2 \times 2 = 8$, what number in the box would make the following TRUE?

$$8^6 = 2^{\square}$$

A. 9   B. 15   C. 18   D. 24

14. Miranda earns $7.50 an hour for the first 40 hours a week she works. She earns time and a half for any hours over 40 she works during the week and double time for hours worked on the weekend. Her time card for one week is shown below. How much did Miranda earn?

Mon.	Tues.	Wed.	Thurs.	Fri.	Sat.
$8\frac{1}{2}$	9	$9\frac{1}{2}$	8	7	$3\frac{1}{2}$

A. $341.25 B. $361.88
C. $375   D. $382.50

15. A fraction is equivalent to $\frac{3}{8}$. The sum of the numerator and denominator is 33. What is the fraction?

16. Suppose you visited Canada and took $325 to spend. The rate of currency exchange was $1.1515 Canadian dollars per U.S. dollar. To the nearest dollar, how many Canadian dollars would you get for the exchange?

17. Helene is paid at the rate of $6.50 an hour for the first 40 hours a week that she works. She is paid time and a half for any hours over 40. How much more will Helene make working 50 hours compared with working 46 hours?

18. If five students share $450 in the ratio 1 : 2 : 3 : 4 : 5, how much is the largest share?

19. A baseball player's batting average is the ratio of the number of hits to the official number of times at bat. A player had 150 hits during a season and wound up with a batting average of .300. What was the total number of times he was at bat for the season?

20. A printer charges 4.2 cents per copy of a standard size original. There is an additional charge of one-half cent for each copy on colored paper. How much would you pay for 100 copies of an original on white paper and 100 copies on blue paper?

21. Ground beef sells for $2.19 per pound. If a package of ground beef costs $4.25, what is the weight of the package to the nearest hundredth of a pound?

22. Because of a printer malfunction, Harold could not read some of the information on the monthly statement from his checking account. From the information given, find the closing balance of Harold's account.

Account Summary		
Number 00-537-387-5		
Beginning balance 08/01	875.45	
3 deposits/credits	xxxxxxx	
3 checks/debits	xxxxxxx	
service charge	xxxxxxx	
Ending balance 08/31		
Date Amount	Date	Amount
08/02 135.00+	08/22	35.92−
08/05 163.50−	08/25	214.35+
08/11 14.75−	08/29 printing checks	11.45−
	08/31 interest	3.45+

23. Mary puts $1,500 in a bank certificate that pays an annual rate of 4.5% compounded annually. No withdrawals or deposits are made. How much will the certificate be worth (to the nearest dollar) at the end of 7 years?

24. If a principal of $1,000 is saved at an annual yield of 8% and the interest is kept in the account, in how many years will the principal double in value?

25. The cost of a hamburger goes from $2.00 to $2.25. Determine the percent of increase. Explain your approach.

26. In York City, the sales-tax rate is increased from 7% to 7.25%. Under this change, how much additional tax would you pay in purchasing an item priced at $800? Show your process in determining the answer.

27. The scale on a map is $\frac{1}{2}$ inch = 80 miles. How far apart are two cities that are $4\frac{3}{4}$ inches apart on the map? Explain your answer and approach.

28. If 4, 5, and 7 are factors of a number, list four other numbers that would also be factors of the number.

29. Your friend applies the Distributive Property to multiplication and determines $2(3 \times 5) = 2(3) \times 2(5)$. Write a paragraph explaining how you would convince your friend that he is incorrect.

30. Every Monday, at Capri Pizza, lucky customers can get free slices of pizza and free soda. Every 10th customer gets a free plain slice of pizza and every 12th customer gets a free cup of soda. On the first Monday of March, Capri Pizza had 211 customers.

    a. How many free pizza slices were given away? How many cups of soda were given away?

    b. When Jackie came into Capri Pizza, the owner told her that she was the first person to get both free items (the free slice of pizza and the free soda). What number customer must Jackie have been? How many other customers (from the 211 customers) would also get both free items?

    c. Suppose that the owner also decides to give away free bag of potato chips to every 7th customer. Would any of the 211 customers be lucky enough to get all three free items? Explain.

31. Your local supermarket offers two brands of cheese sticks:

    Brand A: 12-ounce package for $2.49

    Brand B: 15-ounce package for $3.19

    a. Which is the better buy? Show how you arrived at your answer.

    b. Suppose the one that is a better buy now has a 10% price increase. Is it still the better buy? Explain.

32. Given: $0.4 < A < 0.5$

    $$0.7 < B < 0.9$$
    $$0 < C < 0.1$$
    $$1 < D < 2$$
    $$4 < E < 5$$

    If $X = A + B$, note that the number line shows a possible location of X.

Using the number line below, insert a mark and a capital letter to show one possible location for each of the following:

- P if $P = A \times B$
- Q if $Q = B^2$
- R if $R = 3C - 3D$
- S if $S = \sqrt{E}$

Explain your locations for any two of the four questions.

Spatial Sense and Geometry

Macro A

Recognize, visualize, analyze, and apply geometric properties, relationships, and patterns in real-world and/or problem-solving contexts using models, manipulatives, or technology.

2 A 1 Geometric Terms

Term	Illustration	Definition
point	$\bullet A$	a basic undefined term (A point has no dimensions.)
line ($\overleftrightarrow{AB}$)	A B	a basic undefined term (A line has one dimension.)
ray ($\overrightarrow{AB}$)	A B	the part of line AB that contains point A and all the points of AB that are on the same side of point A as point B
line segment ($\overline{AB}$)	A B	two points and all the points between them that lie on the line containing the two points

Term	Illustration	Definition
midpoint		the point on a line segment that divides it into two equal lengths
plane		a basic undefined term (A plane has two dimensions.)
polygon		a closed figure in a plane formed by three or more sides that are line segments with common endpoints (Each side intersects exactly two other sides, but only at their endpoints.)
vertex of a polygon		a point where two adjacent sides meet
diagonal of a polygon		a segment joining nonconsecutive vertices of the polygon
polyhedron		a closed 3-dimensional figure made up of flat polygonal regions
vertex		in a polyhedron, where 3 or more edges intersect
edge		in a polyhedron, a line segment in which a pair of faces intersect
face		in a polyhedron, the flat polygonal surfaces that intersect to form the edges of the polyhedron
angle (∠ABC)		two rays that share a common endpoint

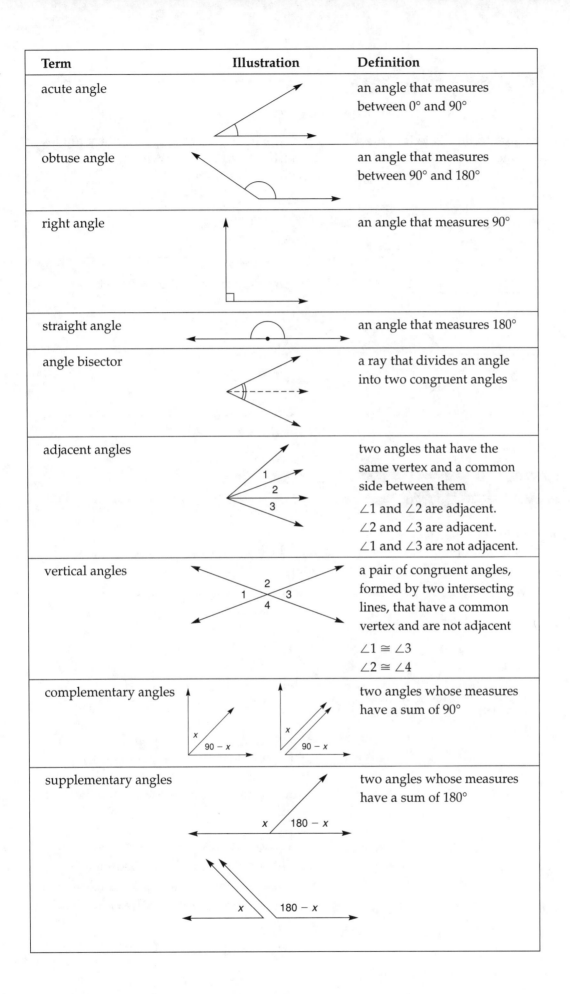

Term	Illustration	Definition
acute angle		an angle that measures between 0° and 90°
obtuse angle		an angle that measures between 90° and 180°
right angle		an angle that measures 90°
straight angle		an angle that measures 180°
angle bisector		a ray that divides an angle into two congruent angles
adjacent angles		two angles that have the same vertex and a common side between them ∠1 and ∠2 are adjacent. ∠2 and ∠3 are adjacent. ∠1 and ∠3 are not adjacent.
vertical angles		a pair of congruent angles, formed by two intersecting lines, that have a common vertex and are not adjacent ∠1 ≅ ∠3 ∠2 ≅ ∠4
complementary angles		two angles whose measures have a sum of 90°
supplementary angles		two angles whose measures have a sum of 180°

MODEL PROBLEMS

1. Draw and label a figure to illustrate the following situation. Planes *A* and *B* intersect. Planes *B* and *C* intersect, but planes *A* and *C* do not intersect.

Solution:

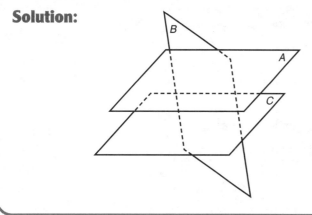

2. The measures of two supplementary angles are in the ratio of 2 : 3. What is the degree measure of the larger angle?

Solution:

$$2x + 3x = 180°$$
$$5x = 180°$$
$$x = 36°$$

The larger angle is $3x$, so $3(36°) = 108°$

PRACTICE

1. What is the measure of the complement of the complement of an angle of 30°?

  A. 30°
  B. 60°
  C. 120°
  D. 250°

2. The measures of two supplementary angles are in the ratio of 4 : 5. What is the degree measure of the smaller angle?

  A. 20°
  B. 80°
  C. 100°
  D. 160°

3. In which of the following diagrams are $\angle a$ and $\angle b$ vertical angles?

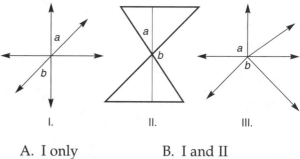

  I.   II.   III.

  A. I only   B. I and II
  C. I and III   D. I, II, and III

4. Which of the following statements is always TRUE?

  A. Vertical angles are supplementary.
  B. The complement of an obtuse angle is acute.
  C. The supplement of an obtuse angle is acute.
  D. Complementary angles are congruent.

5. Draw and label the following figure. Planes P and Q intersect each other. They both intersect plane R.

6. If D is the midpoint of $\overline{AC}$ and C is the midpoint of $\overline{AB}$, what is the length of $\overline{AB}$ if $BD = 12$ cm?

7. If $\overrightarrow{BD}$ is the angle bisector of $\angle ABC$ and $\overrightarrow{BE}$ is the angle bisector of $\angle ABD$, what is m$\angle ABC$ if m$\angle DBE = 36$?

8. If a polyhedron has 8 faces and 12 vertices, how many edges will it have?

9. A polygon has 9 diagonals. How many sides does it have?

10. Find the measure of the angle made by the hands of a clock at 4:30.

2 A 2 Properties of Geometric Figures

Polygons

A *polygon* is a closed figure in a plane formed by three or more sides that have common endpoints. Each side intersects exactly two other sides but only at their endpoints.

Polygons may be classified by number of sides:

3—triangle	7—heptagon
4—quadrilateral	8—octagon
5—pentagon	9—nonagon
6—hexagon	10—decagon

n—n-gon

A *regular polygon* is a convex polygon with all sides congruent and all angles congruent.

The sum of the measures of the interior angles of a convex polygon with n sides is $S = 180°(n - 2)$.

 **MODEL PROBLEM**

ABCDE is a regular pentagon. What is the measure of each interior angle of the figure?

Solution: Since a pentagon has 5 sides, $n = 5$. Therefore, to find the sum of the measures of the interior angles of the pentagon, use the formula $S = 180°(n - 2)$

$$= 180°(5 - 2)$$
$$= 180°(3) = 540°$$

Since the pentagon is regular, all angles are equal. Therefore, to find the measure of each interior angle, divide 540 by 5. Each interior angle equals 108 degrees.

Triangles

In a triangle, the sum of the lengths of any two sides must be greater than the length of the third side. The sum of the interior angles of a triangle is 180°.

Classification of Triangles:

1. *by number of congruent sides:*
   no sides congruent: *scalene triangle*
   two sides congruent: *isosceles triangle*
   all sides congruent: *equilateral triangle*

2. *by types of angles:*
   one right angle: *right triangle*
   one obtuse angle: *obtuse triangle*
   all acute angles: *acute triangle*

 **MODEL PROBLEMS**

1. In $\triangle ABC$, m$\angle A = 52°$ and m$\angle B = 12°$. Classify $\triangle ABC$ as acute, right, or obtuse.

Solution: The sum of the angles of the triangle is 180°.

$52 + 12 = 64$

$180 - 64 = 116$

m$\angle C = 116°$. $\angle C$ is an obtuse angle.

Answer: $\triangle ABC$ is an obtuse triangle.

2. If two sides of a triangle have lengths of 4 cm and 7 cm, what is the range of lengths that is possible for the third side?

Solution: The sum of the measures of any two sides of the triangle must be greater than the third side.

CASE 1: 7 cm represents the longest side.

the third side $+ 4$ cm > 7 cm

the third side > 3 cm

CASE 2: The third side is the longest side.

7 cm $+ 4$ cm $>$ the third side

11 cm $>$ the third side

Answer: 3 cm $<$ the third side $<$ 11 cm

Quadrilaterals

Special quadrilaterals are classified on the basis of lengths of sides, angle measure, and parallel sides.

Name	Illustration	Characteristics
parallelogram		quadrilateral with both pairs of opposite sides parallel and congruent quadrilateral with both pairs of opposite angles congruent
rectangle		parallelogram with right angles
rhombus		parallelogram with all sides congruent
square		rhombus with right angles
trapezoid		quadrilateral with one pair of opposite sides parallel
isosceles trapezoid		trapezoid with congruent legs

MODEL PROBLEMS

1. Which of the following statements is true?

    A. All rectangles are parallelograms.
    B. All parallelograms are rectangles.
    C. All quadrilaterals are trapezoids.
    D. All trapezoids are parallelograms.

Solution: A rectangle is a special parallelogram with right angles. Therefore, any rectangle must be a parallelogram.

Answer: A

2. A quadrilateral *ABCD* has vertices *A*(0, 0), *B*(6, 0), *C*(7, 5), *D*(1, 5). What is the best name for quadrilateral *ABCD*?

    A. Rectangle   B. Trapezoid
    C. Parallelogram   D. Rhombus

Solution: Plot the points (all of which are in the first *quadrant*) and examine the properties of the resulting figure.

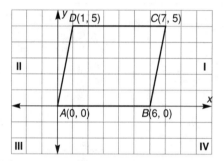

Since both pairs of opposite sides are parallel, the figure is a parallelogram. Since adjacent sides are not congruent, it is not a rhombus. Since there are no right angles, it is not a rectangle.

Answer: C

Circles

A *circle* is a closed plane figure that represents all of the points a specified distance from a point called the *center.*

Key parts of a circle are pictured in the diagram.

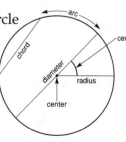

If two or more circles have the same center, they are known as *concentric circles.*

MODEL PROBLEM

A circle with a center at (5, 0) passes through the point (1, 0). What is the length of a diameter of the circle?

Solution: Since the center is at (5, 0) and (1, 0) is on the circle, the length of a radius is the distance from (5, 0) to (1, 0), or 4 units.

Answer: A diameter has a length of 8 units.

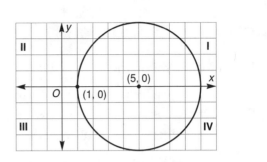

PRACTICE

1. Which of the following sets of lengths does NOT represent a triangle?

   A. 1, 1, 1   B. 3, 4, 5
   C. 4, 4, 8   D. 5, 12, 13

2. If the measure of one angle of a triangle is equal to the sum of the measures of the other two, then the triangle is always

   A. Acute   B. Obtuse
   C. Right   D. Isosceles

3. Which of the following cannot exist?

   A. Isosceles right triangle
   B. Isosceles obtuse triangle
   C. Scalene right triangle
   D. Right obtuse triangle

4. The measures of the angles of a triangle are in the ratio of 2 : 2 : 5. What type of triangle is it?

   A. Isosceles triangle   B. Acute triangle
   C. Right triangle   D. Scalene triangle

5. In parallelogram ABCD, what is the measure of ∠C?

   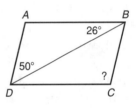

   A. 76°   B. 86°   C. 100°   D. 104°

6. Quadrilateral ABCD has vertices at A(−2, 2), B(−2, −4), C(5, −8), D(5, 6). What is the most specific name for the quadrilateral?

   A. Parallelogram   B. Isosceles trapezoid
   C. Trapezoid   D. Rectangle

7. Triangle ABC has vertices A(1, 6), B(10, 3), C(1, 3). Which of the following must be TRUE concerning ∠A and ∠B?

   A. They are congruent.
   B. They are supplementary.
   C. One is twice as large as the other.
   D. They are complementary.

8. A circle has its center at (4, 0) and a radius of 5 units. Which quadrant(s) does the circle pass through?

   A. I only   B. I and II
   C. I and IV   D. All four

9. Which of the following statements is TRUE?

   I. A rhombus with right angles is a square.
   II. A rectangle is a square.
   III. A parallelogram with right angles is a square.

   A. I only   B. II only
   C. III only   D. I and III

10. A pentagon has two right angles. What is the sum of the measures of the other three angles?

   A. 108°   B. 360°   C. 450°   D. 540°

11. Which of the following could NOT be the sum of the measures of the interior angles of a polygon?

   A. 720°   B. 1,080°   C. 1,900°   D. 1,980°

12. A circle with its center at P has a radius of 5 cm. Line segment PQ measures 6 cm and line segment PR measures 5.1 cm. Which of the following is a TRUE statement?

   A. Points Q and R are inside the circle.
   B. Points Q and R are on the circle.
   C. Points Q and R are outside the circle.
   D. The distance from point R to point Q is 0.9 cm.

13. Three concentric circles are shown. The diameter of the largest circle is 16 units. The diameter of the middle circle is 12 units and the diameter of the smallest circle is 10 units. What is the distance between the smallest circle and the middle circle?

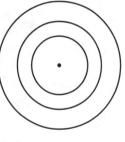

   A. 1.   B. 2   C. 4   D. 6

14. A circular swimming pool has a diameter of 20 feet. Two poles for a volleyball net are each placed 15 feet from the center of the pool and as far apart as possible. What is the length of net needed to be strung tautly between the two poles? (Assume the net extends pole to pole.)

15. In quadrilateral $ABCD$, $A(0, 0)$, $B(0, 5)$, $C(4, 11)$, $D(4, k)$. What value of k will make $ABCD$ a parallelogram?

16. There are 50 paper quadrilaterals in a box. If 18 are rectangles, 30 are rhombuses, and 7 are squares, how many of the quadrilaterals would be of a type other than rectangle, rhombus, or square?

17. Two vertices of a triangle are (0, 0) and (6, 0). List four possible sets of coordinates for the third vertex such that the triangle would be a right scalene triangle.

18. Explain why the measure of $\angle a$ equals the measure of $\angle c$.

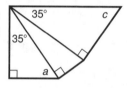

19. Draw the diagram resulting from the following directions. Rectangle $ABCD$ has side AD removed. Segments drawn from A and D meet at point E, outside the rectangle, such that m$\angle E$ = 100. What type of polygon is $ABCDE$? What is the sum of the measures of $\angle EAB$ and $\angle EDC$? Explain your justification for the answer to this last question.

20. Two sides of a triangle each measure 8 cm.

   a. Divide the following list of integers into two groups.

      1, 2, 3, 8, 10, 12, 18, 20, 30

      Group 1: possible lengths for the third side of the triangle

      Group 2: lengths that are not possible for the third side of the triangle.

   b. What is the smallest positive integer that cannot represent the length of the third side?

   c. For the triangles that are possible, with sides of integral lengths, draw and label the lengths of the sides for one acute triangle and one obtuse triangle.

21. One angle of a triangle has a measure equal to half the measure of each of the other two angles.

   a. Classify this triangle according to sides.
   b. Write an equation (using x as a variable) you could use to find the measure of the angles of the triangle.
   c. What are the measures of the three angles of this triangle?
   d. Explain why you cannot find the perimeter of this triangle.

22. If two circles have unequal radii, there are different configurations that can be drawn to show how these circles might intersect. Here is a configuration in which the two circles intersect in two points.

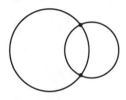

   a. Draw as many different diagrams as necessary to show all other possible ways the two circles can be pictured in terms of points of intersection.
   b. A circle has center at $(0, 0)$ and a radius of 5 units. A second circle has a center at $(0, 7)$ and a radius of 4. Show a sketch of these circles in order to determine the number of points of intersection between them.

2 A 3 Geometric Relationships

Lines

In a plane, distinct lines will either *intersect* or be *parallel*. *Perpendicular lines* intersect at right angles.

Lines will be parallel if certain relationships exist between pairs of angles formed when the lines are cut by a third line, called a *transversal*.

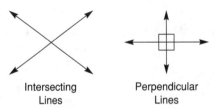

Intersecting Lines   Perpendicular Lines

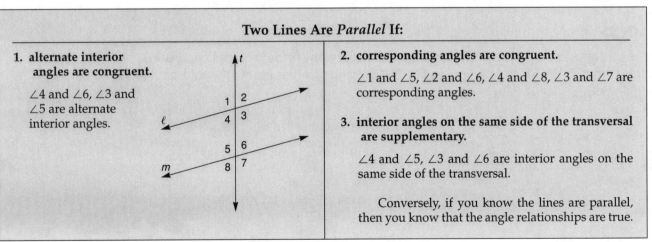

Two Lines Are *Parallel* If:

1. **alternate interior angles are congruent.**

   ∠4 and ∠6, ∠3 and ∠5 are alternate interior angles.

2. **corresponding angles are congruent.**

   ∠1 and ∠5, ∠2 and ∠6, ∠4 and ∠8, ∠3 and ∠7 are corresponding angles.

3. **interior angles on the same side of the transversal are supplementary.**

   ∠4 and ∠5, ∠3 and ∠6 are interior angles on the same side of the transversal.

   Conversely, if you know the lines are parallel, then you know that the angle relationships are true.

Skew lines are lines that do not intersect and are not in the same plane.

1. Line *a* is parallel to line *b*. Line *c* is perpendicular to line *b*. Line *d* is parallel to line *c*. Line *e* is perpendicular to line *d*. How is line *a* related to line *e*?

Solution: Draw a diagram to determine the relationship.

Answer:

Line *e* is parallel to line *a*.

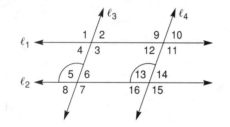

2. In the given diagram, $\angle 5$ is congruent to $\angle 13$ (in symbols, $\angle 5 \cong \angle 13$). Based on that information, what pairs of lines can you conclude are parallel?

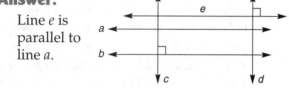

Solution: $\angle 5$ and $\angle 13$ are corresponding angles formed by ℓ_3 and ℓ_4 being cut by ℓ_2. Since $\angle 5 \cong \angle 13$, $\ell_3 \parallel \ell_4$. Since no additional information is provided about angles, you cannot conclude that ℓ_1 is parallel to ℓ_2.

3. $\ell \parallel m$. Find the measure of *x*.

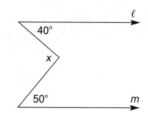

Solution: Draw in line *r* such that $r \parallel \ell$ and $r \parallel m$. $m\angle 1 = 40$ and $m\angle 2 = 50$ by alternate interior angle relations. Hence, $x = 40 + 50 = 90$.

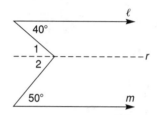

Locus

A *locus* of points is a set of all the points that satisfy one or more given conditions. For example, the locus of points in the plane *r* units from a point *P* would be the circle with center at *P* and radius *r*.

MODEL PROBLEM

On the coordinate plane, what would be the locus of points equidistant from the lines $x = -3$ and $x = 5$?

Solution: Draw the graph to help visualize the situation.

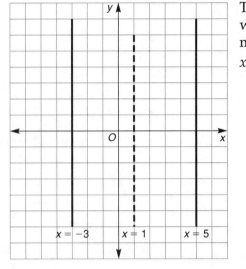

The locus of points equidistant from the two given lines would be a line parallel to the given lines and located midway between them. The locus would be the vertical line $x = 1$.

PRACTICE

1. How many pairs of skew lines are represented by the edges of a cube?

   A. 0   B. 6   C. 12   D. 24

2. Parallel lines s and t are 6 units apart. Point P is on line s. How many points are in the locus of points equidistant from s and t and, at the same time, 3 units from point P?

   A. 0   B. 1   C. 2   D. 4

3. If ray AB is perpendicular to ray AC, what is the measure of $\angle EAG$?

   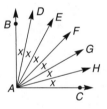

   A. 15°   B. 30°
   C. 36°   D. 60°

4. $ACDF$ is a rectangle divided into two squares. How many pairs of line segments in the diagram are perpendicular?

   A. 3   B. 4
   C. 6   D. 14

5. Given $\overleftrightarrow{AB} \perp \overleftrightarrow{CD}$ and $\overline{FG} \parallel \overline{EH}$, which of the following would be true about triangles EOH and GOF?

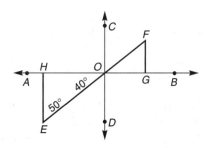

A. The two triangles are congruent.
B. The two triangles are congruent right triangles.
C. The two triangles are isosceles.
D. The two triangles are similar right triangles.

6. Based on the diagram, which of the following may be FALSE?

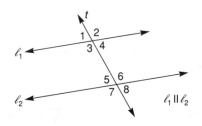

A. $\angle 1 \cong \angle 4$
B. $\angle 1 \cong \angle 5$
C. $\angle 1$ is supplementary to $\angle 3$
D. $\angle 1 \cong \angle 7$

7. In the diagram, if $\ell_1 \parallel \ell_2$, $\ell_2 \parallel \ell_3$, and $\ell_1 \perp \ell_4$, which of the following statements must be true?

   I. $\ell_1 \parallel \ell_3$ II. $\ell_2 \perp \ell_4$ III. $\ell_3 \perp \ell_4$

A. I only
B. II only
C. I and II
D. I, II, and III

8. How many pairs of parallel lines are shown?

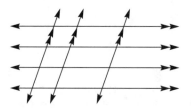

9. Find the coordinates of the point that is equidistant from the points (1, 5) and (9, 5) and, at the same time, equidistant from the points (9, 5) and (9, 12).

10. For this diagram, you are told that $m\angle 3 = m\angle 5$. How does the appearance of the diagram contradict the given information? Write out an explanation.

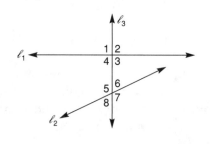

2 A 4 Inductive and Deductive Reasoning

Deductive reasoning is a system of reasoning used to reach conclusions that must be true whenever the assumption on which the reasoning is based is true.

  Inductive reasoning is reasoning that uses a number of specific examples to arrive at generalizations or predictions.

MODEL PROBLEMS

1. Here is a deductive proof that the measure of an exterior angle of a triangle is equal to the sum of the two nonadjacent interior angles.

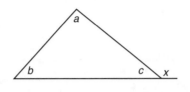

$m\angle a + m\angle b + m\angle c = 180$	measures of angles of a triangle total 180°
$m\angle c + m\angle x = 180$	supplementary angles
$m\angle a + m\angle b + m\angle c = m\angle c + m\angle x$	substitution
$m\angle a + m\angle b = m\angle x$	subtraction property of equality

If you wanted to explore this theorem through inductive reasoning, discuss the approach you would use.

Solution:

Draw several different triangles with one exterior angle shown. Using a protractor measure the exterior angle and the two nonadjacent interior angles in each of the triangles. Compare the sum of the two interior angles with the measure of the exterior angle. Conclude they are the same.

2. Given that $\angle A$ and $\angle C$ are complementary angles and $\angle B$ and $\angle C$ are complementary angles, which of the following conclusions follows?

A. $\angle A$ and $\angle B$ are complementary   B. $\angle A \cong \angle B$ C. $\angle A \cong \angle B \cong \angle C$
D. $\angle A, \angle B, \angle C$ are supplementary

Solution:

If $\angle A$ and $\angle C$ are complementary then $m\angle A + m\angle C = 90$.

If $\angle B$ and $\angle C$ are complementary then $m\angle B + m\angle C = 90$.

It follows that $m\angle A + m\angle C = m\angle B + m\angle C$. Therefore, $m\angle A = m\angle B$ and $\angle A \cong \angle B$.

Answer: B

PRACTICE

1. Using a ruler and grid paper or an automatic drawing program, give evidence of the following theorem:

   "A point on the perpendicular bisector of a line segment is equidistant from the endpoints of the segment."

2. Use induction to show evidence of the following theorem:

   "If two parallel lines are cut by a transversal, then each pair of corresponding angles is congruent."

3. Determine if the given conjecture is true or false. Explain your answer and give a *counterexample* (a false example) if the conjecture is false.

   Given: *ABCD* is a rectangle.
   Conjecture: *AB* = *BC* and *CD* = *DA*

4. If △*PQR* is equilateral then m∠*P* = 60. If m∠*P* ≠ 60, then what can you conclude?

5. Does the conclusion follow from the given argument? If yes, explain why; if no, explain why not.

   If three angles of a triangle are acute, then the triangle is acute. If △*DEF*, angle *D* and angle *F* are acute. Therefore, △*DEF* is acute.

2 A 5 Spatial Relationships

Common Three Dimensional Figures		
Type	**Illustration**	**Description**
pyramid		a polyhedron in which the base is a polygon and the lateral faces are triangles with a common vertex
prism		a solid with 2 faces (bases) formed by congruent polygons that lie in parallel planes and whose other faces are rectangles
cone		a solid consisting of a circular base and a curved lateral surface which extends from the base to a single point called the vertex
cylinder		a solid with congruent circular bases that lie in parallel planes.
sphere		the set of all points a given distance from a given point

To Visualize or Represent a Figure:

1. Make a drawing—use grid paper or isometric dot paper.
2. Think about a physical model.
3. Create a physical model.

1. Which of the following pieces of cardboard cannot be folded along the dotted lines to make a closed box?

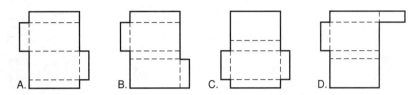

A.   B.   C.   D.

Solution: METHOD 1: Copy the four patterns onto paper or cardboard. Cut them out and fold on dotted lines to determine which would work and which would not work.

METHOD 2: Envision the folds and the relationships of the different faces.

Answer: Choice A would not make a closed box because opposite faces would not turn out to be congruent.

2. A plane passing through a solid gives a cross section of the solid. Determine the cross section of a cone if a plane passes through the cone parallel to the base.

Solution: You can combine the strategy of drawing a diagram with the strategy of thinking about a physical model.

Think of a traffic cone being cut by a piece of cardboard parallel to the base. What do you see when the vertex has been cut off the cone?

Answer: The top of the cone is a circle.

3. From the views given below make a model and then draw a corner view.

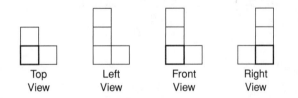

Top
View

Left
View

Front
View

Right
View

Solution: If you use cubes to represent the views, then the top view tells us that the base has 3 blocks and that the figure has columns of different heights. The left view shows blocks flush with the surface. The left back must be three blocks high. From the front and right views it is clear the other columns are one block high. Hence, the figure should look like this:

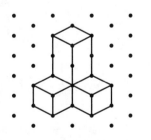

1. Which of the following patterns will NOT fold to form a cube?

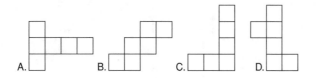

2. Which figure will be formed by folding the given pattern along the dotted lines?

   A. Hexagonal prism
   B. Hexagonal pyramid
   C. Cone
   D. Triangular prism

3. A plane passing through a solid gives a cross section of the solid. Which of the following plane figures can be a cross section of a triangular prism?

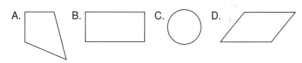

4. If rectangular region *ABCD* is rotated 360° about $\overline{BC}$, which of the following three-dimensional solids is formed?

   A. Cone   B. Pyramid
   C. Prism   D. Cylinder

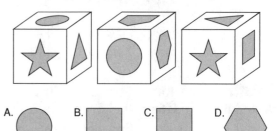

5. Given the three views of the cube below, what shape is opposite the triangle?

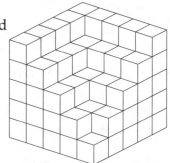

6. How many cubes are needed to build the given figure?

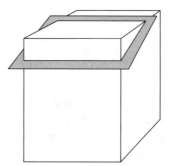

7. What would the cut surface of the following solid look like?

8. Explain why the diagram shown cannot be folded along the dotted lines to make a closed box. Suggest a modification in the diagram to allow the folding to result in a closed box.

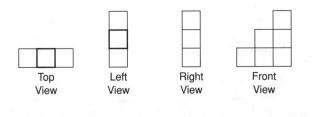

9. Draw the solid figure described by the given views.

Top View   Left View   Right View   Front View

10. For the given solid, sketch the top, left, right, and front views.

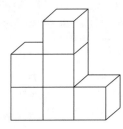

ASSESSMENT MACRO A

1. Two lines are cut by a transversal as shown. As a result, which of the following statements is NOT necessarily true?

   A. ∠1 supplementary to ∠2
   B. ∠1 supplementary to ∠4
   C. ∠5 ≅ ∠7
   D. ∠6 ≅ ∠4

2. The measures of the angles shown are in the ratio of $1 : 2 : 3$. What is the degree measure of the middle angle, ∠2?

   A. 30°   B. 60°   C. 90°   D. 120°

3. The angles of a triangle are in the ratio of $1 : 2 : 6$. What kind of triangle results?

   A. Acute   B. Right
   C. Obtuse   D. Isosceles

4. Which of the following is TRUE?

   A. Every square is a rhombus.
   B. Every rectangle is a square.
   C. Every rhombus is a square.
   D. Every parallelogram is a rectangle.

5. A solid figure was cut by a plane forming a cross section that was a triangle. From which of the following solids would it NOT be possible to obtain a triangular cross section?

   A. Pyramid   B. Cube
   C. Cylinder   D. Prism

6. p is the measure of the vertex angle of an isosceles triangle with base angles measuring 70° each. q is the measure of one of the two acute angles of a right triangle. Which of the comparisons is correct?

   A. $p < q$ B. $p > q$ C. $p = q$
   D. The comparison cannot be completed with the given information.

7. Four straws are going to be used to form quadrilaterals. If two of the straws are each 6 inches long and the other two are each 8 inches long, which of the following quadrilaterals could NOT be formed?

   A. Rectangle   B. Parallelogram
   C. Rhombus   D. Kite

8. *Given:* $\overset{\leftrightarrow}{AC}$ is parallel to $\overset{\leftrightarrow}{DF}$.
       $\overset{\leftrightarrow}{AF}$ is parallel to $\overset{\leftrightarrow}{BE}$.

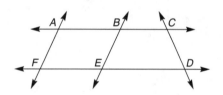

Based on the above, which of the following is TRUE?

   A. *ABEF* and *BCDE* are parallelograms.
   B. *ACDF* and *BCDE* are trapezoids.
   C. *BCDE* is an isosceles trapezoid.
   D. *ABEF* is a rhombus.

9. If you spin this two-dimensional figure about the axis shown, you will generate a solid of revolution. Which solid would you generate?

10. Which of the following patterns folds to give the cube pictured?

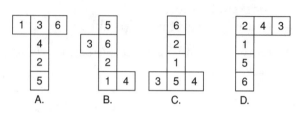

   A.   B.   C.   D.

11. Which pattern can be folded to form a cylinder?

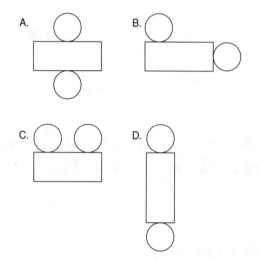

12. In which of the following solids are the top view, front view, and right side view identical?

   A. Pyramid   B. Cylinder
   C. Triangular prism   D. Cube

13. Which of the following are faces of an octagonal prism?

   I. octagon
  II. triangle
  III. rectangle

   A. I only   B. I and II
   C. II and III   D. I and III

14. What is the sum of the measure of the interior angles of a polygon of 32 sides?

15. The diagram contains two squares and an equilateral triangle. What is the degree measure of ∠x?

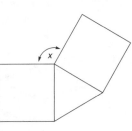

16. The measures of two supplementary angles are in the ratio 1 : 9. Find the degree measure of the smaller angle.

17. One angle of a triangle measures 100°. If the other two angles are in the ratio of 1 to 3, what is the measure of the larger acute angle?

18. *ABCDEF* is a regular hexagon. Three diagonals are drawn as shown. What is the measure of ∠*FBD*?

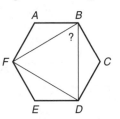

19. In pentagon *ABCDE,* diagonals $\overline{AC}$ and $\overline{AD}$ are drawn. The measures of ∠*B* and ∠*E* are each 100°. What is the sum of the measures of ∠*a*, ∠*b*, ∠*c*, ∠*d*, ∠*e*, ∠*f*, and ∠*g*?

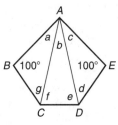

20. How many sides does a polygon have if the sum of the measures of the interior angles is 2,520°?

21. How many sides does a polygon have if the sum of the measures of the interior angles is 1,800°?

22. Find the measure of the angle made by the hands of a clock at 9:30.

23. An equilateral triangle is inscribed in a circle. What is the degree measure of each arc formed?

24. Describe the locus of all points in a plane that are equidistant from the sides of a given angle and are in the interior of that angle.

OPEN-ENDED QUESTIONS

25. A line segment has point *M* as its midpoint. Make a sketch to determine the number of points that are 3 units from the given line segment and, at the same time, 4 units from point *M*. How would the answer change if the second condition asked for points 2 units from point *M*?

26. Explain why a pentagon cannot exist with the following interior angles: one interior angle measures 100° and each additional interior angle measures 15° more than the previous one.

27. In right scalene triangle *ABC*, *B* is the vertex of the right angle. A line segment is drawn from *B* to $\overline{AC}$ forming two triangles. Determine the possible types of triangles formed. Show a diagram for each possible case.

28. Determine if the following conjecture follows from the given information. If it does, explain why. If it does not, explain why not. Provide a counterexample as well.

    Two angles are congruent. ∠1 ≅ ∠2 Therefore, ∠1 and ∠2 are vertical angles.

29. Draw the top, left, right, and front views for the given solid.

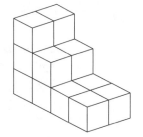

30. The larger cube is built from smaller cubes. The exterior of the large cube is painted red. The larger cube is then separated into the 27 smaller cubes.

a. Copy and complete the table to show the number of smaller cubes containing the indicated red faces.

b. If a large cube is built from 64 smaller congruent cubes and the exterior of the large cube is painted red, how many of the smaller cubes will not have red paint on any faces?

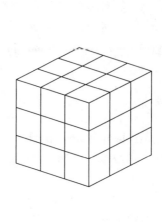

number of red faces	number of small cubes
0	
1	
2	
3	
4	
5	
6	

Macro B

Use coordinate geometry in problem-solving situations and apply the principles of congruence, similarity, and transformations.

2 B 1 Congruence

Congruent figures have the same size and the same shape. The symbol for congruence is ≅ .

Characteristics of Congruent Polygons:

1. Corresponding angles are congruent.
2. Corresponding sides are congruent.

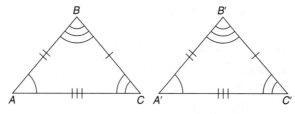

$$\triangle ABC \cong \triangle A'B'C'$$

$\angle A \cong \angle A'$	$\overline{BC} \cong \overline{B'C'}$
$\angle B \cong \angle B'$	$\overline{AC} \cong \overline{A'C'}$
$\angle C \cong \angle C'$	$\overline{AB} \cong \overline{A'B'}$

MODEL PROBLEM

Give a set of coordinates for point Q so that parallelogram $ABCD$ will be congruent to parallelogram $MNPQ$.

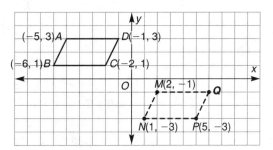

Solution:

If parallelogram $ABCD \cong$ parallelogram $MNPQ$, $\overline{AD} \cong \overline{MQ}$.

Since $AD = 4$ units, MQ must be 4 units.

Answer: Point Q must be located at $(6, -1)$.

PRACTICE

1. Quadrilateral $ABCD \cong$ quadrilateral $PQRS$. Which of the statements below does NOT follow?

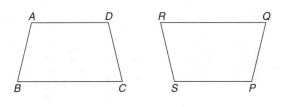

   A. $\overline{AB} \cong \overline{PQ}$
   B. $\overline{AD} \cong \overline{RS}$
   C. $\overline{BC} \cong \overline{QR}$
   D. $\overline{CD} \cong \overline{RS}$

2. Which of the following everyday applications is an illustration of congruence?

   A. Obtaining an enlargement of a picture
   B. Duplicating a key
   C. Preparing a scale drawing
   D. Buying a scale model of a sports car

3. $\triangle DAB \cong \triangle CBA$. Which angle is congruent to $\angle BDA$?

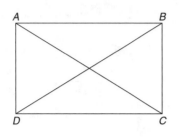

   A. $\angle ACB$
   B. $\angle BAC$
   C. $\angle ABC$
   D. $\angle CAB$

4. Which statement is TRUE?

   I. If two circles have the same area, the circles are congruent.
   II. If two squares have the same area, the squares are congruent.
   III. If two rectangles have the same area, the rectangles are congruent.

   A. II only   B. III only
   C. I and II only   D. II and III only

5. $\triangle ABC \cong \triangle EFG$, $m\angle A = 40$, $m\angle F = 105$. What is the measure of $\angle C$?

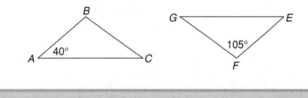

6. What is the x-coordinate of point Z such that trapezoid $ABCD \cong$ trapezoid $WXYZ$?

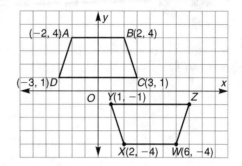

7. Take a regular octagon. Draw all the diagonals from one vertex. How many pairs of congruent triangles are formed?

8. Bob thinks that if the angles of one triangle are congruent to the angles of another triangle, then the two triangles must be congruent. Do you agree with Bob? Explain. Give an example to support your answer.

9. Draw two triangles that meet each of the given conditions. Be sure to label the dimensions on the triangles.

   a. The two triangles have equal areas and are congruent.
   b. The two triangles have equal areas and are not congruent.

2 B 2 Similarity

Similar figures have the same shape. The symbol for similar is ~.

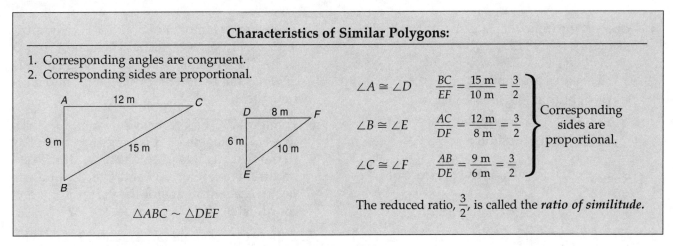

Characteristics of Similar Polygons:

1. Corresponding angles are congruent.
2. Corresponding sides are proportional.

$\angle A \cong \angle D$ $\quad \dfrac{BC}{EF} = \dfrac{15 \text{ m}}{10 \text{ m}} = \dfrac{3}{2}$

$\angle B \cong \angle E$ $\quad \dfrac{AC}{DF} = \dfrac{12 \text{ m}}{8 \text{ m}} = \dfrac{3}{2}$ $\left.\begin{array}{c} \\ \\ \end{array}\right\}$ Corresponding sides are proportional.

$\angle C \cong \angle F$ $\quad \dfrac{AB}{DE} = \dfrac{9 \text{ m}}{6 \text{ m}} = \dfrac{3}{2}$

$\triangle ABC \sim \triangle DEF$

The reduced ratio, $\dfrac{3}{2}$, is called the *ratio of similitude*.

MODEL PROBLEMS

1. Quadrilateral *ABCD* ~ quadrilateral *PQRS*. Find *x, y, z*.

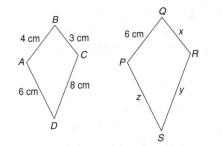

Solution: In similar quadrilaterals, corresponding sides are in proportion.

$\dfrac{AB}{PQ} = \dfrac{BC}{QR}$ $\quad \dfrac{AB}{PQ} = \dfrac{CD}{RS}$ $\quad \dfrac{AB}{PQ} = \dfrac{AD}{PS}$

$\dfrac{4}{6} = \dfrac{3}{x}$ $\qquad \dfrac{4}{6} = \dfrac{8}{y}$ $\qquad \dfrac{4}{6} = \dfrac{6}{z}$

$4x = 18$ $\qquad 4y = 48$ $\qquad 4z = 36$

Answer: $x = 4.5$ cm $\quad y = 12$ cm $\quad z = 9$ cm

Note: Since $\overline{PQ}$ and $\overline{AB}$ are corresponding sides and the length of $\overline{PQ}$ is one and one-half times the length of $\overline{AB}$, the missing sides in the larger quadrilateral must be one and one-half times the corresponding sides in the smaller quadrilateral.

2. A person 6′ tall is standing near a tree. If the person's shadow is 4′ long and the tree's shadow is 10′ long, what is the height of the tree?

Solution: During the day, two objects that are near each other have shadows whose measures are proportional to the heights of the objects, resulting in similar triangles.

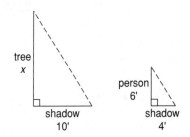

Write a proportion:

$$\dfrac{\text{tree}}{\text{tree's shadow}} = \dfrac{\text{person}}{\text{person's shadow}}$$

$$\dfrac{x}{10} = \dfrac{6}{4}$$

$$4x = 60$$

$$x = 15$$

Answer: The tree is 15′ high.

1. Which of the following statements about similar figures is TRUE?

   A. All squares are similar.
   B. All right triangles are similar.
   C. All rhombuses are similar.
   D. All hexagons are similar.

2. $\triangle ABC \sim \triangle DEF$. What is the measure of $\overline{DF}$?

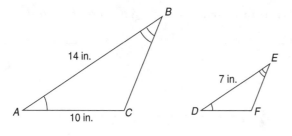

   A. 5 in.   B. 11 in.   C. 17 in.   D. 20 in.

3. Rectangle $ABCD \sim$ rectangle $PQRS$. If $AD = 3$ mi and $PS = 5$ mi, which of the quantities that follow would NOT be in the ratio $3 : 5$?

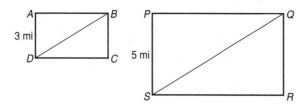

   A. AB and PQ
   B. BD and QS
   C. $m\angle A$ and $m\angle P$
   D. The perimeter of $ABCD$ and the perimeter of $PQRS$

4. A tree casts a 20-m shadow at the same time that a 6-m pole casts an 8-m shadow. Find the height of the tree.

5. The wing of a model of a glider is a right triangle with sides 3 inches, 4 inches, and 5 inches. In the actual glider, the hypotenuse is 35. Find the perimeter of the wing on the actual glider.

6. Triangle ABC has vertices $A(-4, 1)$, $B(-1, 1)$, $C(-4, 3)$. Triangle PQR is to be drawn similar to the first triangle. If two vertices of the second triangle are $P(2, 1)$ and $Q(8, 1)$, find the positive y-coordinate for the vertex R if the x-coordinate is 8.

7. If these two triangles are similar, explain why $m\angle x$ must be equal to $m\angle y$.

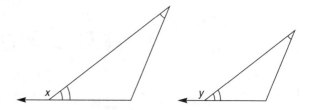

8. After takeoff, a plane ascends at a constant rate. At a ground distance of 240 meters from takeoff, the plane's altitude is 80 meters. Find its altitude at a ground distance of 960 meters from takeoff. Draw a diagram to support your solution.

9. $\triangle ABC$ has vertices $A(0, 0)$, $B(6, 0)$, $C(3, 3)$. If the coordinates of each vertex are multiplied by 2, will the new figure be similar to the original figure? Give the coordinates of the new vertices. Plot the coordinates and draw both triangles on the grid.

10. Jennifer knows that two rectangles are similar and that the ratio of corresponding sides is $2 : 5$. She also knows that the ratio of the perimeters of the two rectangles is $2 : 5$. Because of this, she thinks that the ratio of the areas of the two rectangles is $2 : 5$. Using grid paper, draw approximate rectangles to prove or disprove Jennifer's thinking.

2 B 3 Transformations

Reflection and Line Symmetry

When you look in a mirror, you see your reflected image. A *reflection* is a flipping of a geometric figure about a line to obtain its mirror image.

Note that under a reflection, the **orientation** of the figure is changed. For example, point A is to the left of B in the original figure, or **preimage**, but, in the image, point A' is to the right of B'.

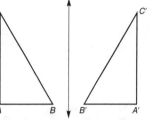

If a line can be drawn through a figure so that the part of the figure on one side of the line is the mirror image of the part on the other side of the line, the figure has **line symmetry**.

MODEL PROBLEMS

1. Draw the reflection of $\triangle ABC$ over the x-axis. State the coordinates of the vertices of the image.

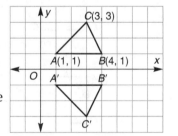

Solution: Point A has coordinates $(1, 1)$. Since point A is 1 unit above the reflecting line, point A' will be 1 unit below the line. Since point $B(4, 1)$ is also 1 unit above the reflecting line, point B' will be 1 unit below the line. Since point $C(3, 3)$ is 3 units above, point C' will be 3 units below.

Answer: point $A(1, 1) \rightarrow$ point $A'(1, -1)$
point $B(4, 1) \rightarrow$ point $B'(4, -1)$
point $C(3, 3) \rightarrow$ point $C'(3, -3)$

2. How many lines of symmetry does a square have?

Solution:

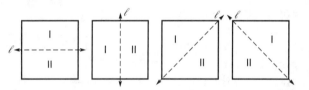

In each of the above figures, line ℓ is a line of symmetry. If the square is folded on line ℓ, then region I will exactly coincide with region II.

Answer: There are four lines of symmetry.

Rotation and Rotational Symmetry

A *rotation* is a turning of an object about a point through a specified angle measure.

A figure will be rotated either clockwise or counterclockwise.

Rotational symmetry exists when a figure is rotated a number of degrees (less than 360°) about a fixed point and the image coincides with the figure.

90° clockwise

MODEL PROBLEMS

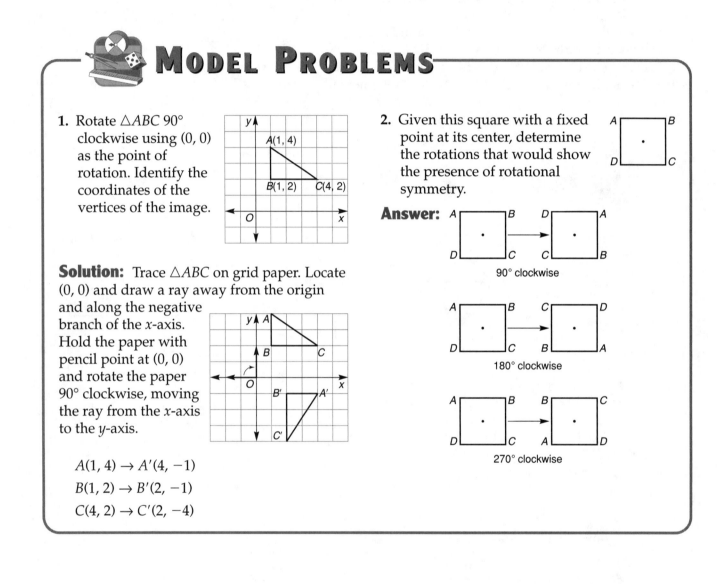

1. Rotate △ABC 90° clockwise using (0, 0) as the point of rotation. Identify the coordinates of the vertices of the image.

A(1, 4)
B(1, 2)   *C*(4, 2)

Solution: Trace △ABC on grid paper. Locate (0, 0) and draw a ray away from the origin and along the negative branch of the *x*-axis. Hold the paper with pencil point at (0, 0) and rotate the paper 90° clockwise, moving the ray from the *x*-axis to the *y*-axis.

$A(1, 4) \rightarrow A'(4, -1)$

$B(1, 2) \rightarrow B'(2, -1)$

$C(4, 2) \rightarrow C'(2, -4)$

2. Given this square with a fixed point at its center, determine the rotations that would show the presence of rotational symmetry.

Answer:

90° clockwise

180° clockwise

270° clockwise

Translation

A *translation* is a sliding of a geometric figure, without turning, from one position to another.

MODEL PROBLEMS

1. Translate △*ABC* right 3 units. State the coordinates of the vertices of the image of △*ABC*.

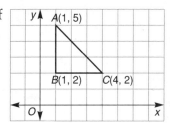

Solution:

The image of *A* under the translation 3 units right is *A'*. Add 3 to the *x*-coordinate of point *A*.

$$A(1, 5) \rightarrow A'(1 + 3, 5) \rightarrow A'(4, 5)$$

Repeat for points *B* and *C*.
$B(1, 2) \rightarrow B'(4, 2)$
$C(4, 2) \rightarrow C'(7, 2)$

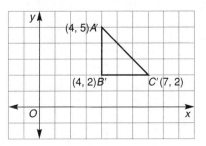

2. Explain the translation used to produce the given image of trapezoid *ABCD*.

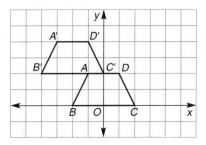

Solution:
$$
\begin{array}{ccc}
A(-1, 2) & \rightarrow & A'(-3, 4) \\
B(-2, 0) & \rightarrow & B'(-4, 2) \\
C(2, 0) & \rightarrow & C'(0, 2) \\
D(1, 2) & \rightarrow & D'(-1, 4)
\end{array}
$$

Both the *x*- and *y*-coordinates changed, indicating that the figure was moved both vertically and horizontally. Since −2 was added to the *x*-coordinates, the *x*-coordinates were moved 2 units left. Since 2 was added to the *y*-coordinates, the *y*-coordinates were moved 2 units up.

Answer: The image of trapezoid *ABCD* was formed by translating the figure left 2 units and up 2 units.

Dilation

A *dilation* is a transformation that reduces or enlarges a figure. In a dilation, every image is similar to its preimage. Every dilation has a point known as the *center of dilation* and a *scale factor k*. If $k > 1$, the dilation is an enlargement. If $0 < k < 1$, the dilation is a reduction. If k is written as a fraction, it represents the ratio of similitude between the image and preimage.

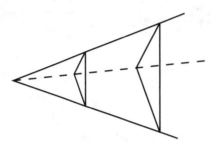

MODEL PROBLEMS

1. Using the diagram, identify the dilation and find its scale factor.

Solution: The dilation is an enlargement because the scale factor is greater than one. $\dfrac{CA'}{CA} = \dfrac{2}{1}$

2. Draw a dilation of rectangle *PQRS* with vertices $P(2, 2)$, $Q(4, 2)$, $R(4, 3)$, $S(2, 3)$. Use the origin as the center and a scale factor of 3. How does the perimeter of the preimage compare to the perimeter of the image?

Solution: With center at $(0, 0)$ you find the image of each vertex by multiplying its coordinates by the given scale factor.

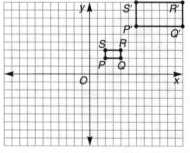

$P(2, 2) \rightarrow P'(6, 6)$

$Q(4, 2) \rightarrow Q'(12, 6)$

$R(4, 3) \rightarrow R'(12, 9)$

$S(2, 3) \rightarrow S'(6, 9)$

From the graph it follows the perimeter of $PQRS = 6$ and the perimeter of $P'Q'R'S' = 18$. The perimeter was enlarged by a scale factor of 3.

1. A figure undergoes a transformation. The preimage and the image are not congruent. What type of transformation took place?

    A. Dilation
    B. Reflection
    C. Rotation
    D. Translation

2. A polygon is dilated with center at the origin and scale factor 3.5. The image is then dilated with center at the origin and scale factor x. What value of x would cause the second image to be congruent to the original polygon?

    A. 3.5   B. 1   C. $\frac{2}{7}$ D. -3.5

3. Which of the following polygons has 36° rotational symmetry?

    A. Equilateral triangle
    B. Regular pentagon
    C. Regular octagon
    D. Regular decagon

4. What would the coordinate of point A' be if $\triangle ABC$ located at $A(1, 1)$, $B(4, 1)$, $C(2, 3)$ was translated left 3 units?

    A. $(4, 1)$ B. $(-2, 1)$ C. $(-2, 2)$ D. $(1, 2)$

5. If the line segment joining $A(-2, 3)$ and $B(1, 6)$ is rotated 90° clockwise about point A, the coordinates of the image of B are:

    A. $(1, 0)$ B. $(1, 6)$ C. $(-2, 0)$ D. $(-2, 6)$

6. Which of the following figures has NO lines of symmetry?

    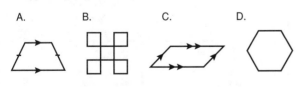

7. What are the coordinates of the image of $(5, 0)$ under a rotation of 90° clockwise about the origin?

    A. $(-5, 0)$ B. $(0, 5)$ C. $(0, -5)$ D. $(5, -5)$

8. Which of the following could be the image of $\triangle ABC$ reflected over the x-axis?

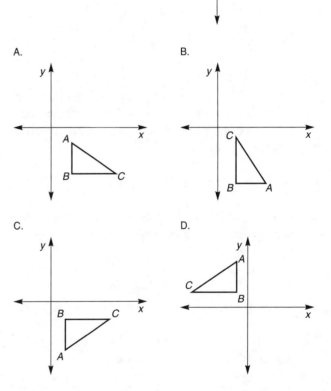

9. Which figure below could be a translation of △ABC?

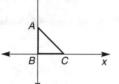

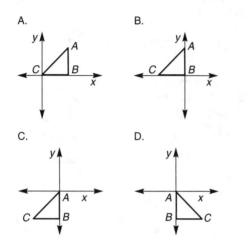

A.

B.

C.

D.

10. If △ABC with vertices A(−2, 0), B(−2, −2), C(−4, −2) is reflected over the x-axis and then the image is reflected over the y-axis, which coordinates would represent the final image of point A?

A. (−2, 0)   B. (2, 0)   C. (0, 2)   D. (0, −2)

11. If the x-axis is the line of reflection, what would be the coordinates of the reflected image of P(6, 1)?

A. (6, −1)   B. (−6, 1)
C. (−6, −1)   D. (6, 1)

12. Which of the following could be the reflected image of **B** over a vertical line?

A. ⌀   B. ⊟   C. **B**   D. ◖

13. Which figure could be a translation of **R**?

A. ꓤ   B. �toⅽ   C. **R**   D. **Я**

14. Which of the following transformations could be a rotation?

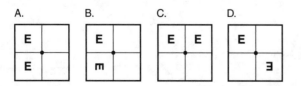

15. Which of the following would NOT represent a translation?

A. $(x, y) \rightarrow (x + 7, y + 1)$
B. $(x, y) \rightarrow (x, y - 3)$
C. $(x, y) \rightarrow (x + 7, y)$
D. $(x, y) \rightarrow (-x, -y)$

16. △ABC has been rotated clockwise about point (0, 0) to produce the image △A'B'C'. Through how many degrees was △ABC rotated?

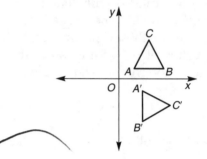

17. Point A is reflected over the x-axis and then the image is reflected over the y-axis, resulting in the point A″ with coordinates (−3, −7). What was the y-coordinate of the original point A?

18. The word MATH when written in column form has a vertical line of symmetry. Find two other words that have a vertical line of symmetry when written in column form.

M
A
T
H

19. The point (2, 1) is rotated 270° clockwise about point (0, 0). What is the y-coordinate of the image?

20. If △RST is translated up 6 units, what will the y-coordinate of point S' be?

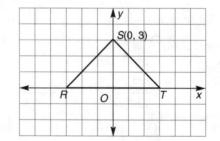

21. Parallelogram *ABCD* was translated down 2 units and right 5 units, resulting in the given image. What was the *x*-coordinate of point *B*?

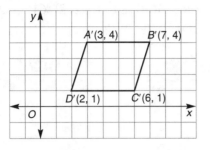

22. Triangle *OAB* with vertices *O*(0, 0), *A*(−3, 0), and *B*(−3, −4) is rotated 180° clockwise about point *O*. Draw the image of triangle *OAB* and state the coordinates of the image.

23. If a line ℓ parallel to the *y*-axis at *x* = 4 is drawn on the given plane and △*ABC* is reflected over the *y*-axis and then over line ℓ, what single transformation could have been used to arrive at the final image?

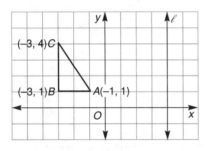

24. △*ABC* with vertices at *A*(−1, 1), *B*(0, 4), and *C*(−3, 3) is rotated 180° clockwise about the origin. What are the vertices of the image of △*ABC*?

25. In △*ABC*, *A*(−1, −2), *B*(0, 3), *C*(1, 1), the image of *A* under a translation is *A*'(−3, 5). What would the image of *B* and *C* be under the same translation?

26. A Ferris wheel's motion is an example of a rotation.

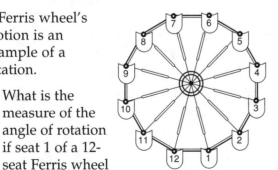

   a. What is the measure of the angle of rotation if seat 1 of a 12-seat Ferris wheel is moved to the seat 6 position?
   b. If seat 1 of a 12-seat Ferris wheel is rotated 240°, find the seat whose position it now occupies.

27. On a coordinate plane, graph the given vertices. Using the origin as the center of the dilation and a scale factor of 2, draw the dilation image. *A*(2, 3), *B*(4, 8), *C*(−3, 5)

28. △*ABC* is mapped onto △*A*'*B*'*C*'. Find the scale factor and state if the dilation is a reduction or an enlargement.

AB = 6 cm	*BC* = 8 cm	*AC* = 10 cm
A'*B*' = 24 cm	*B*'*C*' = 32 cm	*A*'*C*' = 40 cm

29. *AB* = 5 mm. The measure of its dilated image is 7.5 mm. What is the value of the scale factor?

30. △*MNP* was translated down 4 units and right 3 units to form △*M*'*N*'*P*'. △*M*'*N*'*P*' was translated up 6 units and left 6 units to form △*M*"*N*"*P*". Explain how △*M*"*N*"*P*" could have been obtained directly from △*MNP* under a single translation.

31. If the figure on the right is a dilation image of the figure on the left, what is the scale factor for the dilation?

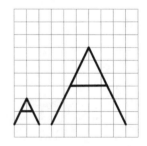

32. A figure *WXYZ*, a dilation center, and an image point *Y*' are given. Copy the diagram and complete the dilation.

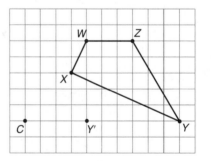

33. A triangle with vertices at (0, 2), (4, 2), and (0, 4) is reflected over the line *y* = 5. The image of the triangle is then reflected over the line *y* = 11.

   a. Give the coordinates of the vertices of the triangle resulting from the second reflection.
   b. What single transformation would also give you the final resulting triangle obtained by the two successive reflections? (Be specific with your answer.)

34. Wrapping paper often consists of a design that is translated over and over to create a pattern. Create an original pattern for wrapping paper by translating a hexagon and an equilateral triangle.

35. Plot the given points to form a figure and its image. Is this an example of a reflection? Explain why or why not.

    figure: $A(-2, 9)$, $B(-2, 2)$, $C(-5, 2)$
    image: $A'(9, 2)$, $B'(2, 2)$, $C'(2, 5)$

2 B 4 Tessellation

A repeating pattern of figures that completely covers a plane region without gaps or overlaps is called a *tessellation*. In any tessellation the sum of the angles about a given point is 360°. For example, a tessellation can be formed using a square.

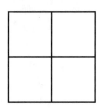

MODEL PROBLEM

Which of the following figures will produce a tessellation? Use diagrams to support your answer.

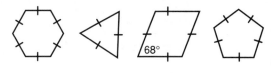

Solution:
hexagon, triangle, rhombus

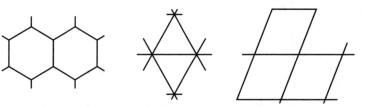

PRACTICE

1. If n represents the number of sides of a regular polygon, which value of n indicates a polygon that will NOT form a tessellation?

   A. 3   B. 4   C. 5   D. 6

2. A dodecagon (12-sided polygon) cannot tessellate by itself. Which of the following figures can be used in combination with the dodecagon to create a tessellation?

   A. Equilateral triangle   B. Square
   C. Regular hexagon   D. Regular octagon

3. The given tessellation illustrates which of the following transformations?

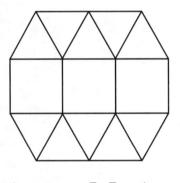

   A. Reflection   B. Rotation
   C. Translation   D. Dilation

4. The given tessellation uses equilateral triangles and regular hexagons. Find another combination of regular polygons that can be used to create a tessellation where each polygon has an even number of sides. Show a sketch of the new tessellation.

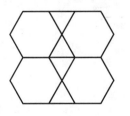

5. Which of the following patterns will NOT tessellate a plane?

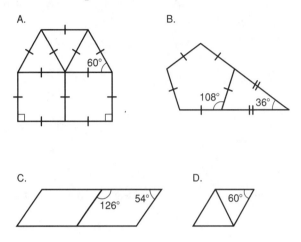

6. An equilateral triangle can be used to create a tessellation. Will other triangles create tessellations? For each of the following situations, if the triangle tessellates, show the tessellation. If it does not tessellate, explain why.

   a. Draw a scalene triangle. Can you create a tessellation using this triangle?
   b. Draw an isosceles triangle. Can you create a tessellation using this triangle?
   c. Draw a right triangle. Can you create a tessellation using this triangle?

   Based on your findings, make a conjecture about triangles and tessellations.

2 B 5 Coordinate Geometry

Every point in the coordinate system can be represented as an ordered pair (x, y).

The rectangular coordinate system can be used to represent geometric situations and solve related problems. Major coordinate geometry topics are midpoint, slope, and distance.

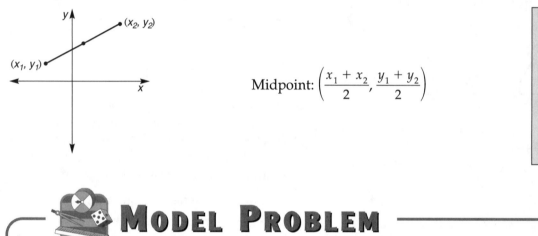

Midpoint of a line segment with endpoints at (x_1, y_1) and (x_2, y_2):

Midpoint: $\left(\dfrac{x_1 + x_2}{2}, \dfrac{y_1 + y_2}{2} \right)$

> **Note:**
>
> The coordinates of the midpoint are the respective averages of the x- and y-coordinates of the endpoints of the segment.

MODEL PROBLEM

A line segment has a midpoint at (3, 4). If one endpoint has coordinates (6, 0), find the coordinates of the other endpoint.

Solution:

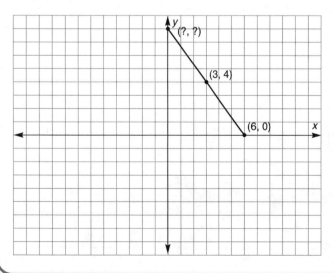

Missing endpoint (x_1, y_1)

Using the midpoint formula

$$3 = \frac{x_1 + 6}{2} \qquad\qquad 4 = \frac{y_1 + 0}{2}$$

$$x_1 + 6 = 6 \qquad\qquad y_1 + 0 = 8$$

$$x_1 = 0 \qquad\qquad y_1 = 8$$

The endpoint has coordinates (0, 8).

Slope, or steepness, of a line with points at (x_1, y_1) and x_2, y_2):

$$\text{slope} = \frac{y_2 - y_1}{x_2 - x_1}$$

To describe the steepness of a roof, you determine the *vertical rise* compared to the *horizontal run*.

To describe the slope of a straight line, you choose two points on the line and determine the rise and run.

$$\text{Slope} = \frac{\text{rise}}{\text{run}} = \frac{\text{vertical change}}{\text{horizontal change}} = \frac{\text{difference of } y\text{-coordinates}}{\text{difference of } x\text{-coordinates}}$$

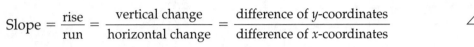

rise

run

MODEL PROBLEM

Show that two different segments on the line $y = x$ have the same slope.

Solution:

Select two points on the line:
  $(0, 0)$ and $(5, 5)$

$$\text{slope} = \frac{5 - 0}{5 - 0} = 1$$

Select two different points on the line:
  $(3, 3)$ and $(-2, -2)$

$$\text{slope} = \frac{3 - (-2)}{3 - (-2)} = \frac{5}{5} = 1$$

The two segments have the same slope, 1.

The slope of the line $y = x$ is the same value, 1, everywhere on the line.

The slope of a line is always a constant value and is the same as the slope of any segment on the line.

If a line is parallel to the *x*-axis, the line has no steepness. Its slope is zero.

If a line is parallel to the *y*-axis, the line has an undefined slope.

If a line rises from left to right, its slope is positive.

If a line falls from left to right, its slope is negative.

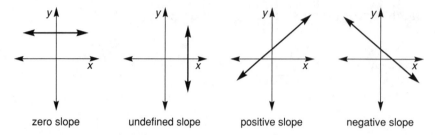

zero slope   undefined slope   positive slope   negative slope

Slopes of parallel lines are equal.

Slopes of perpendicular lines are negative reciprocals of each other.

MODEL PROBLEM

A quadrilateral has vertices at $A(0, 0)$, $B(8, 0)$, $C(11, 3)$, $D(3, 3)$. Show that the quadrilateral is a parallelogram.

Solution: For the quadrilateral to be a parallelogram, both pairs of opposite sides must be parallel. For lines to be parallel, they must have the same slope.

Since $\overline{AB}$ and $\overline{DC}$ are both horizontal lines, the slope of each line is 0. Thus, $\overline{AB} \parallel \overline{DC}$.

$$\text{slope } \overline{AD} = \frac{3-0}{3-0} = 1 \quad \text{slope } \overline{BC} = \frac{3-0}{11-8} = 1 \quad \text{Thus, } \overline{AD} \parallel \overline{BC}.$$

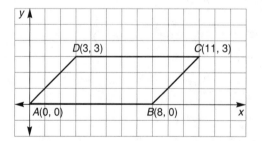

$ABCD$ is a parallelogram because slopes show that both pairs of opposite sides are parallel.

Distance can be determined in one of two ways.

1. If the segment joining the two points is either horizontal or vertical, the distance between the points is found by subtraction.
2. If the two points are the endpoints of an oblique segment, the distance (length) is found by using the Pythagorean Relation ($a^2 + b^2 = c^2$).

 **MODEL PROBLEMS**

1. Find the distance from (2, 0) to (6, 3).

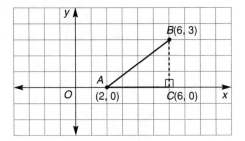

Solution: Draw $\overline{BC}$ to form a right triangle.

$$(AC)^2 + (BC)^2 = (AB)^2$$
$$4^2 + 3^2 = (AB)^2$$
$$16 + 9 = (AB)^2$$
$$25 = (AB)^2$$

Answer: $AB = 5$ units

Note: Using the distance formula,

$$d = \sqrt{(x_2 - x_1)^2 + (y_2 - y_1)^2}$$

is the same as using the Pythagorean Relation.

2. Plot the following points on a grid:

$$A(1, 0), B(1, 3), C(5, 3), D(5, 0)$$

What is the length of $\overline{BD}$?

Solution:

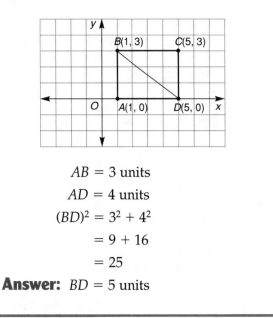

$$AB = 3 \text{ units}$$
$$AD = 4 \text{ units}$$
$$(BD)^2 = 3^2 + 4^2$$
$$= 9 + 16$$
$$= 25$$

Answer: $BD = 5$ units

1. Segment AB is horizontal. What must be the coordinates of point B if the length of $\overline{AB}$ is 10 units?

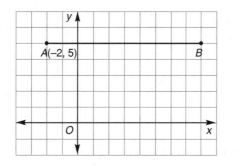

   A. $(10, 0)$ B. $(10, 5)$ C. $(8, 5)$ D. $(12, 5)$

2. If you plot the following points on a grid, what kind of triangle is formed?

   $A(0, 0), B(8, 0), C(10, 5)$

   A. Right   B. Acute
   C. Obtuse   D. Isosceles

3. A rectangle located in the first quadrant has two vertices at $(0, 0)$ and $(0, 6)$. Where would the other two vertices be if the area of the rectangle is 30 square units?

   A. $(0, 5)$ and $(6, 5)$ B. $(5, 0)$ and $(6, 5)$
   C. $(5, 0)$ and $(5, 6)$ D. $(9, 0)$ and $(9, 6)$

4. What is the best name for quadrilateral $ABCD$ defined by $A(0, 0), B(8, 0), C(10, 5), D(2, 5)$?

   A. Rectangle   B. Trapezoid
   C. Isosceles trapezoid   D. Parallelogram

5. If a line passes through the points $(3, 5)$ and $(1, k)$ and has a slope of 2, what must be the value of k?

6. Two vertices of a triangle are $A(0, 0)$, and $B(6, 0)$. The third vertex in the first quadrant is $(6, k)$. The area of triangle ABC is 30 square units. Find the value of k.

7. Find the slope of the line.

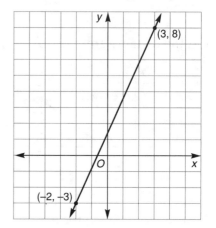

8. Find the coordinates of point C on the line $y = 4$ such that $\overline{CD} \parallel \overline{AB}$. Explain your procedure.

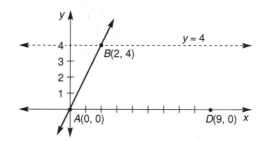

9. Line segment AB has $A(2, 3)$ and $B(10, -3)$. Point M is the midpoint of AB and point P is the midpoint of segment AM. What are the coordinates of point P?

10. Given $A(1, 5), B(1, -1), C(9, -1)$.

   a. Plot the points on a grid, and form a figure.
   b. Give the best name for the figure formed.
   c. Find the area.

 **Vectors**

A *vector* is a directed line segment. It contains a point of origin, an endpoint, and a direction. The length of a vector is the distance between the point of origin and the endpoint. On a coordinate plane direction is measured counterclockwise from the direction of the positive x-axis. On a map, direction is measured clockwise from the north.

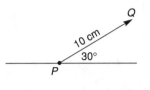

Vector $\overrightarrow{PQ}$ with direction 30° and length 10 cm

One can model a path consisting of two or more components by using a sequence of vectors. Walking three blocks north and then four blocks east and then two blocks north can be represented as:

A vector sum $\overrightarrow{AB} + \overrightarrow{BC}$ means the vector $\overrightarrow{AB}$ followed by the vector $\overrightarrow{BC}$.

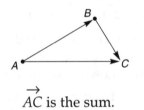

$\overrightarrow{AC}$ is the sum.

A vector can be multiplied by a constant, resulting in a change in the magnitude but not in the direction. For example, if vector $\overrightarrow{AB}$ is represented by (1, 2) then $3\overrightarrow{AB}$ can be represented by (3, 6).

MODEL PROBLEMS

1. Let vector $\overrightarrow{OA}$ be represented by the ordered pair (2, 4). If vector $\overrightarrow{OB}$ is represented by (5, −2), what ordered pair represents vector $\overrightarrow{AB}$?

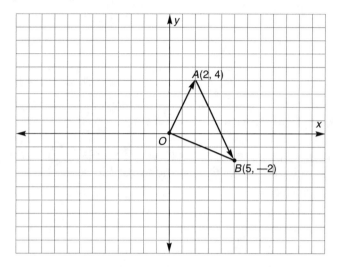

Solution: Vector $\overrightarrow{OA}$ has the origin as one endpoint and the second endpoint at the point (2, 4); 2 over and 4 up. $\overrightarrow{OB}$ is represented by the origin as one endpoint and the second endpoint being located at the point (5, −2); over 5 and down 2. The ordered pair representing $\overrightarrow{AB}$ is determined by the movement needed to go from A to B—over 3 and down 6, which translates to (3, −6).

2. A car starts at point A and travels 5 miles east and then turns and travels 12 miles south reaching point B. Using grid paper, make a scale drawing using vectors to show the car's movement, starting from point A. Draw a vector that would show the direct path from point A to point B.

   What would be the approximate number of miles the car could have traveled along the path?

   Approximately how many degrees from north would this path be? Explain how you arrived at your answer.

Solution:

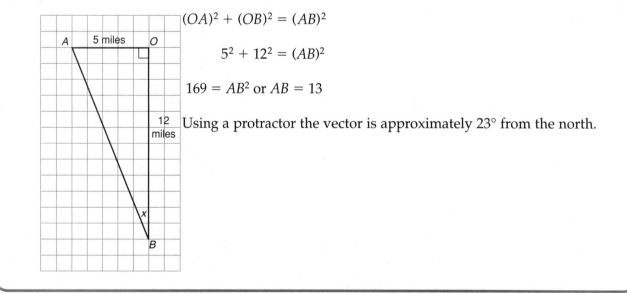

Since a right triangle is formed,

$(OA)^2 + (OB)^2 = (AB)^2$

$5^2 + 12^2 = (AB)^2$

$169 = AB^2$ or $AB = 13$

Using a protractor the vector is approximately 23° from the north.

1. Which vector represents a walk of 5 blocks north followed by 6 blocks west?

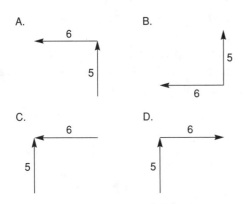

A.

B.

C.

D.

2. Let vector $\overrightarrow{OM}$ be represented by the ordered pair (1, 5). Vector $\overrightarrow{OR}$ is represented by (x, y). Find x and y such that (9, 4) represents vector $\overrightarrow{MR}$.

3. A boat is traveling north at 24 mph. A wind from the west is blowing the boat eastward at 7 mph. Find the speed of the boat and the direction the boat is moving.

4. If vector $\overrightarrow{TM}$ is represented by the ordered pair (1, 7) and $k\overrightarrow{TM}$ is represented by (4, 28), find the value of k.

5. In still water a swimmer's speed is 2 mph. If the swimmer swims perpendicular to a 4-mph current, find the actual speed and direction of the swimmer.

   a. Draw a diagram to illustrate the situation.
   b. Explain how you determine the speed and the angle of the current.

1. Let vector $\overrightarrow{OA}$ be represented by the ordered pair (1, 4). If vector $\overrightarrow{OB}$ is represented by (6, −1), what ordered pair represents vector $\overrightarrow{AB}$?

   A. (7, −3)   B. (5, −5)   C. (5, 3)   D. (5, 5)

2. The vector diagram below models which addition problem? (Note the origin is the starting point.)

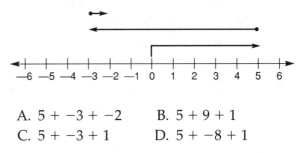

   A. 5 + −3 + −2   B. 5 + 9 + 1
   C. 5 + −3 + 1   D. 5 + −8 + 1

3. Which of the following would NOT represent three consecutive vertices of a rectangle?

   A. (2, 0), (6, 0), (6, 3)
   B. (0, 0), (1, 4), (5, 3)
   C. (0, 0), (3, 3), (2, 4)
   D. (0, 0), (2, 1), (2, 3)

4. Which of the following is NOT true?

   A. Squares with the same perimeter are congruent.
   B. Any two equilateral triangles must be congruent.
   C. Any two isosceles right triangles must be similar.
   D. Noncongruent squares have unequal areas.

5. The coordinates of the image of $P(2, -3)$ after a reflection about the x-axis are:

   A. (2, −3)   B. (−2, −3)
   C. (2, 3)   D. (−2, 3)

6. $\overline{AB}$ has endpoints (0, 0) and (5, 0).
   $\overline{CD}$ has endpoints (−1, −1) and (−6, −1).
   $\overline{EF}$ has endpoints (6, 0) and (9, 4).
   $\overline{GH}$ has endpoints (1, 4) and (−5, 4).

   Which segment does NOT have a length of 5 units?

   A. $\overline{AB}$ B. $\overline{CD}$ C. $\overline{EF}$ D. $\overline{GH}$

7. Right triangle ABC, with the right angle at vertex C, is reflected about the x-axis. Which of the following properties of triangle ABC is changed as a result of the reflection?

   A. The measure of angle A
   B. The orientation of the triangle
   C. The length of the hypotenuse
   D. The area of the triangle

8. Under a translation, which of the following properties of a figure are preserved?

   I. the length of the sides
   II. the measure of the angles
   III. the orientation of the figure

   A. I only   B. II only
   C. I and II   D. I, II, and III

9. Which set of transformations on the white figure below will NOT make the black figure become the image of the white figure?

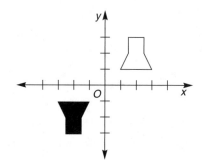

   A. Reflection over the y-axis followed by a reflection over the x-axis
   B. Translation 4 units left followed by a reflection over the x-axis
   C. Translation 4 units left followed by a translation 2 units down
   D. Rotation 180° clockwise about the origin

10. If a triangle in the second quadrant is reflected over the x-axis and its image is next reflected over the y-axis, in which quadrant would the final image appear?

    A. I   B. II   C. III   D. IV

11. Rectangle $PQRS$ is translated 4 units to the left and 3 units down, producing the image of rectangle $PQRS$ with vertices $P'(-3, -2)$, $Q'(-3, 2)$, $R'(3, 2)$, $S'(3, -2)$. What were the original coordinates of point R?

    A. (7, 5)   B. (11, 5)   C. (7, −1)   D. (0, −2)

12. If △PQR with vertices P(3, 2), Q(7, 2), R(5, −1) is reflected over the y-axis and then the image is translated 3 units to the right, which coordinates would represent the final image of point R?

    A. (−8, 1)   B. (−5, 1)
    C. (−2, −1)   D. (8, 1)

13. Which symbol has 90° rotational symmetry?

    A. X   B. H   C. S   D. 8

14. △ABC has a line segment on the x-axis as its base and a point on the y-axis as its third vertex. The reflection of △ABC over the y-axis causes the image to coincide with the original triangle.

    For which of the following triangles would this relationship be true?

     I. equilateral triangle
    II. isosceles triangle
    III. scalene triangle

    A. I only   B. III only
    C. I and II   D. I, II, and III

15. The point (5, 6) is reflected over the y-axis and the image point is then translated 3 units to the left. What are the coordinates of the final image?

    A. (−5, 6)   B. (−8, 6)   C. (−2, 6)   D. (2, 6)

16. Which of the following does NOT show a pair of similar triangles?

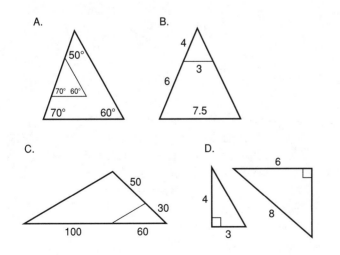

17. Triangle ABC with A(2, 1), B(6, 1), C(8, 2) is transformed to produce an image triangle A'B'C' with A'(−2, 1), B'(−6, 1), C'(−8, 2). Which of the following describes this transformation?

    A. A translation 4 units to the left
    B. A rotation 180° counterclockwise
    C. A reflection over the y-axis
    D. A rotation 270° clockwise

18. Which pair of points determines a line parallel to a line with slope $\frac{2}{3}$?

    A. (1, 4), (2, 5)   B. (4, 5), (6, 8)
    C. (3, 2), (0, 0)   D. (−3, 2), (0, 0)

19. In a circle the coordinates for the endpoints of a diameter are (−3, 2) and (9, −2). Find the coordinates of the center of the circle.

20. Jack wants to use an isosceles triangle with an 18° vertex angle to make a tessellation. How many triangles will have to meet at a vertex to complete the tessellation?

21. Three regular pentagons are similar. Corresponding sides of the three pentagons have lengths in the ratio 1 : 2 : 5. If a side of the smallest pentagon has a length of 6 inches, find the perimeter of the largest pentagon.

22. A tree casts a shadow 20 meters long at the same time that a man 2 meters tall casts a shadow of 5 meters. What is the height of the tree?

23. A ramp that is 50 yards long slopes up from the ground to a height of 15 yards. A vertical support beam is to be built 20 yards from the top of the ramp. How long (in yards) would the support beam be?

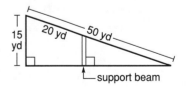

24. Two vertices of a rectangle are A(0, 0) and B(0, 6). The other two vertices in the first quadrant are C(k, 6) and D(k, 0). The perimeter of ABCD is 28 units. Find the value of k.

25. A triangular plot of land is represented by the diagram. $AB = 80$ feet, $BD = 80$ feet, $BC = 80$ feet, and $DF = 160$ feet. Fencing is going to be constructed along the parallel segments BC, DE, and FG. How many total feet of fencing will be needed for the three sections?

OPEN-ENDED QUESTIONS

26. Given $A(-4, 0)$, $B(4, 0)$, $C(1, 8)$, $D(-1, 8)$.

   a. Plot the points and form a figure.

   b. Give the best name for the figure formed.

   c. Find the area. Show the steps involved in your process.

27. Two triangles are each isosceles and have unequal areas. Explain why there is NOT enough information provided to be able to determine if the two triangles are similar. Draw a sketch as part of your explanation.

28. A boat starts at point A and travels 15 mph in a northern direction. A wind from the west is blowing the boat eastward at 8 mph. Find the speed of the boat and the direction the boat is moving.

   a. Draw a diagram to illustrate the situation.

   b. Explain how you determine the speed and the direction of the boat.

29. An equilateral triangle has three lines of symmetry as shown.

Sketch regular polygons with 4, 5, 6, and 8 sides and complete the following table to indicate the number of lines of symmetry for each regular polygon.

number of sides	3	4	5	6	8
number of lines of symmetry	3	?	?	?	?

30. $ABCD$ is a parallelogram. Segments AE and CF are each perpendicular to diagonal BD. There are three pairs of congruent triangles present in the figure.

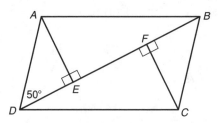

   a. List the three pairs of congruent triangles.

   b. In order to make $\triangle AEB$ similar to $\triangle DEA$, what type of quadrilateral would $ABCD$ have to be? Explain why.

Apply the principles of measurement and geometry to solve problems involving direct and indirect measurement.

2 C 1 Perimeter and Circumference

The *perimeter* of a figure is the total distance around the outside of the figure. Perimeter is measured in linear units.

For a circle, the distance around the outside is called *circumference* instead of perimeter.

Formulas can be used to find the perimeters of common geometric figures.

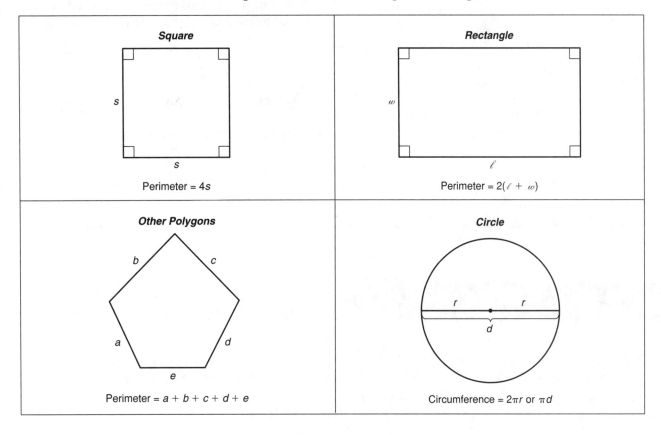

Square

s

s

Perimeter = 4s

Rectangle

w

ℓ

Perimeter = 2($\ell + w$)

Other Polygons

b c

a d

e

Perimeter = $a + b + c + d + e$

Circle

r r

d

Circumference = 2πr or πd

MODEL PROBLEMS

1. A rectangle with a width of 5 cm has the same perimeter as an equilateral triangle with a side of 12 cm. Find the length of the rectangle.

Solution: Draw a diagram to help.

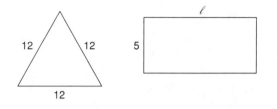

Perimeter is the distance around the outside.

$$P_{triangle} = 12 + 12 + 12 = 36$$
$$P_{rectangle} = 2(\ell + w)$$
$$P_{triangle} = P_{rectangle}$$
$$36 = 2(\ell + 5)$$
$$36 = 2\ell + 10$$
$$26 = 2\ell$$
$$13 = \ell$$

Answer: 13 cm

2. A circle is inscribed in a square with a perimeter of 24 cm. What is the circumference of the circle?

Solution: Draw a picture to help with the solution.

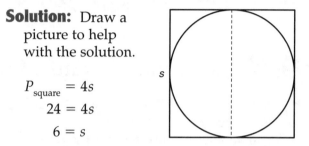

$$P_{square} = 4s$$
$$24 = 4s$$
$$6 = s$$

A side of the square is 6 cm.
The length of a diameter of the circle is equal to the length of a side of the square.

$$C = \pi d$$
$$C = \pi 6$$

Answer: $C = 6\pi$ cm

Note: If a single-number answer is needed, use $\pi = 3.14$ to simplfy:

$$6\pi = 6(3.14) = 18.84 \text{ cm}$$

PRACTICE

1. The perimeter of the rectangle *ABCD* is 40 units and its length is 15 units.

Find the number of units in the perimeter of the square.

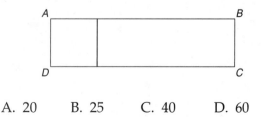

A. 20   B. 25   C. 40   D. 60

2. A rectangle has three vertices at $(-2, 3)$, $(10, 3)$, $(10, 6)$. What is the perimeter of the rectangle?

A. 22   B. 26
C. 30   D. 36

3. If the circumference of a circle is increased from 30π inches to 50π inches, by how many inches is the length of the radius increased?

A. 10   B. 10π C. 20   D. 20π

4. Six congruent squares are shown. Squares added to the figure must share an existing side. What is the minimum number of squares that needs to be added to the diagram in order to increase the perimeter to 18 units?

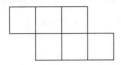

5. A regular pentagon and a regular decagon each have sides with a length of 8 cm. What is the difference between the two perimeters?

6. To the nearest centimeter, what is the perimeter of trapezoid *ABCD*?

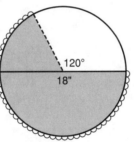

7. A garden hose lies coiled in a circular pile about 2 ft across. If there are 6 coils, estimate the length of the hose.

8. A circular piece of plywood is to be decorated to form a wall hanging. Elena wants to place lace completely around the shaded sector of the circle.

To the nearest inch, how much lace will she need if the diameter of the plywood piece is 18 inches and the measure of the central angle is 120°?

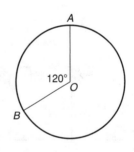

9.

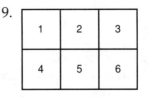

For the given diagram, what happens to the total perimeter of the shape if you remove the following squares? Explain your answers.

a. square 3 only
b. square 2 only
c. Which other square could you remove and have the same effect as in part a?
d. Which other square could you remove and have the same effect as in part b?
e. Draw a diagram to show how you could add three squares to the original figure and thereby change the perimeter from the original 10 units to 14 units.

10. Use a centimeter ruler to determine the length of the radius of the given circle. Using this measurement, find the length of the 120° arc of the circle (to the nearest tenth of a centimeter). Explain how you go about finding the length of this arc.

2 C 2 Area

Area is the number of square units needed to cover a surface.
Formulas can be used to find the areas of common geometric figures.

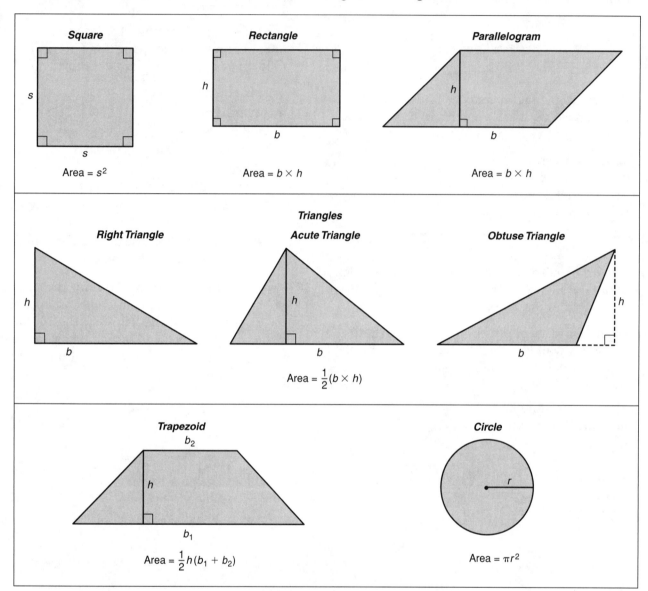

Square

$\text{Area} = s^2$

Rectangle

$\text{Area} = b \times h$

Parallelogram

$\text{Area} = b \times h$

Triangles

Right Triangle

Acute Triangle

Obtuse Triangle

$\text{Area} = \frac{1}{2}(b \times h)$

Trapezoid

$\text{Area} = \frac{1}{2}h(b_1 + b_2)$

Circle

$\text{Area} = \pi r^2$

MODEL PROBLEMS

1. Arrange the three figures in INCREASING order of area.

    I. a rectangle with dimensions of 6 in. by 8 in.
    II. a square with a side of 7 in.
    III. a right triangle with sides of 5 in., 12 in., and 13 in.

    A. rectangle, square, triangle
    B. rectangle, triangle, square
    C. triangle, rectangle, square
    D. square, rectangle, triangle

Solution: Find the areas by using the appropriate formulas.

$$\text{Area (rectangle)} = bh \qquad \text{Area (square)} = s^2$$
$$A = (6)(8) \qquad\qquad A = 7^2$$
$$A = 48 \text{ sq in.} \qquad\qquad A = 49 \text{ sq in.}$$

$$\text{Area (triangle)} = \frac{1}{2}bh$$
$$A = \frac{1}{2}(5)(12)$$
$$A = 30 \text{ sq in.}$$

In increasing order: triangle, rectangle, square

Answer: C

2. A right triangle is inscribed in a circle as shown. Write an expression involving π for the area of the shaded region.

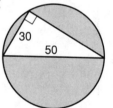

Solution: Since the triangle is a right triangle, the missing leg can be found by the Pythagorean Relation.

$$c^2 = a^2 + b^2$$
$$50^2 = 30^2 + b^2$$

Recognize that these numbers are a multiple of the triple 3, 4, 5.
The missing side is 10(4) or 40 units.

$$\text{area of shaded region} = \text{area of circle} - \text{area of triangle}$$
$$A = \pi r^2 - \frac{1}{2}bh$$
$$A = \pi(25)^2 - \frac{1}{2}(30)(40)$$

Answer: $A = 625\pi - 600$

Using a calculator, you can express the answer as 1,362.5 square units.

1. The area of a rectangle is 200 sq cm and one dimension is 15 cm. Find the length of a diagonal of the rectangle.

   A. 13.3 cm   B. 20.1 cm
   C. 28.3 cm   D. 48.1 cm

2. If a radius of a circle is tripled, then the area is:

   A. Increased by 3
   B. Multiplied by 9
   C. Tripled
   D. Cubed

3. If you draw a square with an an area equal to the area of triangle ABC, how long will each side of the square be?

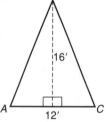

   A. A little less than 7 ft
   B. A little less than 10 ft
   C. A little more than 10 ft
   D. A little less than 14 ft

4. What is the area of the shaded portion of the triangle?

   A. 8 sq in.
   B. 20 sq in.
   C. 36 sq in.
   D. 44 sq in.

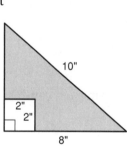

5. If A_L represents the area of the triangle on the left and A_R represents the area of the triangle on the right, which of the following is a correct comparison of the areas?

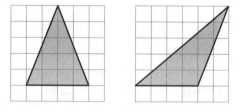

   A. $A_L < A_R$ B. $A_L > A_R$ C. $A_L = A_R$
   D. You cannot make the comparison without additional information.

6. A circle has a diameter with endpoints at $(5, 0)$ and $(-5, 0)$. How many square units are in the area of the circle?

   A. 5π B. 25   C. 25π D. 100π

7. In the figure, each side of the square has been divided into four equal segments. What is the ratio of the shaded area to the total area?

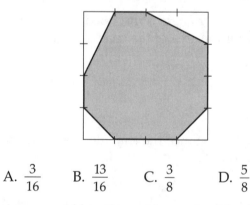

   A. $\dfrac{3}{16}$ B. $\dfrac{13}{16}$ C. $\dfrac{3}{8}$ D. $\dfrac{5}{8}$

8. A trapezoid has three sides each with a length of 5 units. If the height of the trapezoid is 4 units, what is the area of the trapezoid?

9. In a town, the property tax is $0.06 per square foot of land. What would the tax be on the plot of ground pictured?

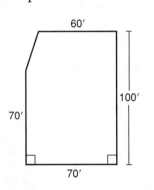

10. If there are 100 square units in the grid, what is the area, in square units, of the shaded figure?

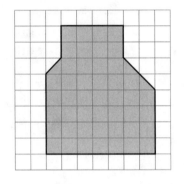

11. The length of a rectangle is increased by 20% and its width is decreased by 10%. Explain how to determine what happens to the area in terms of percent increase or percent decrease. Would the new area be the same if the original length were increased 10% and the original width were decreased 20%? Explain.

12. An isosceles trapezoid in the first quadrant has a lower base with endpoints at (0, 0) and (8, 0). The upper base has endpoints at (r, 6) and (t, 6) where r and t are whole numbers and $r < t$.

   a. What values for r and t would give the largest area for the isosceles trapezoid?

   b. What is this largest area? Show your process in coming up with the area.

   c. Explain why the perimeter of the trapezoid cannot be a whole number. (You may need the Pythagorean theorem to answer part c. See page 88.)

2 C 3 Volume

The *volume* of a solid figure is the number of cubic units that fit inside the solid.
Formulas can be used to find the volumes of common solid figures.

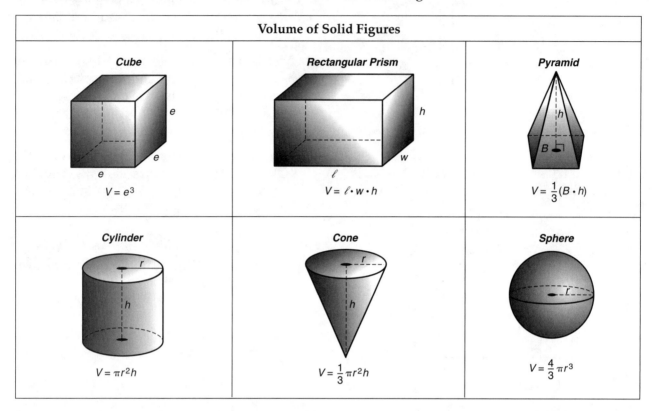

Volume of Solid Figures		
Cube $V = e^3$	**Rectangular Prism** $V = \ell \cdot w \cdot h$	**Pyramid** $V = \frac{1}{3}(B \cdot h)$
Cylinder $V = \pi r^2 h$	**Cone** $V = \frac{1}{3}\pi r^2 h$	**Sphere** $V = \frac{4}{3}\pi r^3$

MODEL PROBLEMS

1. Which of the following rectangular prisms does NOT have a volume of 48 cubic units?

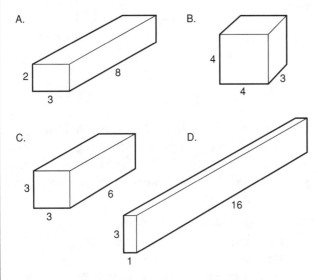

A.

2, 8, 3

B.

4, 4, 3

C.

3, 6, 3

D.

16, 3, 1

Solution: Use $V =$ area of base $\times$ height. For rectangular prism, $V = lwh$.

Prism A: $V = 2 \times 3 \times 8 = 48$ cu units

Prism B: $V = 4 \times 4 \times 3 = 48$ cu units

Prism C: $V = 3 \times 3 \times 6 = 54$ cu units

Prism D: $V = 3 \times 1 \times 16 = 48$ cu units

Answer: C

2. The Air Puff Popcorn Company is considering the three designs shown as new containers for their popcorn.

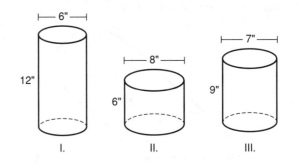

I.   II.   III.

Which container holds the most popcorn?

Solution: The container that holds the most popcorn is the one with the greatest volume.

$$V = \pi r^2 h$$

Container I: $V = 3.14(3)^2 \cdot (12) = 339.12$ in.^{3}

Container II: $V = 3.14(4)^2 \cdot (6) = 301.44$ in.^{3}

Container III: $V = 3.14(3.5)^2 \cdot (9) = 346.185$ in.^{3}

Answer: Container III holds the most popcorn.

PRACTICE

1. If the edge of a cube is doubled, the volume is multiplied by:

A. 2   B. 3   C. 6   D. 8

2. Which of the following has a volume different from the other three volumes?

A. A cylinder with a radius of 4 cm and a height of 9 cm

B. A cylinder with a radius of 5 cm and a height of 6 cm

C. A cylinder with a radius of 2 cm and a height of 36 cm

D. A cylinder with a radius of 6 cm and a height of 4 cm

3. The measure of a radius of a cone is doubled and the measure of the height remains the same. The volume is multiplied by:

A. 2   B. 4   C. 6   D. 8

4. An ice cream log is packaged as a semicircular cylinder as shown. What is the volume of the package in cubic inches?

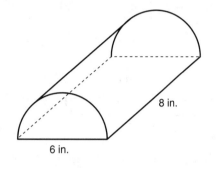

8 in.

6 in.

A. 18π B. 24π C. 36π D. 72π

5. What is the volume of this right triangular prism?

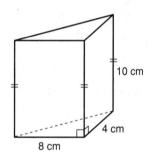

10 cm

4 cm

8 cm

6. Find the number of cubic centimeters in the volume of the solid shown.

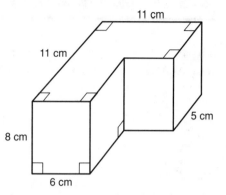

11 cm

11 cm

8 cm

5 cm

6 cm

7. Two cylinders have the same height. If the base of one of the cylinders has a diameter that is three times the diameter of the other base, how do the volumes of the two cylinders compare?

8. A structure is formed with a cone attached to a cylinder. Find the volume of the structure. Show your use of formulas. Give your answer to the nearest cubic inch.

8"

10"

4"

9. You have 80 blocks, each one a cube with a volume of 1 cubic centimeter. List the dimensions of all the different rectangular prisms you can build using all the blocks for each prism. Explain why none of these prisms turns out be a cube.

2 C 4 Surface Area

The *surface area* of a solid is the sum of the areas of all the surfaces of the solid. Surface area is measured in square units.

To find the surface area of a solid:

- Visualize the unfolded pattern made up of the faces of the solid.
- Find the area of each face of the solid.
- Find the sum of the areas.

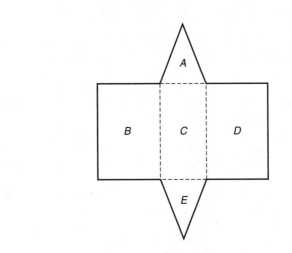

Surface area of the triangular prism = Area A + Area B + Area C + Area D + Area E

MODEL PROBLEMS

1. Find the surface area of the triangular prism shown.

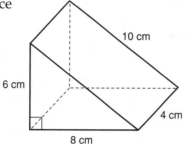

10 cm

6 cm

4 cm

8 cm

Solution: The surface area of the prism equals the area of two triangular faces plus the area of three rectangular faces.

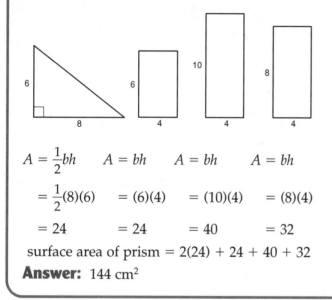

$A = \frac{1}{2}bh$ $A = bh$ $A = bh$ $A = bh$

$= \frac{1}{2}(8)(6)$ $= (6)(4)$ $= (10)(4)$ $= (8)(4)$

$= 24$ $= 24$ $= 40$ $= 32$

surface area of prism $= 2(24) + 24 + 40 + 32$

Answer: 144 cm²

2. If the surface area of the cube is 24 cm², what is the length of an edge of the cube?

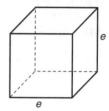

e

e

Solution: Surface area of cube $= 6 \cdot$ area of a face

$$24 = 6 \cdot e^2$$
$$4 = e^2$$
$$2 = e$$

Answer: An edge is 2 cm.

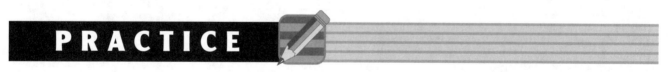

PRACTICE

1. Find the surface area of a cube whose edge has a length of 5 cm.

   A. 100 cm²   B. 120 cm²
   C. 125 cm²   D. 150 cm²

2. Which of the following applications would require finding surface area?

   A. Finding the amount of packing material needed to fill a box
   B. Finding the amount of ribbon needed to tie a bow on a gift box
   C. Determining the amount of wrapping paper needed for a gift box
   D. Determining the amount of water needed to fill a fish tank

3. The diagram shows a structure made with eight cubes. If each cube has an edge of 1 cm, what is the surface area of the structure?

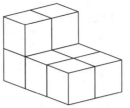

   A. 22 cm²   B. 26 cm²

   C. 28 cm²   D. 30 cm²

4. Of the following solids, which one has the greatest surface area?

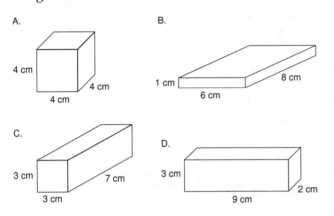

5. The volume of a cube is 27 cubic inches. Find the surface area.

6. The bottom of a box meaures 18 cm by 20 cm. The box is 10 cm high and has no top. What is the surface area of the box?

7. Find x such that the total surface area of the prism is 132 square inches.

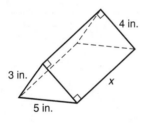

8. Two rectangular prisms have the same volume. Show that it is not necessary for them to have the same surface area. Use a diagram with your explanation.

9. A rectangular solid has a surface area of 42 square units. If the dimensions are each tripled, find the new surface area. Explain your procedure and generalize the relationship between the original surface area and the surface area after the dimensions are tripled.

10. Sketch the figure that the net shown folds into.

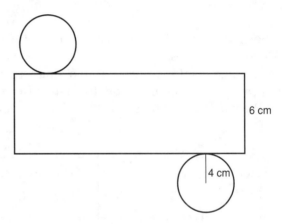

   a. What is the solid called?

   b. Find its volume. Show your process.

   c. Find its surface area. Show your process.

   d. Suppose the "6 cm" and "4 cm" on the figure above were switched. What change would result in the surface area?

2 C 5 Standard and Non-Standard Units of Measure

Measurement Systems

The *metric system* of measurement is a decimal system. The basic unit for length is the *meter*, for weight is the *gram*, and for capacity is the *liter*.

To convert from a larger unit to a smaller unit, multiply the larger unit by an appropriate power of ten. To convert from a smaller unit to a larger unit, divide the smaller unit by an appropriate power of ten.

Here is the relationship of the units in the metric system to the basic unit:

1000	100	10	1	0.1	0.01	0.001
kilo-	hecto-	deka-	unit	deci-	centi-	milli-

The chart shows the most commonly used units of measure in the *customary system* of measures.

To change from a larger unit to a smaller unit, multiply the larger unit by the appropriate conversion factor. To change from a smaller unit to a larger unit, divide the smaller unit by the appropriate conversion factor.

Length	Weight (Mass)	Liquid (Capacity)
Customary System: 1 foot (ft) = 12 inches (in.) 1 yard (yd) = 36 inches 1 yard = 3 feet 1 mile (mi) = 5,280 feet	Customary System: 1 pound (lb) = 16 ounces (oz) 1 ton (T) = 2,000 pounds	Customary System: 1 cup (c) = 8 fluid ounces 1 pint (pt) = 2 cups 1 quart (qt) = 2 pints 1 gallon (gal) = 4 quarts
Metric System: 1 meter (m) = 100 cm 1 kilometer (km) = 1000 m	Metric System: 1 gram (g) = 1000 mg 1 kilogram (kg) = 1000 g	Metric System: 1 liter (l) = 1000 ml

MODEL PROBLEMS

1. A rectangle has a length of 85 cm and a width of 53 cm. What is the perimeter of the rectangle in meters?

Solution:

$P = 2(l + w)$

$P = 2(85 \text{ cm} + 53 \text{ cm}) = 2(138 \text{ cm}) = 276 \text{ cm}$

To change to meters, divide by 100 since 1 cm = 0.01 meter.

Answer: $P = 2.76 \text{ m}$

2. Bob purchased two packages of ground beef for hamburgers. One package weighed 2.5 pounds and the other package weighed 3.75 pounds. How many four-ounce hamburgers can Bob make from the two packages?

Solution: Total number of pounds purchased = 2.5 lb + 3.75 lb = 6.25 lb. Since 1 pound equals 16 ounces, 4 ounces equal $\frac{1}{4}$ of a pound. In 6 pounds, you have 24 four-ounce hamburgers and 0.25 lb equals another 4-ounce hamburger.

Answer: 25 hamburgers can be made.

Converting Units

In the customary measurement system, 60 miles per hour (mph) is considered a unit of rate. Sometimes it is necessary to convert a unit of rate to an equivalent unit.

To convert unit rates:

- Write the given unit in fraction form.
- Write one or more conversion fractions.
- Multiply and cancel.

 **MODEL PROBLEM**

Convert 60 mph to ft/min.

Solution: Since 60 mph can be written as $\frac{60 \text{ miles}}{1 \text{ hour}}$, the conversion can be accomplished by selecting conversion fractions (each equal to 1) to lead to the goal of ft/min.

1 mile = 5,280 feet

1 hour = 60 minutes

$$\frac{60 \cancel{\text{ mi}}}{1 \cancel{\text{ hr}}} \times \frac{5,280 \text{ ft}}{1 \cancel{\text{ mi}}} \times \frac{1 \cancel{\text{ hr}}}{60 \text{ min}} = \frac{5,280 \text{ ft}}{1 \text{ min}} \text{ \textbf{Answer}}$$

Estimating Measurements

In working with measurements, you can judge the reasonableness of results better if you know how common units of measure relate to familiar objects.

Length	
inch:	distance between the joints of your index finger
foot:	length of a sheet of notebook paper
yard:	distance from the tip of your nose to the tip of your middle finger with your arm outstretched
meter:	a little more than a yard
centimeter:	a little less than half an inch
Weight/Mass	
gram:	weight of a paper clip
kilogram:	weight of a hammer
ounce:	weight of a slice of bread
pound:	weight of a loaf of bread

 **MODEL PROBLEM**

Which of the following is the best estimate for the measure of the diameter of an NBA basketball?

    A. 4 in.   B. 8 in.   C. 13 in.   D. 24 in.

Solution: 4 inches and 8 inches would be too small.
           24 inches would be much too large.

Answer: 13 inches is a reasonable estimate.

Accuracy of Measurements

In measuring the length using an inch ruler, it is necessary to determine the degree of precision required.

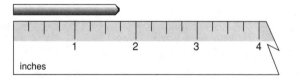

The pencil is 2 inches long to the nearest inch.

The pencil is $1\frac{1}{2}$ inches long to the nearest half-inch.

The pencil is $1\frac{3}{4}$ inches long to the nearest quarter-inch.

MODEL PROBLEM

Find the length of the straw to the nearest half-inch.

Solution: The length of the straw is between 3 and 4 inches. In finding the length to the nearest half-inch, you need to see if it is closer to 3, $3\frac{1}{2}$, or 4. Since it is closer to $3\frac{1}{2}$, the length is $3\frac{1}{2}$ inches.

PRACTICE

1. A tree grows 1.4 cm each day. In 120 days, how many METERS will the tree have grown?

   A. 0.168 m   B. 1.68 m
   C. 16.8 m   D. 168 m

2. Which of the following is a correct measurement of the length of the crayon?

   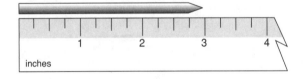

   A. 2 inches to the nearest inch

   B. $2\frac{1}{2}$ inches to the nearest half-inch

   C. $2\frac{1}{2}$ inches to the nearest quarter-inch

   D. 3 inches to the nearest half-inch

3. Which of the conversions below would be done using the following procedure?

$$6 \text{ mi} \times \frac{5{,}280 \text{ ft}}{1 \text{ mi}} \times \frac{12 \text{ in.}}{1 \text{ ft}}$$

   A. Miles to feet
   B. Feet to miles
   C. Miles to inches
   D. Inches to miles

4. Which of the following is a correct reading of the voltage?

   A. 4 volts to the nearest volt
   B. 3.5 volts to the nearest volt
   C. 3.5 volts to the nearest $\frac{1}{2}$ volt
   D. 3.5 volts to the nearest $\frac{1}{4}$ volt

5. Each side of a regular decagon (10-sided figure) has a length of 4.25 inches. Find the perimeter.

   A. 3 ft 6.5 in.   B. 3 ft 8 in.
   C. 3 ft 11 in.   D. 4 ft

6. Approximately what percent of a yard is an inch?

   A. 3%   B. 10%   C. 33%   D. 36%

7. At 6:00 A.M., the temperature in Nome, Alaska was 15° below zero Fahrenheit. The average increase in temperature per hour was 3°. What was the temperature at noon?

   A. −12°F   B. −3°F   C. 3°F   D. 33°F

8. For which of the following objects would 180 cm be a good estimate of its length?

   A. The length of a driveway
   B. The length of a dining room table
   C. The height of a kindergarten child
   D. The length of a city block

9. For which of the following objects would 6 pounds be a good estimate of its weight?

   A. A box of cereal
   B. Three apples
   C. Two math textbooks
   D. A case of 24 packages of copy paper

10. Choose the best comparison of the two indicated weights:

    p = weight of a 5-pound bag of potatoes
    q = the weight of a 1-kilogram box of sugar

    A. $p > q$ B. $p < q$ C. $p = q$
    D. You cannot complete the comparison based on the given information.

11. Using a ruler, measure the sides of the given figure to the nearest $\frac{1}{8}$ in. Record all measurements. What is the perimeter of the figure to the nearest eighth of an inch?

12. Change 88 ft/sec to miles per hour.

13. Change 75 km/hr to m/min.

14. How many times does a person's heart beat in one day if it beats an average of 68 times per minute?

15. Temperature can be measured in either of two systems: *Celsius* (0° freezing point of water; 100° boiling point of water) and *Fahrenheit* (32° freezing point of water; 212° boiling point of water). The two systems are related by the formula:

$$F = \frac{9}{5}C + 32°$$

20°C is considered an appropriate measure for room temperature. Express this measure in degrees Fahrenheit.

16. Use an inch ruler to determine the lengths of the sides of the figure shown. Use your measurements to find the area of the figure.

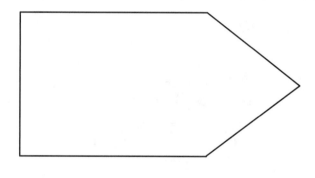

2 C 6 Pythagorean Theorem

If you know the lengths of two sides of a right triangle, a special formula can be used to find the length of the third side.

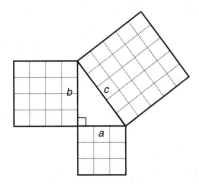

The number of square units in the square on the hypotenuse, c, is equal to the sum of the number of square units in the squares on both legs, a and b.

$$c^2 = a^2 + b^2$$

MODEL PROBLEMS

1. A ladder is 6 meters long. If the ladder is leaning against a wall and the bottom of the ladder is 3 meters from the base of the wall, how far up the wall does the ladder reach?

Solution:
Let h = height of the wall.

$c^2 = a^2 + b^2$
$6^2 = 3^2 + h^2$
$36 = 9 + h^2$
$27 = h^2$
$h = \sqrt{27}$

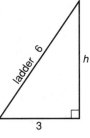

Answer: $h \approx 5.2$ meters

2. Is a triangle with sides of lengths 5, 9, and 10 a right triangle?

Solution: If the triangle is a right triangle, the lengths of the sides must satisfy the Pythagorean Relation. Conversely, if the lengths of the three sides satisfy the Pythagorean Relation, the triangle must be a right triangle.

$5^2 + 9^2 \overset{?}{=} 10^2$
$25 + 81 \overset{?}{=} 100$
$106 \neq 100$

Answer: The triangle is NOT a right triangle.

1. Which of the following represents the lengths of the sides of a right triangle?

   A. 2, 3, 4
   B. 3, 4, 6
   C. 6, 8, 10
   D. 4, 6, 8

2. A rectangle has dimensions 5 cm by 12 cm. How many centimeters long is a diagonal of the rectangle?

   A. 12   B. 13   C. 17   D. 30

3. The two legs of a right triangle have lengths of 5 and 6 units. Between what two integers would the length of the hypotenuse fall?

   A. 5 and 6
   B. 6 and 7
   C. 7 and 8
   D. 8 and 9

4. A right triangle has two sides of lengths 3 and 4. Which of the following could be the length of the third side?

   I. 5   II. $\sqrt{7}$ III. 7

   A. I only
   B. II only
   C. I and II
   D. I and III

5. Pauline walked 4 km due east and then 7 km due north. Which of the following is the most reasonable answer for the distance between Pauline's start and endpoint?

   A. 6.5 km   B. 8.1 km
   C. 9 km   D. 11 km

6. An 8-foot ladder leaning against a wall reaches 6 feet up the wall. How far from the base of the wall is the bottom of the ladder?

   A. 2 ft   B. 5.3 ft   C. 6.2 ft   D. 10 ft

7. Find the value of b in this right triangle.

   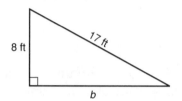

8. Each diagonal of a rectangle has a length of 10 yards. If one dimension of the rectangle is 6 yards, find the perimeter.

9. In circle O, chord $\overline{AB}$ is bisected by segment OM. If $OM = 6$ inches and $AB = 16$ inches, what is the length of a diameter of the circle?

   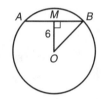

10. Show how you can use the Pythagorean Relation to find the distance from $(0, 0)$ to $(6, 8)$. Use a grid and then write your procedure.

11. Triangle ABC is isosceles with a base of 10 cm and perimeter of 36 cm. Show how you can use the Pythagorean Relation to find the height of the triangle. Give the steps used in your thinking.

    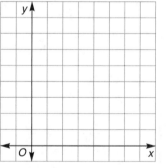

2 C 7 Trigonometric Ratios

A *trigonometric ratio* is the ratio of the lengths of two sides of a right triangle. Trigonometric ratios can be used to find missing measures within right triangles.

Trig Ratio	Definition
sine of A	$\sin A = \dfrac{\text{leg opposite } \angle A}{\text{hypotenuse}} = \dfrac{a}{c}$
cosine of A	$\cos A = \dfrac{\text{leg adjacent to } \angle A}{\text{hypotenuse}} = \dfrac{b}{c}$
tangent of A	$\tan A = \dfrac{\text{leg opposite } \angle A}{\text{leg adjacent to } \angle A} = \dfrac{a}{b}$

Note: A is the measurement of $\angle A$.

MODEL PROBLEMS

1. Find $\sin P$, $\cos P$, $\tan P$. Express each ratio as a fraction and a decimal.

Solution: $\sin P = \dfrac{3}{5} = 0.6$

$\cos P = \dfrac{4}{5} = 0.8$

$\tan P = \dfrac{3}{4} = 0.75$

2. Find the value of each expression. Use a scientific calculator to give the value rounded to the nearest ten-thousandth (Note: Make sure the calculator is in degree mode.)

   a. $\cos 22°$
   b. $\tan 50°$

Solution: $\cos 22 = 0.927183854 = 0.9272$

$\tan 50 = 1.191753593 = 1.1918$

3. A kite is being flown with a 55′ string. If the kite makes a 30° angle with the ground, how high above the ground is the kite? Be sure to show a diagram and the work leading to your solution.

Solution:

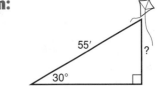

Since you want to know the height of the kite represented by the distance opposite the 30° angle in the given right triangle and you know the adjacent leg, use the trig ratio for sine to find the missing length.

$\sin 30 = \dfrac{x}{55}$

$0.5 = \dfrac{x}{55}$ (use a calculator to find sin 30)

$0.5(55) = x$

$27.5 = x$

Answer: 27.5′ above the ground

1. Find cos A for the given triangle.

   A. 0.3846   B. 0.4167
   C. 0.9231   D. 2.4

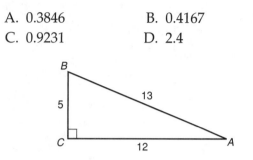

2. Find m$\angle A$ (to the nearest degree) in the right triangle with vertices at $A(6, 0)$, $B(0, 8)$, $C(0, 0)$.

   A. 36°   B. 45°   C. 53°   D. 60°

3. Which of the following would NOT be sufficient information to allow you to complete the task of finding the measures of the three sides and three angles of a right triangle?

   A. The lengths of the two legs
   B. The measures of the two acute angles
   C. The meaure of one acute angle and the length of the hypotenuse
   D. The measure of one acute angle and the length of one leg

4. In right triangle ABC, if $\sin A = \dfrac{5}{13}$, find cos A and tan A.

5. A surveyor needs to find how far away she is from a 200-foot cliff. If the angle of inclination she makes with the top of the cliff is 28°, how far (to the nearest foot) is she from the bottom of the cliff?

6. Find the value of x and y. Round to the nearest tenth of a centimeter. Show your process and explain why it is reasonable that the values of x and y are not equal.

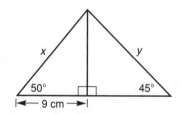

7. An engineer is designing a ramp for wheelchair entry into a building. If the ramp must reach a height of 6 feet and have an angle of elevation of 4°, what should the length of the ramp's base be?

   Draw an illustration to show the situation.

   If the angle of elevation is increased, how will this affect the length of the ramp's base? If the angle is decreased, how will the length be changed?

1. Find x to the nearest tenth of an inch.

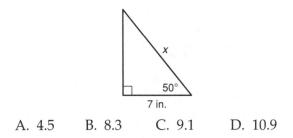

   A. 4.5   B. 8.3   C. 9.1   D. 10.9

2. Which of the following would NOT represent the sides of a right triangle?

   A. $1, 1, \sqrt{2}$ B. $\sqrt{3}, \sqrt{2}, \sqrt{5}$
   C. $8, 15, 17$ D. $5, 6, \sqrt{11}$

3. A rectangle has vertices at $P(3, 10)$, $Q(8, 10)$, $R(8, -2)$, and $S(3, -2)$. How long is the diagonal of this rectangle?

   A. 12   B. $\sqrt{150}$ C. 12.5   D. 13

4. The dimensions of a rectangular park are 66 yards by 88 yards. Juanita needs to walk from the southeast corner of the park to the northwest corner. How many yards longer is it to walk along the edges than to walk along the diagonal?

   A. 4   B. 44   C. 54   D. 110

5. The figure consists of five congruent squares. If the total area is 80 square units, what is the perimeter of the figure?

   A. 12   B. 24
   C. 36   D. 48

6. Which of the following is NOT correct?

   A. $20\ \text{ft} < 7\ \text{yd}$
   B. $100\ \text{in.} < 3\ \text{yd}$
   C. $198\ \text{cm} < 2\ \text{m}$
   D. $2010\ \text{m} < 2\ \text{km}$

7. In which list below are the units of measurement for area arranged in order from LEAST to GREATEST?

   A. $\text{in.}^2, \text{cm}^2, \text{km}^2$ B. $\text{km}^2, \text{m}^2, \text{cm}^2$
   C. $\text{cm}^2, \text{m}^2, \text{km}^2$ D. $\text{cm}^2, \text{km}^2, \text{in.}^2$

8. Two concentric circles are shown. If the radius of the smaller circle is r and the radius of the larger circle is R, which of the following would represent the area of the shaded region?

   A. $\pi R^2 - \pi r^2$ B. $\dfrac{R^2 - r^2}{4}$

   C. $\dfrac{\pi}{4}(R^2 - r^2)$ D. $\dfrac{\pi}{4}R^2 - r^2$

9. Rectangle $ABCD$ is similar to rectangle $WXYZ$, with $\overline{AB}$ corresponding to $\overline{WX}$. If $AB = 24$, $BC = 30$, and $WX = 16$, what is the area of rectangle $WXYZ$?

   A. 20   B. 204.8   C. 320   D. 720

10. The diameter and height of a right circular cylinder are equal. If the volume of the cylinder is 2, what is the height of the cylinder?

    A. 1.37   B. 1.08   C. 0.86   D. 0.85

11. If $\angle A$ and $\angle B$ are complementary angles, which of the following is NOT correct?

    A. $(\sin A)(\tan B) = \cos B$
    B. $(\tan A)(\tan B) = 1$
    C. $\sin(A + B) = 1$
    D. $\sin B = \cos A$

12. Find the area of the rectangle if the radius of each circle is 3 cm.

    A. 48 cm²
    B. 72 cm²
    C. 144 cm²
    D. 288 cm²

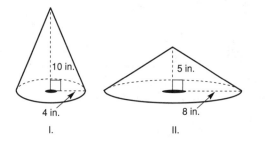

13. In the rectangle $ABCD$, the length of $\overline{DE}$ is one-fifth the length of $\overline{CD}$. If the area of the small right triangle is 21 square units, find the area of the rectangle.

    A. 105
    B. 168
    C. 210
    D. Cannot be
       determined
    with the given information.

14. Which of the following statements is TRUE concerning the capacities of the two containers?

    I.   II.

    A. The capacity of I is greater than the capacity of II.
    B. The capacity of II is greater than the capacity of I.
    C. The capacity of II is the same as the capacity of I.
    D. Based on the given information, it is not possible to determine the comparison between the capacities.

15. The diagram consists of a rectangle and two semicircles. If the rectangle has dimensions of 4 by 10, what is the total perimeter of the figure, to the nearest tenth of a unit?

16. An isosceles trapezoid has vertices at (2, 0), (10, 0), (7, 4), (5, 4). Find the perimeter of the trapezoid.

17. How many circles 1 inch in diameter would it take to have a combined area equal to the area of a single circle 4 inches in diameter?

18. If the volume of a prism is 86.4 cubic centimeters, find the missing dimension. 4.5 cm 8 cm ?

19. A can of paint covers 750 square feet. A parking lot contains 60 cylindrical poles of the kind shown. How many cans of paint are needed to give each pole *two* coats of paint? $d = 1'$ 4'

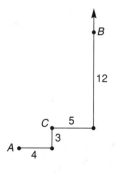

20. A kite string 140 m long makes an angle of 40° with the ground. Determine the height of the kite.

21. A diagonal of a rectangle is 15 cm long and makes a 30° angle with the longer side. Find the width of the rectangle.

22. A wire supporting a 50-meter TV tower joins the top of the tower to an anchor point 25 m from the base. Find the length of the wire and the angle it makes with the ground.

23. An open box is made from a square piece of cardboard by cutting out a 6-inch square from each corner and turning up the sides. If the volume of the box turns out to be 150 cubic inches, what was the length of a side of the original square piece of cardboard?

24. The diagram shows a route from point A to point B in which you start at A, go 4 miles due east, then 3 miles due north, then 5 miles due east, and finally 12 miles due north. When you arrive at point B, how many miles is the direct distance from A to B?

25. How will the surface area of a cylinder change if the height is doubled and the radius is cut in half? Explain your thinking and use a diagram.

26. A baseball diamond is a square with 90-foot sides. The pitcher's mound is exactly 66' 6" from home plate. How far is the pitcher's mound from second base? Show your procedure in doing the problem.

27. As the size of the unit decreases, what happens to the number of units needed to measure the same attribute (such as length)? Show at least two examples to support your answer.

28. A diagonal brace on a wooden gate would look as pictured. In building the gate, Bill has a board that is 7 ft long to use for the brace. If the gate is to be 6 ft by 4 ft, does Bill have a long enough board for the construction of the brace? Explain your answer.

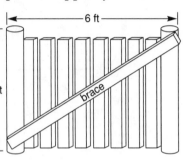

29. For the rectangular solid shown with dimensions (in inches) of 5 × 12 × 2, explain why a diagonal of the entire figure (for example, from vertex X to vertex Y) is longer than 13 inches. You can use a diagram as part of your solution.

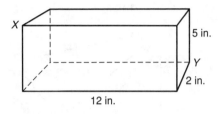

30. A rectangular solid has faces with the following areas (in square inches): 12, 15, 20.

    a. Draw a sketch of a net for this rectangular solid. Indicate the area for each portion of the net.

    b. Find the total surface area for the rectangular solid.

    c. What needs to be done with the given information in order to find the volume of the solid?

    d. Find the volume of the rectangular solid.

1. In using deductive reasoning to show that *a* equals *c*, which of the following would be the major justification?

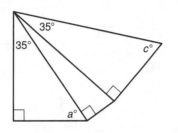

A. Vertical angles have equal measure.

B. Corresponding parts of congruent triangles are congruent.

C. Complements of congruent angles are congruent.

D. An angle bisector divides an angle into two angles of equal measure.

2. Two vertices of a triangle are $(0, 0)$ and $(6, 0)$. Which of the following points would NOT give you a right scalene triangle?

A. $(0, -5)$ B. $(6, 4)$ C. $(-3, 0)$ D. $(6, -4)$

3. Point *A* with coordinates $(8, 15)$ is on a circle with center at the origin. Find the coordinates of point *B* such that *AB* is a diameter of the circle.

A. $(-15, -8)$ B. $(-8, -15)$

C. $(8, -15)$ D. $(4, 7.5)$

4. Which of the following figures shows a line of symmetry for the figure?

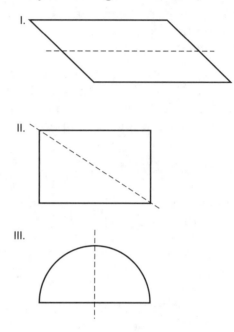

A. II only   B. III only

C. II and III   D. I, II, and III

5. A triangle has vertices at $A(-3, 1)$, $B(3, 1)$, and $C(0, -5)$. How many lines of symmetry does the triangle have?

A. 0   B. 1   C. 2   D. 3

6. If you spin a two-dimensional figure about a vertical axis, a cylinder results. What type of two-dimensional figure did you start with?

   A. Right triangle
   B. Semicircle
   C. Rectangle
   D. Trapezoid

7. How many different isosceles triangles can you find that have sides with integral lengths such that the perimeter of the triangle is 20?

   A. 3   B. 4   C. 5   D. 6

8. A rectangular swimming pool is 72 feet long and 32.5 feet wide. The pool is surrounded by a concrete walkway that is 3.5 feet wide. What is the area of the walkway?

   A. 227.5 square feet   B. 237 square feet
   C. 378 square feet   D. 780.5 square feet

9. If the circumference of a circle is divided by the length of a radius, the quotient is:

   A. $\frac{1}{2}\pi$ B. π C. 2π D. 2

10. Find the height of a trapezoid with an area of 42.5 square centimeters if one base is 5.2 cm and the other base is 3.3 cm.

    A. 4.95 cm   B. 5 cm
    C. 10 cm   D. 38.25 cm

11. Which of the conversions below would be done using the following operations?

    $$\frac{70 \text{ mi}}{1 \text{ hr}} \times \frac{5{,}280 \text{ ft}}{1 \text{ mi}} \times \frac{1 \text{ hr}}{60 \text{ min}}$$

    A. Miles per hour to miles per minute
    B. Feet per minute to miles per hour
    C. Miles per hour to feet per minute
    D. Miles per hour to feet per second

12. If 1 in. ≈ 2.5 cm, then the length of a diagonal of a sheet of paper measuring $8\frac{1}{2}$ in. by 11 in. is closest to:

    A. 35 cm   B. 35 mm   C. 70 cm   D. 70 mm

13. Anytown USA has a cylindrical water tank with dimensions as shown. Due to increased demand for water, the council of Anytown wants to build a new cylindrical tank with twice the volume of the original tank. Which of the following options could be used?

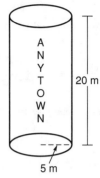

   I. Double the height of the tank and maintain the same diameter.
   II. Double the diameter of the tank and maintain the same height.
   III. Double both the diameter and the height of the tank.

   A. I only   B. II only
   C. III only   D. I and II

14. Which of the lists below shows the three figures P, Q, and R in order of size, from LEAST to GREATEST area?

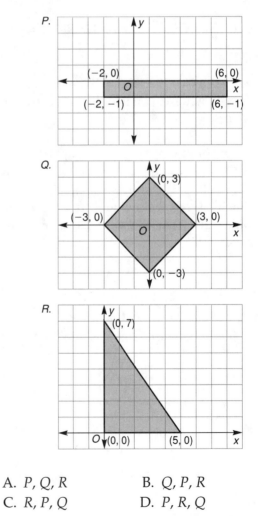

   A. P, Q, R   B. Q, P, R
   C. R, P, Q   D. P, R, Q

15. The Bagel Express uses an average of 2 lb 8 oz of cream cheese per hour. If the Bagel Express is open 7 hours a day for 7 days per week, about how much cream cheese would be used in 3 weeks?

A. 105 lb
B. 122.5 lb
C. 294 lb
D. 367.5 lb

16. Which of the following is NOT possible for some types of triangles regarding the number of lines of symmetry?

A. A triangle can have no lines of symmetry.
B. A triangle can have exactly one line of symmetry.
C. A triangle can have exactly two lines of symmetry.
D. A triangle can have three lines of symmetry.

17. The volume of a cube is at least 6,000 cubic units but no more than 7,000 cubic units. Determine the range of values (rounded to the nearest hundredth) for the length of a side.

A. 6.00–7.00
B. 12.59–13.26
C. 18.17–19.13
D. 77.46–83.67

18. The points $(2, 5)$ and $(2, -5)$ are the endpoints of a diameter of a circle. Find the area of the circle.

A. 4π square units
B. 5π square units
C. 25π square units
D. 100π square units

19. Which of the following sets of coordinates could represent the vertices of an isosceles trapezoid?

A. $\{(0, 0), (6, 0), (7, 4), (0, 4)\}$
B. $\{(0, 0), (6, 0), (6, 4), (0, 4)\}$
C. $\{(-4, 0), (0, 4), (4, 0), (0, -4)\}$
D. $\{(-4, 0), (4, 0), (2, 8), (-2, 8)\}$

20. If the letter **N** is reflected over the y-axis, which of the following represents the image?

A.

B.

C.

D.

21. If the measure of $\angle ECF$ is $15°$, what is the measure of $\angle ACD$?

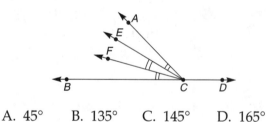

A. $45°$ B. $135°$ C. $145°$ D. $165°$

22. $ABCD$ is a square. If you remove a small right triangle at vertices A and C (with right angles at A and C), what type of figure remains?

A. Octagon
B. Hexagon
C. Pentagon
D. Square

23. Draw a three-dimensional figure that has all three of the following characteristics:

a. an odd number of faces
b. an even number of vertices
c. more vertices than faces

24. *ABCD* is a square and the two triangles are equilateral. What is the measure of ∠*EBF*?

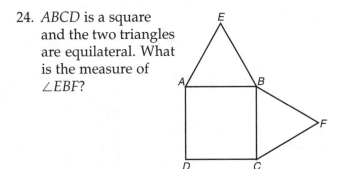

25. Two similar triangles have a ratio of similitude of 2.35 to 1. If the area of the smaller triangle is 8.4 square centimeters, what is the area of the larger triangle?

26. How many revolutions will it take a 24″-diameter bicycle wheel to travel 1 mile? (Give your answer to the nearest whole number.)

27. The diagram shows blocks along First Street and Second Street. If the total frontage on Second Street is 480 feet, find the length of each block along Second Street.

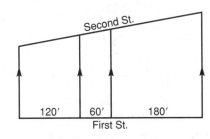

28. The inside of a can of three tennis balls is about 23 cm high and has a diameter of about 7.5 cm. Each ball has an outer circumference of about 23 cm. How much space is left in the can?

29. A piece of wire 106.2 cm long has been bent to form a rectangle. The area enclosed by the rectangle is 623 square centimeters. Find the longer side of the rectangle.

30. A line segment extends from the point (6, 4) to point *P* on the line $y = 8$ such that the slope of the segment is $\frac{1}{4}$. What are the coordinates of point *P*?

31. A wheel rolls along a straight path on the floor. If the diameter of the wheel is 30 centimeters, describe the path followed by the center of the wheel as the wheel rolls along the floor.

32. A pentagon has a perimeter of 50 cm. The shortest side of the pentagon has a length of 3 cm. Find the length of the shortest side of a similar pentagon if the perimeter of the second pentagon is 80 cm.

33. A rectangular solid has a volume of 227.5 cubic inches. If two dimensions are 5 inches and 7 inches, what would the third dimension be?

34. The figure consists of nine small congruent squares. If the area of the figure is 900 square units, find the perimeter of the figure.

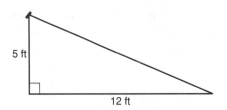

35. A flagpole has cracked 5 feet from the ground and fallen as if hinged. The top of the flagpole hits the ground 12 feet from the base. How tall was the flagpole before it fell?

36. Using the grid, determine the area of the shaded figure.

37. Find the magnitude of $\frac{1}{2}\overrightarrow{TR}$.

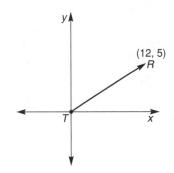

38. A tree on level ground casts a shadow 32 feet long. The angle of elevation from the tip of the shadow to the top of the tree is 60°. Find the height of the tree.

39. Provide a convincing argument that the given triangle is a right triangle.

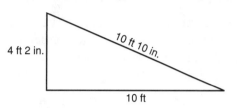

40. Find the area and perimeter of the trapezoid. Show your complete procedure.

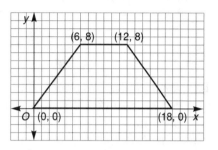

41. Explain why the perimeter of the figure must be greater than 20 units. Also, show how to obtain a good approximation for the perimeter.

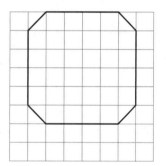

42. a. Explain why a triangle with sides, 5, 10, 12 cannot be a right triangle.
    b. Write an additional set of lengths of sides of a triangle that could NOT serve as the sides of a right triangle.
    c. Write three sets of lengths that could serve as the sides of a right triangle.

43. In the grid, there is a figure with a certain area.

    a. On a separate piece of grid paper, draw a rectangle with an area equal to the area of the figure in the grid.

    b. On a separate piece of grid paper, draw a triangle with an area equal to the area of the figure in the grid.

44. a. Plot the points (8, 6), (8, 2), (14, 2) on grid paper. Connect them to form a triangle. What type of triangle is formed?
    b. Draw the triangle you get when you apply the rule $(0.5x, 0.5y)$ to the three points given above. How are the two triangles related?
    c. The area of the smaller triangle is what percent of the area of the larger triangle? Explain why.

45. Use a set of tangrams to build the rectangle pictured below.

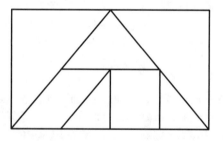

    a. Move one piece of the rectangle to change the figure into a parallelogram with no right angles. Sketch your figure.
    b. Write a paragraph to explain how the area and perimeter of the original rectangle compare to the area and perimeter of the new parallelogram. Be sure to explain how you know this relationship exists. It is not necessary to actually calculate the area and perimeter of the figures.

46. An octagon is shown on the grid.

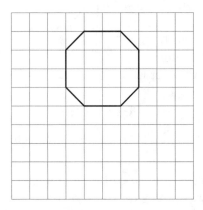

a. Describe any lines of symmetry that are neither horizontal nor vertical.

b. This octagon can be thought of as 4-by-4 square with the corners cut off. The area of the octagon is what percent of the area of the 4-by-4 square? Explain your procedure.

c. Using the blank grid, draw an octagon similar to the original with each side double the length of the original sides.

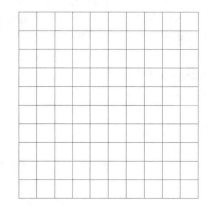

d. Explain what is wrong with the following argument concerning the original octagon and the larger one. Since the sides of the larger octagon are double the original sides, the area of the larger octagon must be double the original area.

CUMULATIVE ASSESSMENT

For Clusters 1 and 2

1. Which of the following would represent all the real numbers at least 7 units away from -3 on the number line?

   A. $|x| \geq 7$ B. $|x + 3| \geq 7$
   C. $|x - 3| \geq 7$ D. $|x + 7| \geq -3$

2. The following numbers represent volumes of a cube. For which value would the cube not have an integral edge?

   A. 125   B. 300   C. 1,000   D. 3,375

3. A college team sweatshirt has a wholesale price of $30.00. The Sports Exchange applies a 20% markup on the wholesale price to obtain the retail price. During a sale, the same sweatshirt is priced at 15% off the retail price. What is the sale price?

   A. $20.40   B. $30.60   C. $31.50   D. $36.00

4. If the area of a rectangle is 10 square units, what is the ratio of the length to the width?

   A. 1 to 10   B. 2 to 5   C. 5 to 2
   D. It cannot be determined from the information given.

5. How many two-digit numbers have all of the following characteristics?

   I. The number is a multiple of 16.
   II. The number is a factor of 144.
   III. The number is divisible by 3.

   A. 0   B. 1   C. 2   D. 3

6. The measures of the angles of a triangle are in the ratio of $3 : 4 : 11$. How many degrees are in the measure of the largest angle of the triangle?

   A. 10   B. 30   C. 55   D. 110

7. A line segment has endpoints at (1, 6) and (4, 6). The segment is translated 4 units to the right and 3 units down, and then reflected over the *x*-axis. After the reflection, what are the coordinates of the endpoints of the final segment?

    A. (5, 3) and (8, 3)
    B. (−5, 3) and (−8, 3)
    C. (4, −2) and (7, −2)
    D. (5, −3) and (8, −3)

8. On a map, 1 centimeter represents 125 kilometers. How many kilometers apart are two cities that are 48 millimeters apart on the map?

    A. 60   B. 600   C. 6000   D. 60,000

9. Which of the following does NOT show a 10% increase?

    A. $100 \rightarrow 110$ B. $50 \rightarrow 60$

    C. $10 \rightarrow 11$ D. $\dfrac{1}{10} \rightarrow \dfrac{11}{100}$

10. If you double the radius of the base of a cylinder and also double the height of the cylinder, what percent increase will there be in the volume of the cylinder?

    A. 200%   B. 400%   C. 700%   D. 800%

11. Using the data from this table, which of the following lists the correct order of the surface areas of the three boxes, from LEAST to GREATEST?

Box	Dimensions (in centimeters)
P	$6 \times 6 \times 6$
Q	$4 \times 10 \times 2$
R	$5 \times 8 \times 3$

    A. P, Q, R B. R, Q, P
    C. Q, R, P D. Q, P, R

12. Triangles *ABC* and *ACD* are right triangles. Determine the perimeter of quadrilateral *ABCD*. Give your answer to the nearest tenth of a unit.

    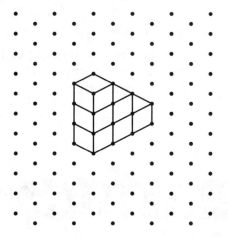

13. If $4^x = 32^y$, write an expression relating *x* and *y*.

14. Sketch two additional views from different perspectives for the figure shown.

15. Two similar rectangles have areas of 12 square units and 108 square units. If the perimeter of the smaller rectangle is 14 units, what is the perimeter of the larger rectangle?

16. As a back-to-school incentive on Wednesdays, Supply Warehouse plans to give every fifteenth customer a free pen and every twenty-fifth customer a free notebook. On a particular Wednesday, Supply Warehouse had 300 customers.

    a. How many free pens were given away on that Wednesday?

    b. How many free notebooks were given away on that Wednesday?

    c. Did any customers receive a free pen and a free notebook? If so, how many customers?

    d. If pens sell for 79¢ and notebooks sell for $1.19, how much did the Supply Warehouse lose in income by giving away these items?

    Justify your answers.

17. Using the diagram, solve for *x*. Explain why you need to know that the two segments indicated are parallel in order to do the problem.

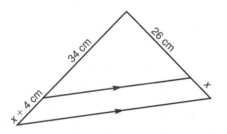

18. An isosceles triangle *ABC* has vertices at *A*(0, 0), *B*(6, 0), and *C*(3, −8). A median of a triangle joins a vertex to the midpoint of the opposite side. Median *AM* intersects side *BC* at point *M*. Graph the triangle and the median. What are the coordinates at point *M*?

19. The formula for the volume of a cylinder is $V = \pi r^2 h$. If the height of a cylinder is 10 cm, what is the smallest whole number of centimeters for the length of the radius that would produce a volume of at least 500 cubic centimeters? Explain your procedure.

20. A rhombus has diagonals of length 16 inches and 20 inches.

    a. Draw a reasonable sketch of this rhombus.

    b. In order to find the perimeter of the rhombus, indicate two properties of the diagonals of a rhombus you would need to know. Find the perimeter of the rhombus.

    c. Using trigonometric ratios, find the degree measure of the obtuse angle of this rhombus. Show your work.

21. A square on a coordinate grid has horizontal and vertical sides. The upper left vertex of the square is located at (−3, 4). The perimeter of the square is 32 units.

    a. Draw a sketch of the square and indicate the coordinates of the other three vertices.

    b. What percent of the area of the square is in each quadrant?

    c. Suppose you next translate the square one unit to the right. Does this translation change the percent of the area now existing in the third quadrant? Explain.

Data Analysis, Probability, Statistics, and Discrete Mathematics

Macro A

Determine, interpret, and use probabilities of simple and compound events.

3 A 1 Probability of Simple Events

The *probability* of an event is the ratio of the number of favorable outcomes to the total number of possible outcomes.

$$\text{probability} = \frac{\text{number of favorable outcomes}}{\text{total number of possible outcomes}}$$

The probability of an event can be expressed as a fraction, decimal, or percent with a value greater than or equal to zero and less than or equal to one. $(0 \leq P \leq 1)$

If $P(A) = 0$, then it is impossible for A to occur.

If $P(A) = 1$, then it is certain the event will occur.

MODEL PROBLEM

A standard die is rolled. Find each of the following:

   a. the probability of rolling a 5
   b. the probability of rolling an even number
   c. the probability of rolling a number less than 3
   d. the probability of rolling a number greater than 7
   e. the probability of rolling a number less than 7

Solution: With the sample space consisting of 1, 2, 3, 4, 5, 6, the simple probabilities can be determined by applying the definition of probability.

   a. $P(5) = \dfrac{1}{6}$ (since 5 is the only favorable outcome)

   b. $P(\text{even}) = \dfrac{3}{6}$ (since 2, 4, and 6 are favorable outcomes)

   c. $P(<3) = \dfrac{2}{6}$ (since 1 and 2 are favorable outcomes)

   d. $P(>7) = 0$ (since there are no favorable outcomes)

   e. $P(<7) = \dfrac{6}{6} = 1$ (since all outcomes are favorable)

Odds

In addition to expressing a probability by the above definition, you can also find the *odds* in favor of or against a particular event.

$$\text{odds in favor} = \frac{\text{number of favorable outcomes}}{\text{number of unfavorable outcomes}}$$

$$\text{odds against} = \frac{\text{number of unfavorable outcomes}}{\text{number of favorable outcomes}}$$

A box contains 9 red balls and 1 white ball.

    a. What are the odds in favor of picking red when picking one ball from the box?

    b. What are the odds in favor of picking white when picking one ball from the box?

Solution:

    a. odds in favor of red $= \dfrac{\text{favorable}}{\text{unfavorable}} = \dfrac{9}{1}$; 9 to 1

    b. odds in favor of white $= \dfrac{\text{favorable}}{\text{unfavorable}} = \dfrac{1}{9}$; 1 to 9

Note: While a probability must be a fraction less than or equal to 1, odds can turn out to be greater than 1 $\left(\text{such as } \dfrac{9}{1} \text{ as in example a}\right)$.

Experimental and Theoretical Probabilities

Experimental probability results from conducting an experiment, making observations, or performing a simulation. For example, if you toss a coin 50 times and obtain 30 heads, the experimental probability of obtaining heads would be $\dfrac{30}{50}$ or $\dfrac{3}{5}$. Each time you toss the coin 50 times, the experimental probability of heads may vary.

In contrast with experimental probability, ***theoretical probability*** represents what you would expect from the "theory" or description of the situation. When we say that the probability of obtaining heads on the toss of a coin is $\dfrac{1}{2}$ or 50%, or the probability of obtaining an ace is $\dfrac{4}{52}$ or $\dfrac{1}{13}$, we are giving the theoretical probability.

MODEL PROBLEMS

1.

Girls in Families of Four Children	
Number of Girls	Frequency
0	10
1	15
2	49
3	19
4	7

The above table shows the results of data gathering on the number of girls in 100 families with four children.

    a. Based on the data, what is the experimental probability that exactly two children will be girls?

    b. Explain why your answer would most likely be different if you collected data from another group of 100 families consisting of four children.

Solution:

    a. From the information in the table, the experimental probability is $\frac{49}{100}$.

    b. The probabilities are based on the frequencies. As the data are gathered, it is not likely that you would get the same frequencies.

2. What is the theoretical probability of having exactly two girls in a family of four children?

Solution:

The sample space shows a total of 16 possibilities for combinations of boys and girls in a family with four children.

    BBBB   BGBB   GGGG   GBGG

    BBBG   BGBG   GGGB   GBGB

    BBGB   BGGB   GGBG   GBBG

    BBGG   BGGG   GGBB   GBBB

Since 6 of the sequences above represent exactly two girls (and two boys), the theoretical probability is $\frac{6}{16}$ or $\frac{3}{8}$ or 37.5%.

PRACTICE

1. Which of the following cannot be the answer to a probability question?

   A. 0   B. 30%   C. $\frac{11}{10}$ D. $\frac{10}{11}$

2. You flip a fair coin. The first eight flips come up heads. What is the probability that the ninth flip of the coin will be a tail?

   A. $\frac{1}{2}$ B. 1   C. $\frac{8}{9}$ D. $\frac{1}{9}$

3. Consider the following events:

   I. Obtaining a sum of 2 in rolling two dice
   II. Obtaining 5 heads when tossing five coins
   III. Obtaining a red with one spin of the spinner shown

   Arrange the events in order from LEAST probable to MOST probable.

   A. III, II, I
   B. I, II, III
   C. I, III, II
   D. II, I, III

4. Two events, A and B, are considered *complementary* if $P(B) = 1 - P(A)$. For example, in tossing a coin, P(heads) $= \frac{1}{2}$ and P(tails) $= \frac{1}{2}$, which is equal to $1 - P$(heads). Which of the following would NOT represent complementary events?

   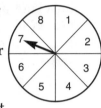

   A. Spinning an odd number on the spinner shown
      Spinning an even number on the spinner shown
   B. Picking a number divisible by 3 from the set of whole numbers between 1 and 30
      Picking a number not divisible by 3 from the set of whole numbers between 1 and 30
   C. Obtaining a sum less than 7 when tossing two dice
      Obtaining a sum greater than 7 when tossing two dice
   D. Picking a red card from a regular deck of cards
      Picking a black card from a regular deck of cards

5. For the spinner shown, the probability of landing on each color is $\frac{1}{4}$ or 25%.

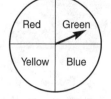

A different spinner has 3 sectors each with a different color (red, green, or yellow). If the ratio $P(\text{red}) : P(\text{green}) : P(\text{yellow})$ is $1:4:7$, draw the resulting spinner. Show your work and use a protractor.

6. A coin-toss game at a carnival has a board as shown. To win, the coin must land in the shaded area. What is the probability of winning the game, expressed to the nearest percent?

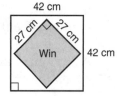

7. A dice game is played by two students using a pair of dice.

Player 1 gets a point if the product of the numbers rolled on the dice is even.

Player 2 gets a point if the product of the numbers rolled on the dice is odd.

The player with more points after 20 rounds wins.

Is the game, as outlined, fair or not? Explain.

8. Mary rolled a die 600 times. The results are shown below.

odd 252   even 348

Calculate the experimental probability for rolling odd as shown by the results given. Determine the theoretical probability for rolling an odd number on a die. Compare the experimental and theoretical probabilities. What could Mary have done to see if the experimental results would come closer to the theoretical results?

3 A 2 Probability of Compound Events

Compound events consist of two or more events. If the outcome of one event does not affect the outcome of the other event, the events are *independent*.

For two independent events,

$$P(A \text{ and } B) = P(A) \cdot P(B)$$

If the outcome of one event affects the outcome of the other event, the events are *dependent*.

For two dependent events,

$$P(A \text{ and } B) = P(A) \cdot P(B \text{ after } A \text{ occurs})$$

MODEL PROBLEMS

1. Suppose a number cube is rolled twice. What is the probability that an odd number will occur both times?

Solution: Since the first and second rolls of the number cube are independent of each other, P(rolling 2 odd numbers) = P(first roll odd) $\cdot$ P(second roll odd)

outcomes: 1, 2, 3, 4, 5, 6   total 6

odd numbers: 1, 3, 5   total 3

$$P(\text{odd}) = \frac{3}{6} = \frac{1}{2}$$

$$P(\text{rolling 2 odd numbers}) = \frac{1}{2} \cdot \frac{1}{2} = \frac{1}{4}$$

2. A jar contains 3 red balls, 2 white balls, and 1 green ball. What is the probability of picking two white balls if the first ball is not replaced?

Solution:

$$P(\text{first white}) = \frac{2}{6} = \frac{1}{3}$$

Since the first ball selected was white and not replaced,

$$P(\text{second white}) = \frac{1}{5}$$

$$P(\text{two whites}) = \frac{1}{3} \cdot \frac{1}{5} = \frac{1}{15}$$

Probability of *A* or *B*

Sometimes you want to find the probability that either of two events will occur. This calculation depends on whether or not the events are mutually exclusive, that is, events that cannot occur at the same time.

For mutually exclusive events,

$$P(A \text{ or } B) = P(A) + P(B)$$

If the events are not mutually exclusive because it is possible for both to occur at the same time, the probability of *A* or *B* requires you to subtract the $P(A \text{ and } B)$ from the sum of $P(A) + P(B)$, because of the overlapping components of the sample space.

For non–mutually exclusive events,

$$P(A \text{ or } B) = P(A) + P(B) - P(A \text{ and } B)$$

MODEL PROBLEM

For the spinner shown, find the following probabilities:

   a. P(a 2 or a 5)

   b. P(a multiple of 2 or a multiple of 3)

Solution:

   a. Since obtaining a 2 and obtaining a 5 are mutually exclusive, P(a 2 or a 5) = $P(2) + P(5) = \frac{1}{8} + \frac{1}{8} = \frac{2}{8} = \frac{1}{4}$

   b. Since there is an overlapping condition, P(mult. of 2 or mult. of 3) = P(mult. of 2) + P(mult. of 3) − P(mult. 2 and 3) = $\frac{4}{8} + \frac{2}{8} - \frac{1}{8} = \frac{5}{8}$

PRACTICE

1. A coin is tossed and a die with numbers 1–6 is rolled. What is P(heads and 3)?

   A. $\frac{1}{12}$ B. $\frac{1}{4}$ C. $\frac{1}{3}$ D. $\frac{2}{3}$

2. Two cards are selected from a deck of cards numbered 1 through 10. Once a card is selected it is not replaced. What is P(two even numbers)?

   A. $\frac{1}{4}$ B. $\frac{2}{9}$ C. $\frac{1}{2}$ D. 1

3. Which of the following is NOT an example of independent events?

   A. Rolling a die and spinning a spinner
   B. Tossing a coin two times
   C. Picking two cards from a deck with replacement of first card
   D. Selecting two marbles one at a time without replacement

4. A club has 25 members, 20 boys and 5 girls. Two members are selected at random to serve as president and vice president. What is the probability that both will be girls?

   A. $\frac{1}{5}$ B. $\frac{1}{25}$ C. $\frac{1}{30}$ D. $\frac{1}{4}$

5. One marble is randomly drawn and then replaced from a jar containing two white marbles and one black marble. A second marble is drawn. What is the probability of drawing a white and then a black?

   A. $\frac{1}{3}$ B. $\frac{2}{9}$ C. $\frac{3}{8}$ D. $\frac{1}{6}$

6. Maria rolls a pair of dice. What is the probability that she obtains a sum that is either a multiple of 3 OR a multiple of 4?

   A. $\frac{5}{9}$ B. $\frac{7}{12}$ C. $\frac{1}{36}$ D. $\frac{7}{36}$

7. Greg rolls a pair of dice. What is the probability that he obtains a sum of 2 OR 12?

8. Jack never pairs his socks after doing laundry. He just throws the socks into the drawer randomly. If the drawer contains 14 white socks and 12 grey socks, what is the probability he will select a pair of grey socks when selecting two socks at random? Give your answer as a decimal rounded to the nearest thousandth.

9. Find the probability of spinning red AND even given the spinners pictured.

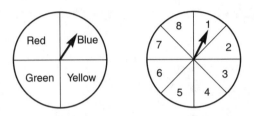

10. A basketball player is given two free throws for a foul committed against him. During the season, he has made 36 out of 50 free throws attempted. Using this experimental probability, find the probability of each event as a percent.

   a. Making both free throws
   b. Making neither free throw
   c. Making one free throw

11. Events A and B are independent. The probability of event A occurring is $\frac{3}{5}$ and the probability of event B not occurring is $\frac{2}{3}$. What is $P(A \text{ and } B)$?

12. Suppose E and F are independent events. The probability that event E will occur is .7 and the probability that event F will occur is .6.

   a. Find the probability of E and F both occurring.
   b. Explain why the answer should be less than each of the individual probabilities.
   c. Suppose E and F are independent events with the probability of E being p and the probability of F being q. If $P(E \text{ and } F) = .36$ and $P(E) \neq P(F)$, find a pair of possible values for p and q.

---

3 A 3 The Counting Principle

In finding theoretical probabilities, it is often necessary to have an efficient method for finding the total number of possible outcomes.

If special license plates require two letters followed by two digits (with all letters and digits possible), the product $26 \times 26 \times 10 \times 10$ will give the total number of possible license plates. The *counting principle* says that if there are 26 possible letters for the first letter and 26 for the second letter, and 10 choices for the first digit and 10 choices for the second digit, the product will yield the total number of possibilities.

> **The Counting Principle:**
>
> The total number of ways that a multipart event can happen is the *product* of the number of ways that the individual parts can happen.

Factorial Notation

Use of the counting principle often results in the need to indicate products of consecutive descending factors where 1 is the last factor. A notation used for this purpose is called *factorial*.

$$5 \times 4 \times 3 \times 2 \times 1 = 5! \quad \text{read as 5 factorial}$$

Most scientific and graphing calculators contain a factorial key.

Note: 0! is defined as equal to 1.

 **MODEL PROBLEMS**

1. In how many different ways can five students be seated on a five-seat bench?

Solution: Any of the 5 students may be seated in the first seat. After a student is seated in the first seat, there are 4 choices for the second seat. For each successive seat, the number of choices decreases by 1.

Use the counting principle:

$$\underset{\substack{\text{1st} \\ \text{seat}}}{5} \cdot \underset{\substack{\text{2nd} \\ \text{seat}}}{4} \cdot \underset{\substack{\text{3rd} \\ \text{seat}}}{3} \cdot \underset{\substack{\text{4th} \\ \text{seat}}}{2} \cdot \underset{\substack{\text{5th} \\ \text{seat}}}{1}$$

Answer: = 120 possibilities

2. From the digits 0–9, how many different four-digit numbers are possible if the number must be an odd multiple of 5 with no repeated digits in the number?

Solution: Since the number must be an odd multiple of 5, there is only one choice for the units digit: it must be a 5.

For the digit in the thousands place, you cannot use a 5 or a 0, leaving you with 8 possibilities.

For the digit in the hundreds place, you cannot use a 5 or the digit used in the thousands place. As a result, you have 8 possibilities.

It then follows that you will have 7 possibilities for the digit in the tens place.

Answer: Using the counting principle, you get $8 \cdot 8 \cdot 7 \cdot 1$ or 448 possible numbers.

3. Find the value of $\dfrac{10!}{6!}$.

Solution:

$$10! = 10 \times 9 \times 8 \times 7 \times 6 \times 5 \times 4 \times 3 \times 2 \times 1$$
$$6! = 6 \times 5 \times 4 \times 3 \times 2 \times 1$$

Therefore, as a result of reducing the fraction,

$$\frac{10!}{6!} = 10 \times 9 \times 8 \times 7 = 5{,}040$$

4. How many pizzas can be made using 0, 1, 2, 3, or 4 of the following toppings: pepperoni, onion, mushroom, green pepper?

Solution:

Although it is possible to try to make systematic listing, this process is too time consuming. It is better to apply the counting principle by indicating the number of choices regarding each topping.

$$\underset{\text{pepperoni}}{2} \quad \underset{\text{onion}}{2} \quad \underset{\text{mushroom}}{2} \quad \underset{\text{green pepper}}{2}$$

Using this approach, you are saying that there are 2 possibilities for pepperoni (either it will be on the pie or not), and the same for the other toppings.

$$2 \times 2 \times 2 \times 2 = 2^4 = 16 \text{ total possible pizzas}$$

PRACTICE

1. Marcia, Doris, Roberta, and Carmen are running a race. If there are no ties, in how many different ways can they finish the race?

    A. 6　　B. 12
    C. 24　　D. 36

2. The track team needs to select a four-person team from among Mike, Dan, Steve, Robert, Richard, and John. How many different four-person relay teams can be made from the six runners?

    A. 24　　B. 256
    C. 360　　D. 720

3. A true/false quiz has 10 questions. How many different sets of answers are possible?

    A. 10!　　B. 20　　C. 2^{10}　　D. 100

4. How many different batting orders are possible for a nine-player softball team if the lead-off batter is always Tom Jones; the clean-up hitter (4th in the batting order) is always Sal Rivera; and the pitcher, Sandy Carlton, always bats in the ninth spot?

Lineup	
1. Tom Jones	Left Fielder
2.	
3.	
4. Sal Rivera	Center Fielder
5.	
6.	
7.	
8.	
9. Sandy Carlton	Pitcher

5. Four roads go from town A to town B. Three roads go from town B to town C. In addition, there are two roads that go from A to C without going through B. In how many ways can you go from A to C?

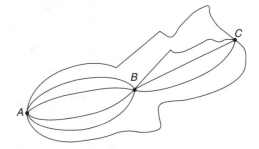

6. If $k \times 8! = 10!$, find the value of k.

7. Observe that $8 \times 7! = 8!$ and $5 \times 4! = 5!$. Write the generalization that follows.

8. Using the digits 5, 6, 7, 8, with repetition of digits possible, how many four-digit numbers can be formed if the number must be greater than 8,000 and also a multiple of 5?

9. Suppose a state's license plates have three digits, then a picture of the state bird, and then three more digits.

    a. If any digit (including zero) can go in any position, how many license plates are possible?

    b. If the state expects to use up all of the license plate numbers within the next year, it needs to have a plan to develop more numbers. If it decides to replace the first three digits with letters of the alphabet, how many license plate numbers are now possible? Show your process.

    c. A member of the state transportation board suggested that one additional digit (for a total of 7 digits) would be better than 6 spaces with the three letters and three digits. Is this suggestion accurate? Explain.

1. One marble is randomly drawn, and then NOT REPLACED, from a jar containing two white marbles and one black marble. A second marble is drawn. What is the probability of drawing a white one and then a black one?

   A. $\frac{1}{3}$ B. $\frac{2}{9}$ C. $\frac{3}{8}$ D. $\frac{1}{6}$

2. From a club of 21 students, 12 girls and 9 boys, two students will be randomly selected to serve as president and vice president. What is the probability that two girls will be selected?

   A. $\frac{1}{4}$ B. $\frac{9}{35}$ C. $\frac{11}{35}$ D. $\frac{4}{7}$

3. In rolling two dice, the probability of obtaining a sum of 12 (the largest possible sum) is $\frac{1}{36}$. What is the probability of obtaining the largest possible sum when you roll five dice?

   A. $\frac{5}{36}$ B. $\frac{1}{1,296}$ C. $\frac{1}{216}$ D. $\frac{1}{7,776}$

4. Assume that there is an equal probability that a baby will be born on a given day of the week and that there is also an equal probability that a baby will be either male or female. What is the probability that a baby will be a male born on a Sunday?

   A. $\frac{1}{49}$ B. $\frac{1}{14}$ C. $\frac{1}{7}$ D. $\frac{1}{2}$

5. The Smith family plans to have three children. Assume that male children and female children are equally likely. What is the probability that the oldest child will be a girl?

   A. $\frac{1}{3}$ B. $\frac{1}{8}$ C. $\frac{1}{2}$ D. $\frac{3}{8}$

6. In how many ways can seven different books be arranged on a bookshelf?

   A. 7^2 B. $7!$ C. $7\frac{1}{2}$ D. 7^7

7. License plates are assigned three-digit numbers followed by a group of three letters. Zero is not allowed to be the first digit in the number, and Q, X, O, P, Z, D are not allowed to be the first letter in the letter group. Repeats of digits and letters are allowed. How many different license plates are possible?

   A. 5,832,000   B. 8,424,000
   C. 12,168,000   D. 17,576,000

8. Mel's success record in achieving basketball free throws is 60%. With no time left on the clock, Mel's team is losing by 1 point, and Mel has a free throw in a 1-and-1 situation (that is, if Mel makes the first free throw, he is given another free throw). What is the probability that Mel's team will win the game?

   A. 24%   B. 36%   C. 40%   D. 60%

9. Which of the following pairs of probabilities would NOT represent complementary events?

   A. $\frac{1}{5}$ and $\frac{4}{5}$ B. $\frac{1}{2}$ and $\frac{1}{2}$
   C. .01 and .9   D. .01 and .99

10. Dimitri is asked to find the probability that a die will show an even number or a number greater than 1 on a single roll of the die. He adds the individual probabilities and comes up with a probability of $\frac{8}{6}$. Explain why this result is NOT reasonable.

11. The digits 2, 3, 4 are used to form three-digit whole numbers, without any repetition of digits. What is the probability that a randomly selected number, from among all those generated by the above, is NOT an even number?

12. For the spinner shown, the probability of landing on each color is 25% or $\frac{1}{4}$.

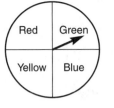

Draw a spinner so that the probabilities (P) would be as follows:

P(Red)   = .5
P(Yellow) = .25
P(Orange) = .2
P(Brown) = .05

13. Find the value of $\frac{7 \times 6!}{7!}$.

14. If the probability of an event E is $\frac{2}{17}$, what are the odds against E happening?

15. An ice cream store has 8 flavors of ice cream and the following toppings: whipped cream, chocolate sauce, nuts, and marshmallow. A junior ice cream sundae consists of one scoop of ice cream and one or more toppings. How many junior sundaes are possible?

16. A box contains 15 marbles: 6 green, 4 red, and 5 blue. Name a compound event that would have a probability of $\frac{4}{15} \times \frac{3}{14} \times \frac{2}{13}$.

17. Three dice are rolled. Obtaining a sum of 3 is not very likely. What other sum would have the same probability as a sum of 3?

18. Suppose a dress code survey that included 200 men and 200 women had results as indicated in the table.

	For Stronger Dress Code	Against Stronger Dress Code	Total
Men	80	120	200
Women	110	90	200
Total	190	210	400

Find the probability that a person chosen at random, from among the 400 people, is a male against a stronger dress code.

OPEN-ENDED QUESTIONS

19. a. Find the probability that an object landing randomly on the figure will land in the shaded circle. Express the probability as a percent.

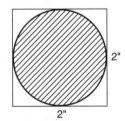

2"

2"

b. Would the probability change if we used this double diagram? Explain your answer.

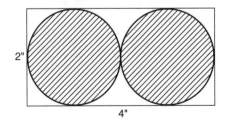

2"

4"

20. In a family of three children there are 8 possibilities for the boy-girl combinations, such as BBG, GBG, etc.

a. The probability of all boys equals the probability of all girls. What would each of these be?

b. The probability of 2 boys and 1 girl is equal to $\frac{3}{8}$. Explain why it is $\frac{3}{8}$ and not $\frac{1}{8}$.

c. For this family of three children, what other situation would have a probability equal to $\frac{3}{8}$?

d. If the family had four children, how would the answer to part a change?

Understand and interpret statistical distributions and apply to real-world situations.

3 B 1 Relationships Involving Data

A *scatter plot* is a graph used to show a relationship or *correlation* between sets of data. In a scatter plot, we plot the data as ordered pairs, represented by unconnected points. The pattern of the data points shows the correlation, if any, between the two data sets. If most of the data points are clustered together along an imaginary line, the two data sets are correlated.

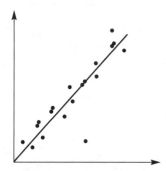  

Positive Correlation
both sets of data
increase together

Negative Correlation
one set of data
decreases as the
other set increases

No Correlation
the data sets are
not related

A *line of best fit* or *trend line* can be drawn near where most of the points cluster on a scatter plot. If the line slopes upward, there exists a positive correlation. If the line slopes downward, there exists a negative correlation. Graphing calculators can be used to determine an equation for a line of best fit.

Outliers are points that lie far from the overall linear pattern.

1. Plot the data given in the table on a graph. Draw the trend line that best fits the data. Does the graph show a positive or negative correlation?

Height (in.)	60	62	63	65	68	69	70	70	72	74	75	75
Weight (lb)	120	122	125	130	132	142	158	147	150	152	160	156

Solution:

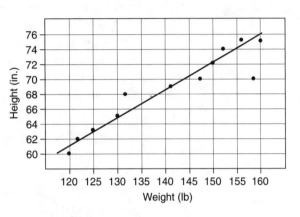

Answer: The trend line slopes upward, showing a positive correlation.

2. Describe the correlation that would exist in each of the following:

a.

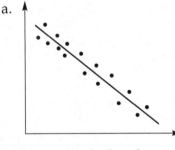

b. Hours worked and earnings

c.

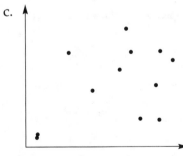

Solution:

a. The scatter plot suggests a line that slopes downward to the right. The two data sets would have a negative correlation.

b. You would expect to earn more if you worked more hours. Therefore, a positive correlation exists.

c. The points are very spread out. There appears to be no correlation.

1. For which of the following situations would you expect the scatter plot to show a negative correlation?

    A. The number of students in a high school and the average temperature of the city
    B. The age of the car and the resale value
    C. The price of an item and the amount of tax on the item
    D. The speed of a car and the distance traveled in a fixed time

2. Which scatter plot shows a positive correlation?

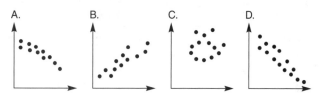

3. For which of the following situations would you expect the scatter plot to show no correlation?

    A. Miles driven and gallons of gas used
    B. Driving speed and driving time on a 5-mile stretch of highway
    C. Number of pages in a book and number of copies sold
    D. Oven temperature and cooking time for a 12-pound turkey

4. Which of the following could be the equation for the line of best fit for the scatter plot shown?

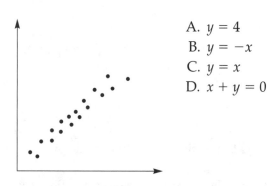

    A. $y = 4$
    B. $y = -x$
    C. $y = x$
    D. $x + y = 0$

5. Display the data in a scatter plot and describe the type of correlation present.

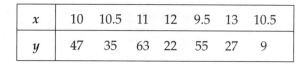

x	10	10.5	11	12	9.5	13	10.5
y	47	35	63	22	55	27	9

6. Two students in a geometry class made a scatter plot to show the relationship between diameter and circumference of circular objects. For each object (such as the top of a coffee can), they plotted the points (diameter on the horizontal axis and circumference on the vertical axis) and drew the line of best fit.

    a. Draw a possible scatter plot to go along with this situation.
    b. What type of correlation did they find? Why does this make sense?
    c. Explain why you would not expect your data to include any outliers.

7. Explain why you would not need to gather data and draw a scatter plot in order to determine the type of correlation between the length of the sides of a square and the perimeter of the square. What type of correlation exists?

8. Using the scatter plot, estimate what the value of new-home sales in the region might have been for 1995. Can you extrapolate a reasonable value for sales in 1997? Explain.

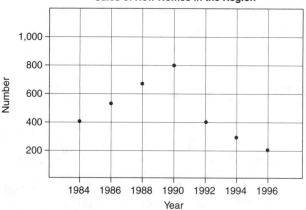

Sales of New Homes in the Region

3 B 2 Direct and Inverse Variation

Direct Variation

Jamal works at a store after school and is paid $5 per hour. He knows that the more hours he works, the more money he makes. The relationship between hours worked and wages paid is described as a *direct variation*, and the wages *vary directly* with the hours worked.

A relationship is a **direct variation** if it can be expressed as:

$$y = kx, \text{ where } k \neq 0$$

Inverse Variation

A car traveling 50 mph will take 6 hours to go 300 miles. However, a car traveling 60 mph will take only 5 hours to go the same 300 miles. The relationship between rate and time is called an *inverse variation*, and time is said to *vary inversely* with rate.

A relationship is an **inverse variation** if it can be expressed by the equation:

$$y = \frac{k}{x} \quad \text{or} \quad xy = k$$

Note: k is called the **constant of variation** for both types of variations.

 **MODEL PROBLEMS**

1. The annual interest on a loan varies directly with the amount borrowed. The interest on a loan of $600 is $27. What is the interest on a loan of $800?

Solution: Since the interest varies directly with the amount borrowed,

$$\frac{600}{27} = k \text{ and } \frac{800}{\text{interest}} = k$$

Therefore: $\dfrac{800}{x} = \dfrac{600}{27}$

$$21{,}600 = 600x$$

Answer: $x = \$36$

2. For a constant area, the width of a rectangle varies inversely with the length. If the length of one rectangle is 12″ and its width is 3″, how long is a rectangle with the same area and a width of 4″?

Solution: The width varies inversely with the length.

$$\ell w = A$$

$$(12)(3) = A = 36$$

Since the areas are the same, using dimensions of 4 and ℓ for the second rectangle,

$$4\ell = 36$$

Answer: $\ell = 9''$

3. Do the data in each table represent direct or inverse variation? Write an equation to model the data.

a.
x	y
3	15
5	25
6	30
8	40

b.
x	y
1	12
2	6
3	4
4	3
6	2

Solution:

a. As x increases, y increases. The data show direct variation. The equation would be $y = 5x$.

b. As x increases, y decreases. The data show inverse variation. The equation would be $xy = 12$.

PRACTICE

1. Which of the following is NOT an example of a direct variation?

   A. The number of gallons of gasoline purchased and the total cost
   B. If speed is constant, the distance traveled and the time traveled
   C. The value of a used car and the age of the car
   D. The circumference of a circle and the length of the diameter

2. y is directly proportional to x. If $y = 20$ when $x = 16$, find the constant of variation.

   A. 0.8   B. 1.25   C. 32   D. 320

3. For which table do the data NOT represent direct variation?

   A.
x	y
-2	-4
-1	-2
0	0
3	6

   B.
x	y
0	0
1	10
3	30
6	60
10	100

   C.
x	y
0	2
1	3
3	5
10	12

   D.
x	y
0	0
2	0.5
4	1
8	2
20	5

4. If y varies inversely with x, what is the missing value in the table?

x	y
1	36
2	18
2.5	?
3	12
4	9

   A. 16   B. 15.5   C. 15   D. 14.4

5. x varies inversely as y. If $x = 70$ when $y = 8$, find x when $y = 28$.

6. The perimeter of a square varies directly with the length of a side.

   The perimeter is 16 feet when the side measures 4 feet.

   What is the perimeter when the side measures 5.25 feet?

7. If it takes 2.5 hours to make a trip traveling at 50 mph, how long would it take to make the same trip at a speed of 40 mph?

8. In a relationship y varies inversely with x. What happens to the value of y if x is doubled?

9. The depth of water in a tub varies directly as the length of time the taps are on. If the taps are left on for four minutes, the depth of the water is 24 cm.

a. Find the depth of the water if the taps are left on for 5 minutes.
b. Find the length of time the taps were left on if the depth of the water is 42 cm.
c. Write an equation relating depth to time.
d. Graph the relation between depth and time.

10. Given the graph shown.

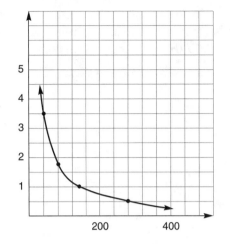

a. Does the graph illustrate a direct or inverse variation? Explain.
b. Give two additional ordered pairs that would appear on the graph if the graph were extended.
c. Suggest a practical situation represented by the given graph.

3 B 3 Probability Distributions

Discrete Probability Distribution

A discrete probability distribution lists the values associated with the outcomes of an event and the probabilities associated with the values. The discrete probability distribution for the outcomes in tossing three coins is as follows:

Number of heads	0	1	2	3
Probability	.125	.375	.375	.125

It should be noted that the sum of the probabilities must be one.

Continuous Probability Distribution

In a continuous probability distribution, the area under portions of a curve corresponds to probabilities. A familiar continuous probability distribution is the *normal distribution* or normal curve.

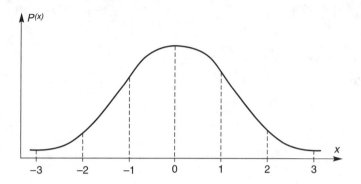

The normal curve distribution is symmetric and bell shaped and has the following properties:

- About 68% of the area (or data) is within 1 standard deviation of the mean.
- About 95% of the area (or data) is within 2 standard deviations of the mean.
- About 99.7% of the area (or data) is within 3 standard deviations of the mean.

The area under the standard normal curve between two data values is closely related to probability. The area under the curve between two values (along the horizontal) is equal to the probability that an outcome (data value) falls between the two limits.

It should be noted that the total area under the curve must be one.

MODEL PROBLEMS

1. The local Sneaker Pro store needs to make a decision concerning the inventory required of sneakers in mens' sizes greater than 14. Assuming that mens' sneaker sizes are normally distributed with a mean of 9 and a standard deviation of 1.5, show a graph and explain what decision should be made by the store.

Solution:

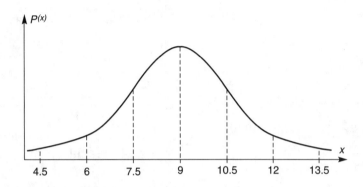

Since you are told that the mean size is 9 and the standard deviation is 1.5, a size of 14 would be more than 3 standard deviations above the mean (9 + 3 × 1.5 = 13.5). As a result, the normal curve properties would say that there is greater than a 99.7% probability that a sneaker size would be 13.5 or smaller. Therefore, the store should not worry about having much of an inventory in sizes greater than 14.

2. The professor of a large class gives 15% each of A's and D's, 30% each of B's and C's, and 10% F's. What is the probability that a student got a B or better?

Solution:

The table shows the probability distribution as stated in the problem.

Grade (X)	A	B	C	D	F
Probability	.15	.30	.30	.15	.10

The probability that the student got a B or better is the sum of the probabilities of an A or a B.

$$P(\text{B or better}) = .30 + .15 = .45$$

1. A number cube has the following faces: 2, 3, 3, 4, 4, 4. Complete the table to show the discrete probabilities for the outcomes of rolling the number cube.

Outcome	2	3	4
Probabilities			

2. Given a normal distribution that has a mean of 10 and a standard deviation of 2, complete the following statements.

   a. Approximately 68% of the data will be between ___ and ___.
   b. Approximately 95% of the data will be between ___ and ___.
   c. Approximately 2.5% of the data will be greater than ___.

3. The graph shows a set of normally distributed test scores. What percentage of the people taking the test scored between 400 and 600?

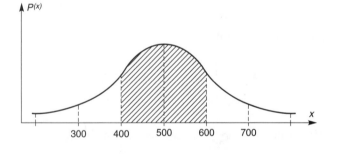

4. What percent of the area under the normal curve shown is shaded if the standard deviation is 150?

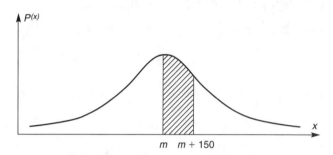

5. A game involves selecting three cards, with replacement, from a deck of 16 cards: ace, 2, 3, and 4 of each suit. Let x represent the number of aces selected. Find the distribution of x. That is, what values can x take, and what are the probabilities for each value?

6. The heights of U.S. males from 18 to 24 years old are approximately normally distributed with a mean of about 70 inches and a standard deviation of about 3 inches.

   a. What is the approximate probability that a randomly selected male in this age group is over 76 inches tall?

   b. Suppose you see a group of 5 males in this age group who are all over 76 inches tall. What is the probability of this happening randomly?

Collect, organize, represent, analyze, and interpret data.

Note:

The Assessment for Macro B is combined with and follows Macro C.

3 C 1 Populations and Samples

The entire group of objects or people involved in a statistical study is called a *population*. However, it is usually impossible to study a very large group. Hence a subset representative of the population, called a *sample*, is usually used in the study. The process of choosing the sample is called *sampling*. It is important to make sure the sample collected is unbiased and representative of the entire population. A random sample will give everyone or everything the same chance of being selected.

 **MODEL PROBLEMS**

1. The Cake Box surveyed people about the type of frosting they preferred on cakes. Use the results to predict how many of the 952 students at Washington High School would choose whipped cream.

Type of Frosting	Percent
whipped cream	55%
butter cream	40%
no preference	5%

Solution: Since 55% of the sample preferred whipped cream, finding 55% of 952 students allows you to make the prediction.

Answer: 0.55(952) = 523.6 or approximately 524 students

2. A quality tester finds three faulty batteries in a sample of 60 batteries. If there is a 2% margin of error, estimate the interval that contains the number of faulty batteries in a group of 3,000.

Solution: Let x = the number of faulty batteries in the group.

$$\frac{\text{faulty in sample}}{\text{total in sample}} = \frac{3}{60} = \frac{x}{3,000} = \frac{\text{faulty in group}}{\text{total in group}}$$

$$3(3,000) = 60x$$
$$9,000 = 60x$$
$$150 = x$$

Use the margin of error to estimate:

$$2\% \text{ of } 3,000 = (0.02)(3,000) = 60$$
$$\text{interval is } 150 - 60 \text{ to } 150 + 60$$

Answer: The interval is 90 to 210 batteries in the total group are faulty.

1. A sporting goods company surveyed 800 baseball players to see what type of bat they preferred. Aluminum bats were preferred over wood by 300 players. Which statement is true?

   A. More than $\frac{1}{2}$ of the players surveyed preferred aluminum.

   B. More than 40% of the players surveyed preferred aluminum.

   C. More than 75% of the players surveyed do not prefer aluminum.

   D. More than $\frac{1}{3}$ of the players surveyed prefer aluminum.

2. Which of the following samples is an example of an unbiased survey?

   A. A random sample of 500 teens in the Northeast to determine the favorite music group for teens ages 13–15

   B. A random sample of 500 men over 50 years of age to determine which brand of vitamins men over 50 prefer

   C. A random sample of 250 women aged 18–35 to determine the favorite brand of ice cream of people 18–35

   D. A random sample of 150 zoo visitors to determine if taxpayers feel that federal money should be used to help run the zoo

3. An office supply store surveyed a group of 200 students to determine their preference for backpack colors. Backpacks come in green, black, blue, and red. Based on the survey results the store will determine the color distribution for its order of 1,000 backpacks. If 75 chose black, 25 chose red, 40 chose green, and the rest chose blue, how many green backpacks will they order?

4. A television rating service found that 945 households out of a sample of 3,340 households watched the Super Bowl. Estimate to the nearest million how many of the 94 million households with a television watched the Super Bowl.

5. Biologists captured 400 deer, tagged them, and released them back into the same region. Later that season, the deer population was sampled to estimate the size of the population that lived in the region. If a sample of 150 deer contained 45 tagged deer, what would be a good estimate for the deer population in the region?

6. A quality tester finds two broken bulbs in every lot of 100. Suppose the margin of error is 3%. Estimate the interval that contains the number of broken bulbs in a lot of 5,000.

3 C 2 Statistical Measures

A set of data, or values, can be described by using the *mean, median, mode,* or *range.* The mean, the median, and the mode are called ***measures of central tendency***.

- The *mean* is the arithmetic *average*. It is found by dividing the sum of the values by the number of values.
- The *median* is the middle value when the values are listed in order. (*Note:* If the set contains an even number of values, the median is the average of the two values in the middle.)
- The *mode* is the value occurring most frequently.
- The *range* is the difference between the largest value and the smallest value.
- The *frequency* of a value is the count of the value—that is, how many times the value appears.

data: 36 36 36 43 43 51 54 58 61

mean = 418 ÷ 9 = 46.4   median = 43   mode = 36   range = 61 − 36 = 25

The frequency of 36 is 3, of 43 is 2, and of the other values is 1.

 **MODEL PROBLEMS**

1. Debbie has the following scores on five math tests:

    88 84 80 90 84

    What score must she get on the sixth test in order for her average to fall between 85 and 87?

    Solution: The sum of the six scores must be 6 times the average.

    $$6 \times 85 = 510$$
    $$6 \times 87 = 522$$

    The sum of the first five scores is 426.

    Answer: The sixth score must fall between 84 [510 − 426] and 96 [522 − 426].

2. Give a set of five scores such that the data would have (a) a median of 60, (b) a mode of 52, and (c) a mean of 65.

    Solution:

    a. __ __ 60 __ __
        If the median for five scores is 60, the third score must be 60. **Answer**

    b. 52 52 60 __ __
        Since the mode is 52, the lowest two scores must each be 52. **Answer**

    c. Since the mean is 65, the sum of the five scores must be 5 × 65 = 325. With 164 as the sum of the first three scores, the highest two scores must total 325 − 164 or 161. Hence, the remaining two scores must be any two distinct numbers above 60 that total 161. For example, one solution is: 52, 52, 60, 80, 81. The solution is not unique. **Answer**

1. During a baseball season, the National League home-run champion had the following home-run statistics by month:

April	May	June	July	August	September	October
5	13	7	11	6	8	6

Which month contains the median for the player's home-run statistics?

A. June
B. July
C. August
D. September

2. For each number shown in the box, the units digit is hidden. Which of the following could NOT be the mean of the set?

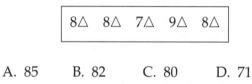

A. 85   B. 82   C. 80   D. 71

3. The following data represent morning temperatures for the month of July in Washington, D.C. What are the mean and median of the data?

89 87 85 88 93 93 93 89 90 91 90 89 88 89 87 90
91 92 92 92 90 89 87 85 86 84 84 83 85 86 88

A. Mean 84.3, median 91
B. Mean 82.9, median 90
C. Mean 88.5, median 89
D. Mean 83.9, median 88

4. For the given scores, the mean is 40.

Scores: 20, 30, 40, 50, 60

If the 20 is changed to a 17, which of the following would have to be done in order for the mean to remain at 40?

A. Change the 50 to a 47.
B. Change the 60 to a 57.
C. Change the 50 to a 53.
D. Change the 30 to a 27.

5. For a set of 6 scores, the following can be noted:

> Score #1 is 6 points below the mean.
>
> Score #2 is 10 points below the mean.
>
> Score #3 is 4 points below the mean.
>
> Score #4 is equal to the mean.

Which of the following could be TRUE about the remaining two scores?

A. Scores #5 and #6 are both equal to the mean.
B. Score #5 is 12 points above the mean and Score #6 is 8 points above the mean.
C. Score #5 is 10 points above the mean and Score #6 is 10 points below the mean.
D. Score #5 is 20 points above the mean and Score #6 is 4 points above the mean.

6. Which of the following statements will always be TRUE?

   I. The mode is always close to the median.
   II. The median is sometimes not included in the data.
   III. The mean is always included in the data.

   A. I only
   B. II only
   C. III only
   D. I and II only

7. The list shows the prices for several different concerts:

   $40 $45 $50 $58 $60 $67 $80 $90

   If an additional concert price of $16 is added to the list, which measure of central tendency is affected most?

8. Edgardo had the following test scores in his science class:

   90   73   86   89   97

   What score must he get on the sixth test in order for his average to turn out to be 89?

9. The mean for a set of 5 scores is 60. The mean for a different set of 10 scores is 90. What is the mean for all 15 scores?

10. Give three different values for x so that 80 would be the median.

Score	Number of Students
90	4
85	2
80	3
75	x
70	4

11. Mr. Abbott asked his math students to use the following data to find average test scores.

Mr. Abbott's Classes		
Period	No. of Students	Test Average
1 Algebra	20	80
2 Algebra	20	70
3 Geometry	30	84
5 Geometry	10	80

In computing the average test score for the combined algebra classes, Bill suggested that Mr. Abbott take the average of 80 and 70 to get 75. For the two combined geometry classes, however, using the same approach gives a wrong result of 82. Explain why the first average (75) was correct but the second average (82) was NOT correct. Find the correct average for the two geometry classes. Explain your approach.

3 C 3 Data Displays

Data can be organized and displayed by using a variety of different graphs. Tables, charts, matrices, and spreadsheets are also commonly used to display data. The type of graph or device used is determined by the nature of the data and what the data are intended to communicate.

A *circle graph* is used to compare parts of a whole. It is sometimes called a *pie chart*.

Profits From Local Carnival

A *bar graph* compares amounts of quantities.

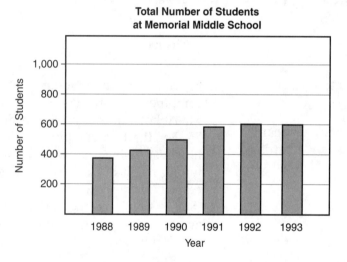

A *pictograph* also compares amounts. A symbol is used to represent a stated amount.

Number of Townhouses in Condominium Complexes

A *histogram* is a bar graph used to show frequencies. In a histogram, the bars, which usually represent grouped intervals, are adjacent.

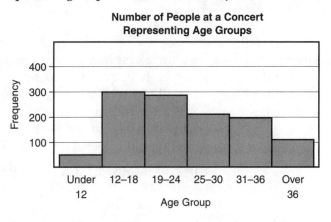

A *line graph* shows continuous change and trends over time.

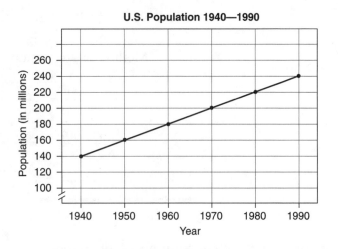

A *line plot* is another way to organize frequency data. A line plot is a picture of the data on a number line corresponding to the range of the data.

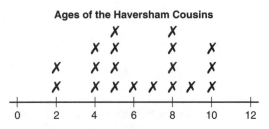

As is shown in the example above, in a line plot you place an x (or a dot) above the appropriate number to indicate each occurrence.

1. You need to construct a graph showing the trend in the price of a gallon of gasoline each month over a five-year period of time. Which of the following types of displays would be most appropriate?

    A. Circle graph
    B. Histogram
    C. Line plot
    D. Line graph

    Solution: Since the situation depicts changing prices over a period of time, the most appropriate display would be the line graph.

    A circle graph is not appropriate since you are not looking at parts of a whole.

    A histogram is not appropriate since you are not comparing intervals of prices.

    A line plot is not appropriate since you are not organizing frequency data.

2. In a circle graph involving a monthly budget, the family in question spends $800 on housing out of a total budget of $2,500. In using a protractor for this sector of the graph, how many degrees (to the nearest tenth of a degree) would correspond to housing?

    Solution: Method 1: finding a percent:

    $$\frac{\text{housing}}{\text{total}} = \frac{800}{2,500} = 0.32$$

    Therefore, we need 32% of 360°, which equals 115.2°.

    Method 2: proportion:

    $$\frac{800}{2,500} = \frac{x}{360}$$

    $$\frac{360(800)}{2,500} = x$$

    $$115.2° = x$$

A *matrix* (plural: *matrices*) is a rectangular arrangement of numbers corresponding to a real-world situation involving data. In a matrix the numbers are arranged in rows and columns. The 3-by-2 matrix below displays the sales of a particular new car by three dealers in June vs. July.

$$\begin{pmatrix} 20 & 12 \\ 3 & 11 \\ 10 & 7 \end{pmatrix}$$

One can add or subtract matrices containing the same number of rows and columns. You add or subtract matrices by adding or subtracting corresponding values. Graphing calculators may be used to perform matrix operations.

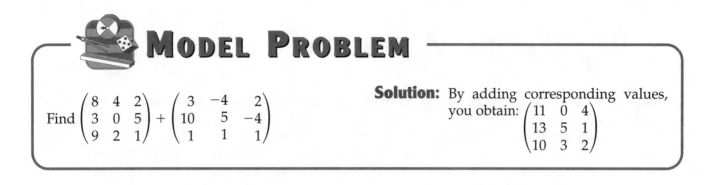
Find $\begin{pmatrix} 8 & 4 & 2 \\ 3 & 0 & 5 \\ 9 & 2 & 1 \end{pmatrix} + \begin{pmatrix} 3 & -4 & 2 \\ 10 & 5 & -4 \\ 1 & 1 & 1 \end{pmatrix}$

Solution: By adding corresponding values, you obtain: $\begin{pmatrix} 11 & 0 & 4 \\ 13 & 5 & 1 \\ 10 & 3 & 2 \end{pmatrix}$

Scalar multiplication of a matrix involves multiplying each element of a matrix by a real number.

$$2\begin{pmatrix} 2 & 7 \\ 5 & 0 \end{pmatrix} = \begin{pmatrix} 4 & 14 \\ 10 & 0 \end{pmatrix}$$

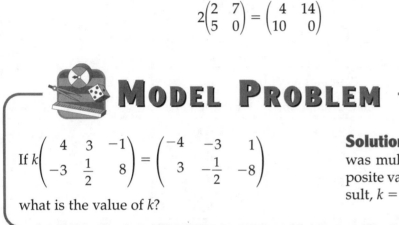
MODEL PROBLEM

If $k\begin{pmatrix} 4 & 3 & -1 \\ -3 & \frac{1}{2} & 8 \end{pmatrix} = \begin{pmatrix} -4 & -3 & 1 \\ 3 & -\frac{1}{2} & -8 \end{pmatrix}$

what is the value of k?

Solution: Each entry in the matrix on the left was multiplied by a factor to result in the opposite values in the matrix on the right. As a result, $k = -1$.

A *spreadsheet* also organizes data in rows and columns. Typically, spreadsheets are accessed through computers. In working with a spreadsheet, one considers the spreadsheet to be a large rectangular array of boxes or cells, each of which is identified by a unique address. The address consists of a letter to indicate the column in which the cell is located and a number to indicate the row in which the cell is located. A spreadsheet giving dimensions (in inches) for different rectangular solids might look like:

	A	B	C	D
1	length	width	height	volume
2	5	3	10	150
3	20	10	10	2,000
4	10	10	10	1,000

The address A3 indicates the cell being referred to is located in column A, row 3. In the spreadsheet shown the number 20 is found at that address.

The power of the spreadsheet lies in the fact that each cell can contain a numerical value determined either by direct entry of the value from the keyboard or by a mathematical formula using information obtained from cells anywhere in the spreadsheet under consideration.

For example, the value in D2 was calculated using the formula A2*B2*C2. If the values in any of the cells A2, B2, or C2 were changed, then the value in D2 would also change.

MODEL PROBLEM

The population of two towns has remained stable for many years. Oak Brook has maintained a population of approximately 25,000 and Westville has a population of approximately 40,000. Suddenly, 20% of Oak Brook's population starts moving to Westville each year, while the rest remains in Oak Brook. At the same time, 15% of Westville's population starts moving to Oak Brook each year with the rest of the population staying in Westville. Refer to the spreadsheet given for population figures (rounded to nearest whole number).

a. What is the change in Oak Brook's population over five years?
b. What is the percent of increase in population for Oak Brook over that period?
c. What formula was used to generate the values in A4, B4, C4?

	A	B	C
1	Moving	Population	
2	Year #	Oak Brook Pop.	Westville Pop.
3	0	25,000	40,000
4	1	26,000	39,000
5	2	26,650	38,350
6	3	27,073	37,928
7	4	27,348	37,653
8	5	27,526	37,475

Solution:

a. To determine the change in Oak Brook's population find the difference between the values in B3 and B8.

$$27,526 - 25,000 = 2,526$$

b. The percent of increase = increase ÷ original population

$$2,526 ÷ 25,000 = 10\% \text{ approximately}$$

c. The formulas used were:
   For A4, add one to the prior year: A4 = A3 + 1.
   For B4, 80% of Oak Brook's population stayed and 15% of Westville's is added, so B4 = 0.80*B3 + 0.15*C3.
   For C4, 85% of Westville's population stayed and 20% of Oak Brook's is added, so C4 = 0.85*C3 + 0.20*B3.

1. Which of the following types of graphs would NOT be an appropriate representation to depict the way a family budgets its September income?

   A. Bar graph   B. Pictograph
   C. Circle graph D. Line graph

2. Using the given pictograph, what percent of the total number of cars sold at Thrifty's in September did Dan sell?

   A. 60%   B. 40%   C. 30%   D. 20%

   Number of Cars Sold at Thrifty's in September

   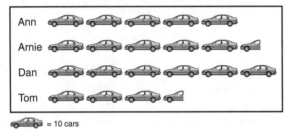

   = 10 cars

3. Use the given circle graph to determine what percent of Tim's exercise program is devoted to running.

   A. 25%

   B. 40%

   C. 60%

   D. $66\frac{2}{3}\%$

   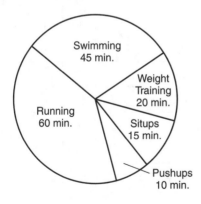

4. For which of the following situations would it NOT be appropriate to use a line graph to represent the data?

   A. Show the population of the U.S. from 1900 to 1990

   B. Show the sale of CD's during a five-year period

   C. Show survey results of how students spend one hour of their time

   D. Show the heating time for water at various altitudes

5. Given

   $$A = \begin{pmatrix} 56 & 73 \\ 69 & 84 \end{pmatrix} \quad B = \begin{pmatrix} 29 & 41 \\ 37 & 52 \end{pmatrix}$$

   what is the value of 2A + B?

   A. $\begin{pmatrix} 85 & 114 \\ 106 & 136 \end{pmatrix}$ B. $\begin{pmatrix} 114 & 155 \\ 143 & 188 \end{pmatrix}$

   C. $\begin{pmatrix} 141 & 187 \\ 175 & 220 \end{pmatrix}$ D. $\begin{pmatrix} 170 & 228 \\ 212 & 272 \end{pmatrix}$

6. Two 4-by-2 matrices have exactly the same values in the corresponding positions. Show what the matrix looks like representing the difference of the two matrices.

7. Assuming that this circle graph applies to the city of Metropolis, which has 42,000 homes, how many homes are NOT heated by natural gas?

   How We Heat Our Homes

   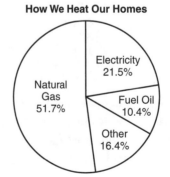

8. The South Side High School annual fund-raiser involved the sale of tins of cookies. The freshmen class sold 2,586 tins of cookies; the sophomore class 3,014 tins; the junior class 3,274 tins; and the senior class 3,326 tins.

   Construct a graph to show how the classes compared in amounts of cookies sold. Explain why you selected that type of graph to represent the data.

9. Test scores in a biology class are as follows: 83, 78, 94, 93, 87, 86, 83, 94, 99, 90, 87, 79, 65, 87, 93, 96, 88, 84, 82, 93, 85.

   a. Construct a line plot for the data.
   b. State the median score for the data.

10. This graph shows the percentages of pickle buyers who selected various types of pickles.

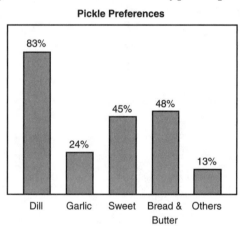

Pickle Preferences

   a. Explain why the data cannot be used to construct a circle graph.
   b. Explain what is wrong or misleading in the given graph.

11. The line plot displays scores on an 80-point mathematics test.

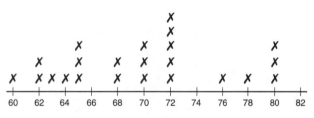

   a. Which measure of central tendency (mean, median, or mode) is most easily observed from this line plot? Explain why.
   b. What is the median test score? Explain how you find it from this line plot.

c. Suppose the teacher finds six scores that need to be added to the line plot: 72, 76, 76, 78, 80, 80.
   (i) Does the median change? If so, what is the new median?
   (ii) Does the mode change? If so, what is the new mode?
   (iii) In a general way, how does the mean change and why? (Do not actually calculate the mean.)

12. Matrix A represents the number of tickets sold for a performance of a musical play on Saturday. Matrix B represents the number of tickets sold for the performance of the same musical play on Wednesday. The columns represent matinees and evening performances. The rows represent orchestra, mezzanine, and balcony seats.

$$A = \begin{pmatrix} 275 & 295 \\ 143 & 158 \\ 65 & 87 \end{pmatrix} \quad B = \begin{pmatrix} 220 & 251 \\ 133 & 140 \\ 52 & 45 \end{pmatrix}$$

   If orchestra seats cost $50, mezzanine seats $45, and balcony seats $30, how much more did the theater make on the two evening performances compared to the two matinee performances?

13. The spreadsheet shown represents data collected from five students who were asked five questions about changes proposed to the school. A score of 1 indicated a least favorable response, while a score of 5 indicated a most favorable response. To find out the average response for question 4, which cell would you look in?

	A	B	C	D	E	F
1	NAME	Q#1	Q#2	Q#3	Q#4	Q#5
2	Alice	2	1	3	4	5
3	Bill	3	5	2	1	4
4	Dave	4	5	3	2	1
5	Jennifer	2	3	4	1	5
6	Franco	5	2	3	1	4
7						
8	AVERAGE	3.2	3.2	3.1	1.8	3.8

A. E8   B. B8   C. C8   D. D8

3 C 4 Interpreting Data

To use a graph to interpret data:

- Pay attention to the scale. Check to see if the scale has a broken line between zero and the first interval.
- Know what the numbers mean.
- Read the title and the labels on the axes.
- Check graphs with multiple lines or bars for relationships between points.
- Be able to make predictions about the relation that *goes beyond* what is displayed. This is called **extrapolation**.

To use a table to interpret data:

- Read the title and labels.
- Know what the numbers mean.
- Be able to estimate values *between* given entries. This is called **interpolation**.

When interpreting data, be alert for misuses and abuses of statistics. Statistics can be misleading if:

- An inappropriate scale is used to display data.

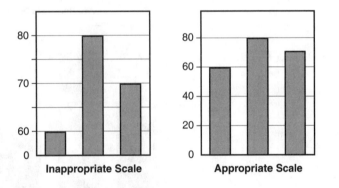

- The wrong measure of central tendency is used to describe the data.
  In a small company of six people, the salaries of individuals are $80,000; $20,000; $25,000; $19,000; $22,500; $23,500. The average salary is about $32,000. Using the average would be inappropriate to describe the set. A better descriptor of the data would be the median, $23,000.

- Insufficient titles or labels are used on the axes or chart.

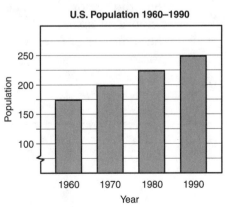

The vertical axis doesn't indicate that the numbers are in millions.

- The graphic has a visual distortion to suggest a disproportionate relation, thus not accurately illustrating the numerical relationship.

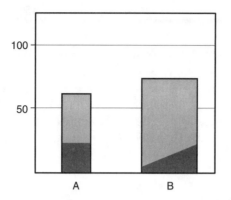

MODEL PROBLEMS

1. The graph displays the average monthly temperatures for two different years. How do the temperatures for Year A compare to those for Year B? Explain.

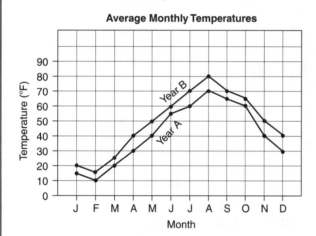

Solution: The graph of the average monthly temperatures for Year B is above the graph for Year A, indicating that the average monthly temperatures for Year B were greater than those for Year A. Since the two graphs never intersect, it is clear that at no time did a month in Year B record a temperature less than or equal to the same month for Year A.

2. What impression is given by the graph? How is this impression created?

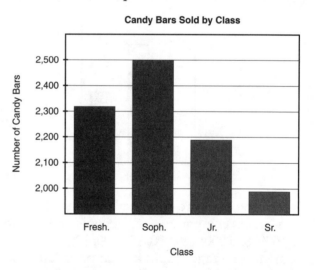

Solution: The graph suggests that the sophomore class sold significantly more candy bars than the senior class. The scale gives the same amount of space to the interval 0–2,000 as to the intervals of one hundred. This is inappropriate.

1. The following graph shows the average monthly 6:00 A.M. and 6:00 P.M. temperatures (°F) recorded at Newark Airport.

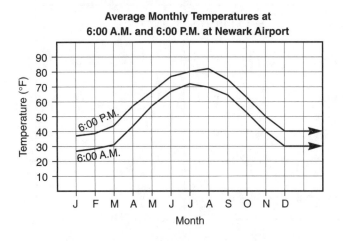

Average Monthly Temperatures at 6:00 A.M. and 6:00 P.M. at Newark Airport

a. How do you know that the graph does NOT show a situation in which the September temperatures at 6:00 A.M. and 6:00 P.M. were the same?

b. According to the graph, was there any month when the average 6:00 A.M. temperature was greater than the average 6:00 P.M. temperature? Explain your response.

2. The circle graphs show how Sally and Michele spend their earnings. How is it possible that Michele can spend a greater dollar amount on recreation than the dollar amount spent by Sally?

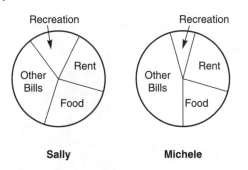

Sally   **Michele**

3. The graph shows the volume of sales of cassette tapes and compact discs (CD's) at a local music store over a six-year period. Explain the trend shown separately in Line A and Line B. Discuss the significance of the point of intersection of Line A and Line B.

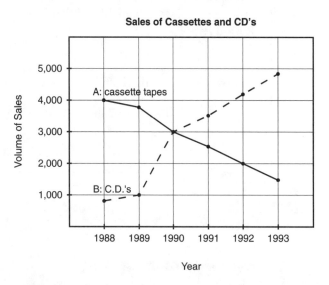

Sales of Cassettes and CD's

4. The graph is intended to compare morning coffee sales at two convenience stores in the same town. Is the visual message depicted in the graph accurate? Explain your response.

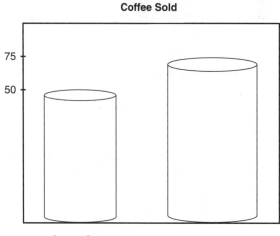

Coffee Sold

Corner Store   Java Jack's

5. Mrs. Mendez is giving a dinner party. She plans to serve a $5\frac{3}{4}$-pound standing rib roast that she plans to cook in a microwave oven. She knows that her guests prefer the meat to be cooked medium. Using the information shown, what is the minimum amount of time (in minutes) needed to cook the roast?

BEEF	Microwave Time		Internal Temperature	
	Step 1 HIGH (100%)	Step 2 MED-HIGH (70%)	At Removal	After Standing
Standing or Rolled Rib	Less than 4 lb: $6\frac{1}{2}$ min	Rare: 9–13 min/lb	120°	140°
	More than 4 lb: $10\frac{1}{2}$ min	Medium: 10–$13\frac{1}{2}$ min/lb	135°	150°
		Well Done: $10\frac{1}{2}$–15 min/lb	150°	160°
Tenderloin	Less than 2 lb: 4 min	Rare: 8–11 min/lb	120°	140°
	More than 2 lb: $6\frac{1}{2}$ min	Medium: 9–13 min/lb	135°	150°
		Well Done: $10\frac{1}{2}$–$14\frac{1}{2}$ min/lb	150°	160°

ASSESSMENT MACRO B and MACRO C

1. Suppose that the time needed to do a job varies inversely with the number of people working on the job. If it takes 8 hours for 3 people to load a moving van, how long would it take for 4 people?

   A. 4   B. 6   C. 7   D. $10\frac{2}{3}$

2. A set of data is normally distributed with a mean of 24 and a standard deviation of 7. What percent of the data values lies between 17 and 31?

   A. 34.1%   B. 47.7%   C. 68.2%   D. 95.4%

3. Given the set of data: 92, 80, 79, 75, 75, 58, 55. If the 58 and 55 were dropped from the data, which measure would remain unchanged?

   A. Median   B. Mode
   C. Mean   D. Range

4. This histogram shows final averages of the students enrolled in Algebra 1 at the North End High School.

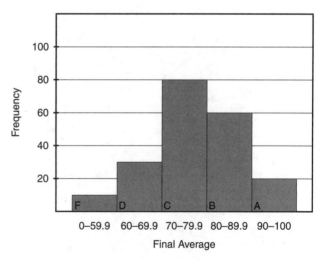

What percent of the students scored B or better in the course?

A. 20%   B. 40%   C. 60%   D. 80%

5. For which of the following situations would you use the entire population rather than a sample?

   A. A cook making sauce wants to know if there is enough salt in it.
   B. The president of the company wants to know how many people are going to the company Holiday Party.
   C. A statistical research company wants to know how many households watched the Academy Awards show.
   D. A medical research group wants to study the blood cholesterol levels of women in the United States over age 50.

6. For which of the following situations would you use the mean to analyze the data?

   A. The preferred color marker students buy
   B. The day of the week on which most students were born
   C. The grades a class received on a test
   D. The difference between the age of the oldest and youngest students in the class

7. The following graphs are used to depict the enrollment of South Side H.S. from 1985 to 1992.

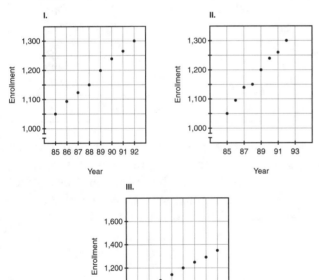

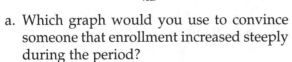

   a. Which graph would you use to convince someone that enrollment increased steeply during the period?
   b. Between which two years did the enrollment show the most growth?

8. Use this bus schedule to answer the question that follows:

Sundays								
HACKENSACK · Sears Main & Anderson Sts.	TEANECK Cedar Lane & Queen Anne Rd.	TEANECK Queen Anne Rd. & DeGraw Ave.	RIDGEFIELD PARK Main & Mt. Vernon Sts.	PALISADES PARK · Morsemere Broad & Columbia Aves.	RIDGEFIELD Traffic Circle	FAIRVIEW Nungessers	NORTH BERGEN Blvd. East & 74th St.	NEW YORK Port Authority Bus Terminal
A.M.	A.M.	A.M.	A.M.	A.M.	A.M.	A.M.	A.M.	A.M.
7.23	7.27	7.32	7.37	7.42	7.44	7.50	7.54	8.10
8.23	8.27	8.32	8.37	8.42	8.44	8.50	8.54	9.10
9.23	9.27	9.32	9.37	9.42	9.44	9.50	9.54	10.10
10.23	10.27	10.32	10.37	10.42	10.44	10.50	10.54	11.10
-	-	-	-	-	-	-	-	P.M.
11.23	11.27	11.32	11.37	11.42	11.44	11.50	11.54	12.10
P.M.	P.M.	P.M.	P.M.	P.M.	P.M.	P.M.	P.M.	-
12.23	12.27	12.32	12.37	12.42	12.44	12.50	12.54	1.10
1.23	1.27	1.32	1.37	1.42	1.44	1.50	1.54	2.10
2.23	2.27	2.32	2.37	2.42	2.44	2.50	2.54	3.10
3.23	3.27	3.32	3.37	3.42	3.44	3.50	3.54	4.10
4.23	4.27	4.32	4.37	4.42	4.44	4.50	4.54	5.10
5.23	5.27	5.32	5.37	5.42	5.44	5.50	5.54	6.10
6.23	6.27	6.32	6.37	6.42	6.44	6.50	6.54	7.10
7.26	7.32	7.37	7.42	7.47	7.49	7.55	7.59	8.15
8.26	8.32	8.37	8.42	8.47	8.49	8.55	8.59	9.15
9.26	9.32	9.37	9.42	9.47	9.49	9.55	9.59	10.15
10.26	10.32	10.37	10.42	10.47	10.49	10.55	10.59	11.15
-	-	-	-	-	-	A.M.	A.M.	A.M.
11.37	11.41	11.46	11.51	11.56	11.58	12.04	12.06	12.24

Mr. and Mrs. Norton are taking a bus from Teaneck to New York City on Sunday in order to see a Broadway show. The show begins at 3:00 P.M. and it normally takes 20 minutes to go from the bus terminal in NYC to the theater.

If they plan to board the bus at the corner of Cedar Lane and Queen Anne Road, what is the latest time they can board the bus?

   A. 12:27 P.M.   B. 1:27 P.M.
   C. 1:32 P.M.   D. 2:27 P.M.

9. Using the spreadsheet shown, what was the approximate percent of increase of $100 after it was invested at the rate of 6% componded annually for five years?

	A	B	C	D	E
1	Compound Interest				
2	Original Price	Rate	Period/Yr	Year	New Balance
3	$100	6.00	1	1	$106.00
4				2	$112.36
5				3	$119.10
6				4	$126.25
7				5	$133.82
8				6	$141.85
9				7	$150.36

A. 6%   B. 30%   C. 34%   D. 42%

10. The appraised values of seven houses on the same block are given in the following chart.

Appraised Values: Block B	
#326	$350,000
#331	$378,500
#338	$343,800
#343	$355,900
#347	$363,500
#354	$358,000
#365	$786,500

a. What is the difference between the mean and median values of the houses?

b. Which measure, mean or median, is a better representation for the data and why?

11. There are 20 students in a class. The average grade for that class on a test was computed as 74, but one student's grade was read mistakenly as 50 instead of 90. What will the average grade for that class be when it is recomputed using the correct score?

12. A random sample of 50 fish in a lake were captured and tagged. Two weeks later, a random sample of 27 fish contains 3 with tags. Estimate the number of fish in the lake.

13. The chart below indicates the costs at a local copy center. Martina, a member of the center, needs to have 75 copies made of a packet containing 22 pages. She needs the packets collated and stapled. Furthermore, she wants the copies run on three-hole-punch paper. What will be the cost of the job?

Copying		
# SETS PER ORIGINAL	PRICE PER COPY	
	MEMBER	NON-MEMBER
1	0.05	0.06
2–49	0.04	0.05
50–499	0.03	0.04
500–999	0.025	0.035
1,000+	0.02	0.03
ADDITIONAL SERVICES (add to copy charges)		
Collating	Free	
Stapling	0.02/Staple	
Hand Feeding	0.10/Page	
Reducing	0.25/Setting	
OTHER STOCK (add to copy charges)		
Legal Size Paper	0.01/Page	
3-Hole-Punch Paper	0.01/Page	
Pastel #20 Paper	0.01/Page	
Bright #60 Paper	0.02/Page	
Resume Stock	0.05/Page	
Card Stock	0.05/Page	
Mailing Labels	0.30/Page	
Transparencies	0.40/Page	
Minimum order $1.00		

14. The matrices show the high and low temperatures in degrees Fahrenheit for selected towns for the months of June and December. The columns represent the high and low temperatures. The rows show the three cities.

	June		December	
Frost	70	56	28	5
Wayne	95	75	40	18
Hale	87	65	35	22

Create a matrix that indicates the changes in the high and low temperatures for the three towns from June to December.

15. The double-bar graph below compares the number of gold medals won by different countries at the 1988 Winter Olympics in Calgary, Canada vs. the 1984 Winter Olympics in Sarajevo, Yugoslavia.

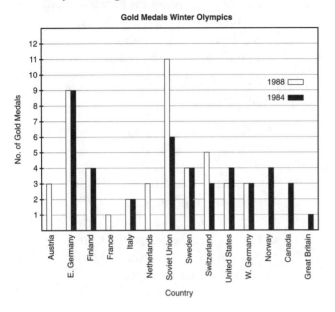

Gold Medals Winter Olympics

a. Based on the data in the graph, can you assume that since East Germany won the same number of gold medals at each of the two Olympics, it won the same percentage of the gold medals awarded?

b. What country in 1988 won approximately the same percentage of gold medals as East Germany won in 1984?

16. Matrix A represents the enrollment at Lincoln High School. Matrix B represents the enrollment at Central High School. The columns represent the grades 9–12 and the rows represent male and female.

$$A = \begin{pmatrix} 155 & 211 & 168 & 198 \\ 173 & 194 & 165 & 181 \end{pmatrix}$$

$$B = \begin{pmatrix} 211 & 204 & 176 & 188 \\ 179 & 209 & 167 & 193 \end{pmatrix}$$

a. How many 9th graders are there at Lincoln High School?

b. How many male 11th graders are at the two high schools combined?

c. How many more female 10th graders are there than female 12th graders at the two schools combined?

d. Which school has the greater total enrollment?

17. Complete the chart. Is it an example of direct or inverse variation?

x	y
32	96
12	36
[ ]	49.5
40	120

OPEN-ENDED QUESTIONS

18. Miguel's scores in chemistry this quarter are 90, 30, 78, 75, 40, 54, 70. He decided to use the median grade to report his grade in chemistry to his parents. What advantage is there to his using the median rather than the mean?

19. A teacher gave two quizzes. The average score on both was 85. Scores on the first quiz ranged from 55 to 100, while scores on the second ranged from 73 to 93. Sketch a possible histogram of the scores in each of the two quizzes. Describe how these histograms differ.

20. For each of the given situations, state whether or not you can find the mean from the information given. Explain your response.

a. You know the scores of five individual students.

b. You know the sum of the scores of five individual students.

c. You know the range of the scores of five students.

21. The table lists the life expectancies in years of males as estimated in 1992.

Age in Years	Expected Years Until Death
0	72.2
10	63.1
20	53.4
30	44.2
40	34.9
50	26.1
60	18.2
70	11.8

a. Make a scatter plot of the data on graph paper.
b. Draw a trend line for the scatter plot.
c. Use your trend line to predict the life expectancy of males age 80.

22. Using an example of five scores, show an illustration to support each of the following:

a. If you change one number, the mean of the data will change.
b. If you change one number, the median of the data may or may not change.
c. If you change one number, the mode of the data may or may not change.

23. The annual salaries for five major-league baseball players are:

$120,000 $110,000 $140,000
$120,000 $1,000,000

a. Find the mean for the salaries.
b. What is the median salary?
c. Which of the two measures (mean or median) gives a better indication of the annual salary for the group of baseball players? Explain your response.

Macro D

Apply the concepts and methods of discrete mathematics to model and explore a variety of practical situations.

3 D 1 Methods of Counting

Counting of discrete or individual items is a major part of the topic of discrete mathematics.

The counting process often involves making an organized list of the items to be counted. For example, in counting the number of rectangles of any size in the picture shown,

it is necessary to organize to count the number of each different size rectangle present.

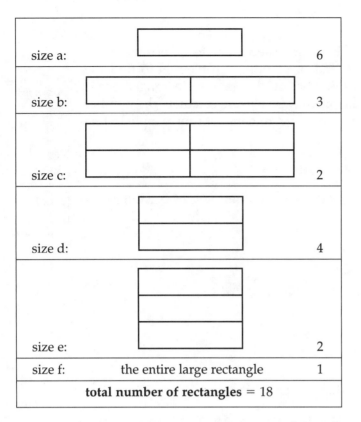

size a:		6
size b:		3
size c:		2
size d:		4
size e:		2
size f:	the entire large rectangle	1
total number of rectangles = 18		

Tree diagrams A graphic called a tree diagram can be used to show all of the possibilities in a counting situation involving a sequence of components, parts, or stages.

MODEL PROBLEM

A restaurant offers a soup-and-sandwich lunch. There are 2 possible soups (tomato and chicken); for the sandwich, 3 breads (white, rye, wheat) and 4 meats (roast beef, ham, turkey, salami).

How many different lunches are possible?

Solution:

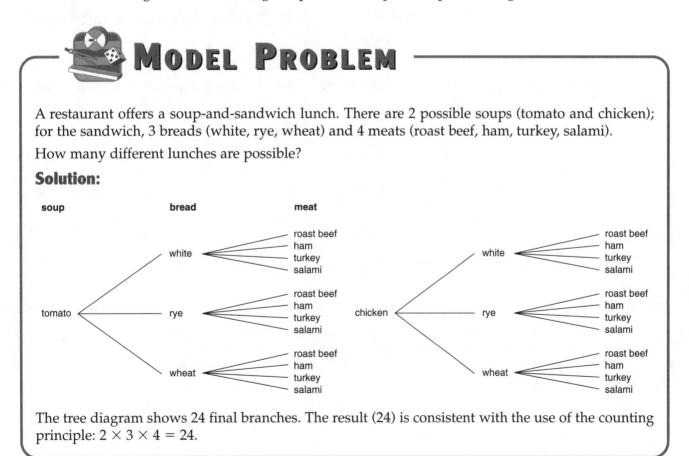

The tree diagram shows 24 final branches. The result (24) is consistent with the use of the counting principle: $2 \times 3 \times 4 = 24$.

Note: To review the counting principle, see page 111.

Permutations

In situations involving counting possibilities, it is necessary to determine if the order of the items matters. A common kind of counting problem is to find the number of arrangements of some or all of a set of objects. Each arrangement is called a *permutation*. The counting principle may be used to calculate the number of permutations. For example, the number of arrangements of four people in line to buy a concert ticket would be:

$$4 \times 3 \times 2 \times 1 = 4! = 24$$

If only two of the individuals were arranged in line, the number of permutations would be $4 \times 3 = 12$.

> Permutations of n objects at a time:
>
> $$_nP_n = n!$$
>
> Permutations of n objects r at a time:
>
> $$_nP_r = \frac{n!}{(n-r)!}$$

MODEL PROBLEMS

1. Find the value of $_7P_3$.

Solution:

$_7P_3$ (the number of permutations of 7 things taken 3 at a time)

$$\frac{7!}{(7-3)!} = \frac{7!}{4!} = \frac{7 \times 6 \times 5 \times 4 \times 3 \times 2 \times 1}{4 \times 3 \times 2 \times 1} = 7 \times 6 \times 5 = 210$$

2. Using the digits 2, 3, 4, 5, 6, how many 3-digit numbers can be formed if repetition of digits is not permitted?

Solution:

Since order does matter (245 and 452 are different numbers), this is a straightforward permutation problem.

$$_5P_3 = \frac{5!}{(5-3!)} = \frac{5!}{2!} = \frac{5 \times 4 \times 3 \times 2 \times 1}{2 \times 1} = 5 \times 4 \times 3 = 60$$

Note: If it is possible to repeat digits, there would be additional numbers possible (such as 445, 333, etc.). With repetition possible the solution would be:

$$5 \times 5 \times 5 = 5^3 = 125$$

Combinations

Combinations involve selecting from among a given number of people or objects where order does not matter. For example, if you are selecting two girls out of a group of four to be on a committee, a listing would show that there are six committees (or combinations) possible:

Alice (A), Bonita (B), Celine (C), Donna (D)

AB	BC	CD
AC	BD	
AD		

The number of combinations of n things r at a time is always smaller than the corresponding number of permutations. This is due to each combination yielding a number of permutations (two for each combination: for example, AB and BA).

As with permutations, there are formulas for calculating the number of combinations.

Special cases include:

$_nC_n = 1$ (only 1 combination possible in selecting n things n at a time)

$_nC_1 = n$ (n combinations possible in selecting n things 1 at a time)

$_nC_0 = 1$ (1 combination possible in selecting n things 0 at a time)

> Combinations of n things r at a time:
> $$_nC_r = \frac{n!}{(n-r)!r!}$$

 **MODEL PROBLEMS**

1. Find the value of $_{10}C_2$.

Solution:

$_{10}C_2$ (the number of combinations of 10 things 2 at a time)

$$\frac{10!}{8! \times 2!} = \frac{10 \times 9}{2}$$ (after reducing the fraction because numerator and denominator each contain 8! as a factor)

$$= \frac{90}{2} = 45$$

2. For a history report, you can choose to write about 3 of the original 13 colonies. How many different combinations exist for the colonies you will be writing about?

Solution:

Since you are making a selection where order does not matter, this is a combinations problem.

$$_{13}C_3 = \frac{13!}{10!3!} = \frac{13 \times 12 \times 11}{3 \times 2 \times 1} = 13 \times 2 \times 11 = 286 \text{ combinations}$$

3. How many pizzas can be made using 0, 1, 2, 3, or 4 of the following toppings: pepperoni, onion, mushroom, green pepper? (*Note:* This is a repeat of a model problem from section 3-A-3 with a different solution strategy.)

Solution: Make the assumption that a pizza with pepperoni and onion is the same as one with onion and pepperoni; therefore order does not matter and we can use combinations.

$_4C_4 = 1$ (only 1 pizza possible with all toppings)

$_4C_3 = \dfrac{4!}{1!3!} = 4$ $\qquad$ $_4C_1 = 4$

$_4C_2 = \dfrac{4!}{2!2!} = 6$ $\qquad$ $_4C_0 = 1$

Total number of possible pizzas = $1 + 4 + 6 + 4 + 1 = 16$

Pascal's Triangle

Pascal's Triangle can be used to solve problems involving combinations. A portion of Pascal's Triangle is as follows:

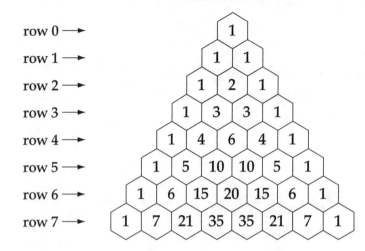

The elements or entries in a given row represent combinations. For example, in row 3:

$$_3C_0 = 1$$
$$_3C_1 = 3$$
$$_3C_2 = 3$$
$$_3C_3 = 1$$

It should be noted that the sum of the entries in a given row involves powers of 2:

$$1 + 2 + 1 = 4 = 2^2$$
$$1 + 3 + 3 + 1 = 8 = 2^3$$
$$1 + 4 + 6 + 4 + 1 = 16 = 2^4$$

MODEL PROBLEMS

1. A row of Pascal's Triangle starts with the numbers 1 and 12. What is the next number in this row?

Solution:

The 1 and 12 would indicate the 12th row involving combinations of 12 things a certain number at a time. $_{12}C_1 = 12$; therefore the next value in the row would be $_{12}C_2$ which is equal to $\frac{12!}{10!2!} = 66$.

2. Find the value of $_6C_3$.

Solution:

In addition to using the formula for combinations, one can simply take the fourth number of the sixth row of Pascal's Triangle:

$$1 \quad 6 \quad 15 \quad 20 \quad 15 \quad 6 \quad 1$$

The fourth value is 20. *Note:* You use the fourth number because the first number would be $_6C_0$; as a result, the fourth number would be $_6C_3$.

3. Starting at M and proceeding downward on a diagonal either left or right each time, how many different paths spell the word MATH?

Solution:

One approach to finding the solution to this problem is to trace the spellings of MATH through the array in a systematic approach. There is always a danger that one or more of the spellings may be missed. A more efficient solution involves the use of Pascal's Triangle. The array of letters is completed in row 3 of Pascal's Triangle. The sum of entries for row 3 is

$$1 + 3 + 3 + 1 = 8$$

where the 1 represents the spelling of MATH on the diagonal indicated in figure 1 and the 3 represents the spellings of MATH on the diagonal paths indicated in figure 2. These two figures show the solution for paths to the left of the M at the top of the triangle. Corresponding solutions exist if you move right of the top M. Hence, 1 is added twice and 3 is added twice to obtain the answer of 8.

figure 1   **figure 2**

1. Which of the following is a combinations problem or situation?

   A. In how many ways can 5 different books be arranged on a shelf?
   B. How many subsets exist from the set {a, b, c, d}?
   C. How many three-digit numbers are possible using the digits 1, 4, 7, and 9?
   D. A school needs to schedule 4 classes—English, Spanish, math, and science—in the first 4 periods. How many different schedules are possible?

2. Which has the greatest value?

   A. $_8C_6$ B. $_9C_4$ C. $_9P_4$ D. $_8P_6$

3. Which of the following is a true statement?

   I. $_nP_n$ for $n > 1$ must be even
   II. $_nP_{n-1} = {_nP_n}$ for $n > 1$
   III. $_nP_1 = n$

   A. III only   B. I and II
   C. II and III   D. I, II, and III

4. A customer in a computer store can choose one of four monitors, one of two keyboards, and one of four computers. If all the choices are compatible, how many different systems are possible?

   A. 10   B. 16   C. 32   D. 10!

5. The numbers 1 and 10 are the first two numbers of the tenth row of Pascal's Triangle. What is the third number in this row?

6. If $k(_{10}C_3) = {_{10}P_3}$, what is the value of k?

7. A school committee consists of the Student Council president, 5 other students, the principal, and 3 other teachers. In how many ways can a subcommittee be selected if the subcommittee is to consist of the Student Council president, 2 other students from the committee, the principal, and 1 other teacher from the committee?

8. A restaurant offers a soup-and-sandwich lunch. There are 3 possible soups, 3 breads possible for the sandwich, and k types of meat available for the sandwich. If the tree diagram constructed yields a total of 45 different lunches possible, find the value of k.

9. How many triangles (of any size) are in the diagram below?

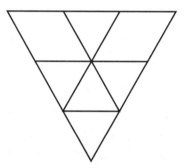

10. From a club with 12 members, a committee of 4 members is needed. The club secretary, a math major, tries to convince everyone that the number of committees of 4 is the same as the number of committees of 8.

    a. Is this correct? Explain.
    b. Using standard notation for combinations, show a generalization of the above.
    c. If $_{15}C_6 = {_{15}C_r}$, $r \neq 6$, what is the value of r?

11. The traveling squad for a college basketball team consists of two centers, five forwards, and four guards. The coach is interested in determining the number of ways she can select a starting team of one center, two forwards, and two guards.

a. Find the number of ways to select one center.

b. In finding the number of ways to select two forwards, are permutations or combinations used? Explain.

c. Find the number of ways to select the two starting forwards.

d. Find the number of ways to select the two starting guards.

e. In using answers to questions a, c, and d, is the answer to the number of possible starting teams a + c + d or a × c × d? Explain.

12. If you wanted to determine the number of diagonals in a convex polygon of n sides, you might try to develop a pattern resulting in a formula.

a. For an octagon *ABCDEFGH*, *AC*, *CE*, *AG* are a few of the diagonals. Why are *AB*, *CD*, *GH* (and possibly others) not diagonals?

b. In finding the number of diagonals, explain why you would use combinations and not permutations.

c. For a pentagon *ABCDE*, you can easily count to verify that there are five diagonals. However, when you take the five vertices, two at a time, you get $_5C_2 = 10$. Since this doesn't quite work, what should the formula be for the number of diagonals in a pentagon?

d. See if your formula works when you extend the problem to a hexagon.

e. Using n for the number of sides (or vertices), what would be the general formula?

3 D 2 Networks

The eighteenth-century European town of Königsberg included two islands and seven bridges as shown below. The question existed of whether or not a person could begin anywhere, and walk through town crossing all seven bridges without crossing any bridge twice.

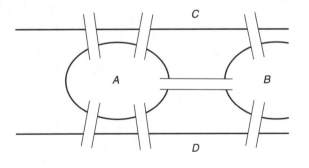

The Swiss mathematician Euler proved that such a walk was impossible. Euler created a geometric model known as a graph or network. In this graph (shown below), the segments or arcs (edges) represent the bridges and the lettered points (vertices) represent the land regions.

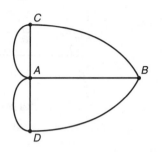

Euler discovered that the ability to carry out the "walk" as described (or traverse the network) was based on analyzing vertices as being even or odd. Odd vertices have an odd number of paths going to them and even vertices have an even number of paths going to them. In the diagram above, vertex A is odd (5 paths), vertex B is odd (3 paths), vertex C is odd (3 paths), and vertex D is odd (3 paths). It turns out that a network is traversable (traceable) if all of the vertices are even or if exactly two of the vertices are odd. Hence, the network pictured is not traversable.

Whenever a collection of things is joined by connectors, the mathematical model employed is a network or graph. A *network* is a figure or graph consisting of points (vertices or nodes) and edges (segments or arcs) that join various vertices to one another.

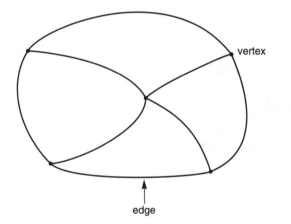

MODEL PROBLEM

For the following network, discuss why the network is traversable. List a sequence that demonstrates a traceable path.

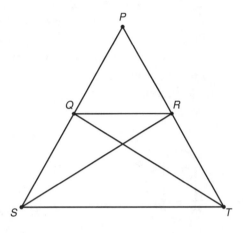

Solution:

The numbers in parenthese indicate if a vertex is odd or even.

$$P(2) \quad Q(4) \quad R(4) \quad S(3) \quad T(3)$$

Since exactly two of the vertices are odd, the network is traversable. The sequence $S \to T \to Q \to R \to S \to P \to T$ would be one traceable path.

PRACTICE

1. For the network below, how many of the vertices are considered odd?

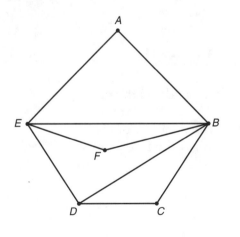

A. 0 B. 2 C. 3 D. 4

2. Which of the following networks would NOT be traversable?

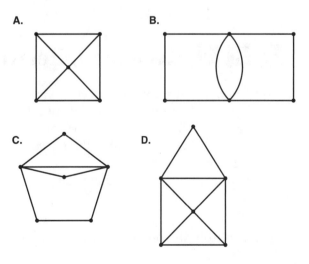

A.

B.

C.

D.

3. For the network below, how many of the vertices are even?

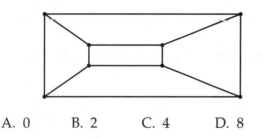

A. 0   B. 2   C. 4   D. 8

4. A complete network has at least one path or edge between each pair of vertices. Which of the following are complete networks?

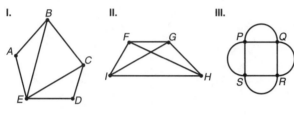

A. I and III
C. II and III
B. II only
D. I, II and III

5. Draw a sketch of a network of five towns that would not be traversable.

6. A salesperson starts in Philadelphia (*P*) and must travel to Newark (*N*), Baltimore (*B*), and Scranton (*S*) before returning to Philadelphia. The distances between these cities are shown below. Find the shortest route the salesperson can take. Explain your approach. You may want to use a tree diagram to analyze the different routes.

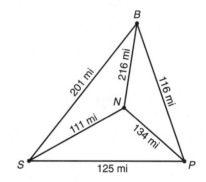

Note:

The Assessment for Macro D is combined with and follows Macro E.

Macro E

Use iteration and recursive patterns and processes to model a variety of practical situations and problems.

3 E 1 Recursion, Iteration, and Fractals

An *iteration*, or *recursion*, is a process where each new result depends on the preceding results. Iterations may involve numbers or geometric figures. An iteration will contain an initial value (or seed) or geometric figure, a rule, and an output value or geometric figure, which then becomes the initial value for the next iteration of the rule.

An example of a numerical iteration:

Start with 5.

Rule: Multiply the previous value by 2.

Result: 5, 10, 20, 40, . . .

An example of a geometric iteration:

Start with a square.

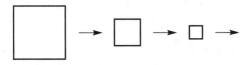

Rule: Form a new square where the new perimeter is
half as long as the previous perimeter.

Result:

MODEL PROBLEMS

1. An iterative process is used in which the rule is "multiply by 5, and then add 2." If the seed value is 3, find the next four values obtained through the iterations.

Solution:

$$3$$
$$5 \times 3 + 2 = 17 \text{ (applying the rule)}$$
$$5 \times 17 + 2 = 87 \text{ (applying the rule a second time)}$$
$$5 \times 87 + 2 = 437 \text{ (applying the rule a third time)}$$
$$5 \times 437 + 2 = 2{,}187 \text{ (applying the rule a fourth time)}$$

2. Write a recursive formula (rule) for the following sequence:

$$1, 3, 4, 7, 11, 18, \ldots$$

Solution:

Except for the first two terms, notice that each value is the sum of the two preceding terms. T_n represents the nth term.

$$T_n = T_{n-1} + T_{n-2}$$

3. If Robin puts $1,000 in a bank that gives 5.5% interest per year figured once a year, how much will she have in the bank at the end of five years? How is this considered an iteration?

Solution:

End of year 1: $1,000.00 + 0.055(1,000) = $1,055.00
End of year 2: $1,055.00 + 0.055(1,055) = $1,113.03
End of year 3: $1,113.03 + 0.055(1,113.03) = $1,174.25
End of year 4: $1,174.25 + 0.055(1,174.25) = $1,238.83
End of year 5: $1,238.83 + 0.055(1,238.83) = $1,306.97

As a result, Robin will have $1,306.97 in the bank at the end of five years. This process is an iterative process since each calculation is exactly the same as the previous calculation, except that the new calculation uses the result from the previous calculation as its starting value.

A *fractal* is a figure obtained through iteration in which you can see self-similarity. That is, the closer you look at a fractal, the more you see the same image. An extremely well-known fractal is the Sierpinski Triangle. To construct the Sierpinski Triangle you start with an equilateral triangle as the initial figure and apply the iteration rule: Remove from the middle of this triangle a smaller equilateral triangle whose side measures one-half of the original side length so that three congruent triangles remain.

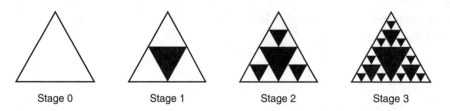

| Stage 0 | Stage 1 | Stage 2 | Stage 3 |

The iteration produces a limiting figure. In looking at the stages, the smaller and smaller details of a shape have the same properties as the original, larger shape. This means that the fractal has self-similarity.

MODEL PROBLEM

The diagram below shows stages 0, 1, and 2 for a fractal tree. Draw the next stage.

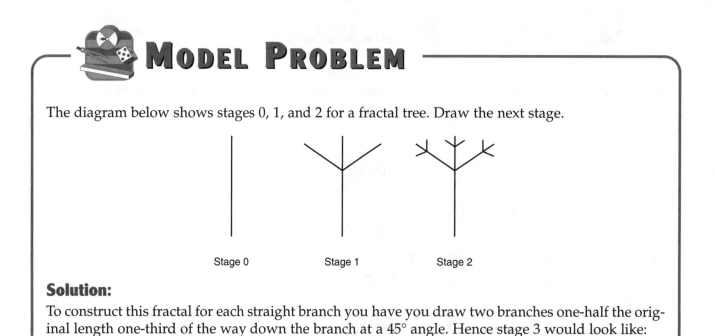

| Stage 0 | Stage 1 | Stage 2 |

Solution:

To construct this fractal for each straight branch you have you draw two branches one-half the original length one-third of the way down the branch at a 45° angle. Hence stage 3 would look like:

1. The first three stages of a fractal are shown:

    How many of the smallest circles will appear in the fourth stage?

    A. 4   B. 8   C. 12   D. 15

2. In working with iterations, arrow notation can be used to indicate the rule. For example, $x \rightarrow 2x$ means "to get the new value, you multiply by 2." Which of the following iterations will produce a sequence of zeros?

    A. $x \rightarrow -x$ with seed of -2
    B. $x \rightarrow \sqrt{x}$ with seed of 1
    C. $x \rightarrow 3x$ with seed of 0
    D. $x \rightarrow x + 5$ with seed of -5

3. An iterative process is used in which each term, after the first term, is found by adding 10 to 10 times the previous term. If the first term has a value of 5, what are the next three values obtained through the iteration?

4. A square has vertices at $(0, 0)$, $(9, 0)$, $(9, 9)$, and $(0, 9)$. A fractal is formed by trisecting the sides of a square, forming nine smaller squares, and then removing the middle square. Stage 1 is shown:

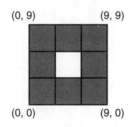

(0, 9)   (9, 9)

(0, 0)   (9, 0)

    In stage 2, what are the coordinates of the vertices of the square removed that is closest to the origin?

5. Use the iteration rule $x \rightarrow x^2$ (to get a new value, square the current value) to investigate what happens for two different initial values: 2 and 0.5.

    a. Show the first five terms based on each initial value.
    b. What can you conclude about the limiting values that each sequence approaches?

6. Apply the following geometric iteration rule: Start with a unit square (side length of 1 unit). Split the square horizontally into two congruent rectangles. Remove the top rectangle, leaving behind the bottom rectangle.

    a. Show the first four stages of this iteration.
    b. What are the dimensions of the remaining rectangle in each stage?
    c. If we carry out the iterations indefinitely, do we generate a fractal? Explain your response.

7. Start with a 45°-45°-90° triangle. The iteration rule is to draw the altitude to the hypotenuse, thereby forming two new isosceles right triangles.

    a. Draw the next three figures based on this iteration rule.
    b. How many small isosceles right triangles appear in the picture after you perform the third iteration?
    c. Describe the appearance of the figure resulting from more and more iterations with the rule stated.

3 E 2 Algorithms and Flow Charts

An *algorithm* is a finite, step-by-step procedure for accomplishing a task. Familiar examples of algorithms include:

- doing long division
- computing percent increase
- writing the prime factorization of a composite number
- applying the quadratic formula
- constructing the perpendicular bisector of a given line segment
- adding two matrices
- alphabetizing a list of words
- following a recipe

An *iteration diagram* is a pictorial representation of the algorithm associated with an iterative process.

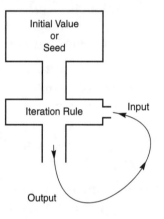

MODEL PROBLEM

If 8 iterations are performed based on the diagram shown, complete a table indicating an output value for each term.

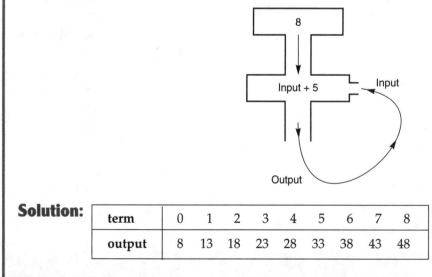

Solution:

term	0	1	2	3	4	5	6	7	8
output	8	13	18	23	28	33	38	43	48

Note: The output value 8 is associated with term 0 since this value exists prior to the iterations.

A *flow chart* is a diagram illustrating a procedure or process. Flow charts are useful in illustrating complicated procedures involving multiple steps, repetition, and decision making. The following flow chart illustrates the process of determining if a whole number is divisible by 3.

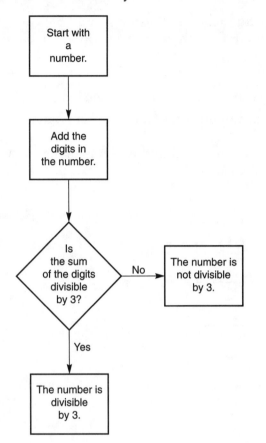

MODEL PROBLEM

The Sieve of Eratosthenes is a procedure for identifying the prime numbers in a certain range (from 1 to n) of positive integers. The algorithm (for numbers from 1 to 50) has the following steps:

Step 1: Cross out 1.

Step 2: Circle 2 and cross out every second number past 2 on the list.

Step 3: Circle 3 and cross out every third number past 3 on the list.

Continue the processions from below. The unmarked numbers remaining in the list are the prime numbers. Draw a flow chart illustrating this algorithm.

Solution:

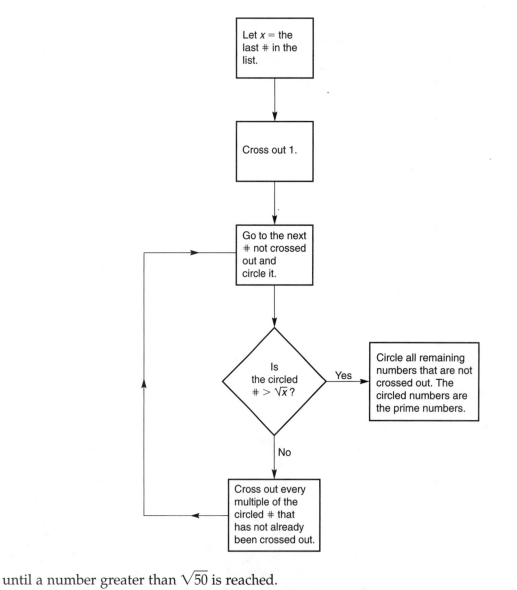

until a number greater than $\sqrt{50}$ is reached.

1. An algorithm has the following steps (for use with natural numbers greater than 1):

   a. If n is odd, replace n by $7n - 5$.

   b. If n is even, then replace n by $\frac{n}{2}$.

   c. If $n = 100$, then stop; otherwise go to step a.

   If $n = 10$, show the list of numbers produced by the algorithm.

In 2–3, suppose that when one shape is inside another, you follow the inside direction first.

2. Given the following definitions:

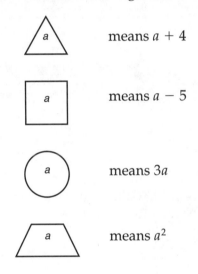

   means $a + 4$

   means $a - 5$

   means $3a$

   means a^2

   Which of the following are true?

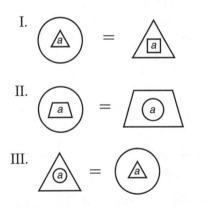

   I.

   II.

   III.

   A. I only
   B. I and II
   C. II and III
   D. I, II, and III

3. Suppose that

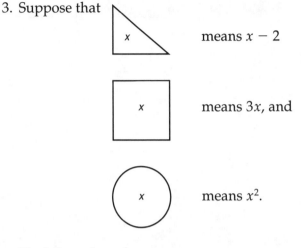

   means $x - 2$

   means $3x$, and

   means x^2.

   Find the value of

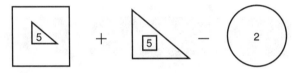

4. Write the expression indicated by the following flowchart.

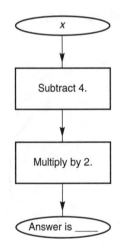

5. Describe the steps of an algorithm which will produce the following sequence of figures:

6. Produce a diagram resulting from the following algorithm:

Step 1: Start with a square having side lengths of 3 inches.

Step 2: Trisect each side of the square.

Step 3: Remove or erase the middle portion of each side of the square.

Step 4: Construct a smaller square on the exterior of each side of the original square where the middle portion has been removed.

a. Draw the figure obtained by following the algorithm.

b. What is the perimeter of the final figure?

c. What is the area of the final figure?

ASSESSMENT MACRO D and MACRO E

1. Which of the following networks is traversable?

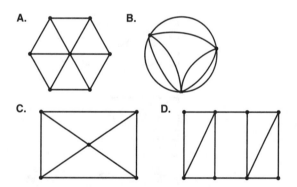

2. Using the digits 5, 6, 7, 8, how many four-digit numbers can be formed if repetition of digits is allowed, except for not allowing four of the same digit?

  A. $_4P_4$ B. $(_4P_4) - 4$

  C. $4^4 - 4$ D. $_4C_4$

3. How many arrangements are possible of all of the letters in ALGEBRA if each arrangement must begin and end with A?

  A. 5!   B. 6!   C. $\dfrac{7!}{2}$ D. $7! - 2$

4. Given the iteration rule "multiply by 2," what would be the value after the rule is applied 5 times starting with a seed value of 5?

  A. 10   B. 40   C. 160   D. 640

5. Draw the next stage in the given fractal.

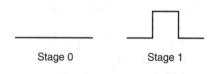

     Stage 0   Stage 1

6. Write a recursion formula for the following sequence:

$$1, 2, 2, 4, 8, \ldots$$

7. For the letters A, B, C, D, E, F, there are 6! or 720 arrangements of all the letters. For the letters AAACCC, determine the number of different arrangements of all six letters.

8. If four teams A, B, C, D were playing in a single-elimination tournament, the following diagram would illustrate the progress of the tournament.

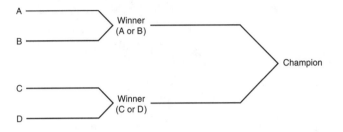

In this tournament, there were a total of three games. How many games would exist in a field of 64 teams for a single-elimination tournament?

9. A box fractal is formed by the following rule:

Start with a square.
Divide the square into 9 smaller squares.
Remove 4 middle squares from each side.
Continue the same procedure with each remaining square.

Stages 0 and 1 are shown.

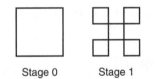

Stage 0   Stage 1

How many squares are there in stage 2?

10. Write the rule that is defined by the operation * if

$$4 * 2 = 12$$
$$3 * 1 = 8$$
$$10 * 9 = 19$$
$$a * b = \underline{\quad\quad}$$

11. Many members of the Student Council are on more than one subcommittee as shown in the chart. An X indicates that these two subcommittees have at least one member in common. If the subcommittees must all meet and the only time slot available each day is 2:30 P.M. to 3:30 P.M., what is the minimum number of days necessary for all of the subcommittees to meet?

	Special Events	Home-coming	Dances	Fund-Raising	School Policy	Publi-city
Special Events						X
Home-coming			X		X	
Dances		X		X	X	X
Fund-Raising			X			X
School Policy		X	X			X
Publicity	X		X	X	X	

12. Sketch the next 3 pictures using the iteration rule "change the previous rectangle so that each figure is one half as long and twice as wide."

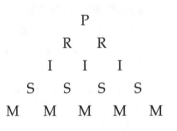

width 2"

length 4"

13. Starting at P and proceeding downward on a diagonal either left or right each time, how many different paths spell the word PRISM?

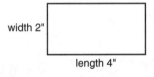

```
          P
        R   R
      I   I   I
    S   S   S   S
  M   M   M   M   M
```

14. Find the starting number for the given flow-chart.

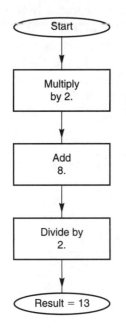

15. A map company has been contracted to design a map representing the state of New Jersey. Each region of the state must be colored with one color. Regions that share a common boundary, except at a corner, may not be the same color. What is the least number of colors needed?

16. A coin is flipped 5 times.

a. How many possible sequences of heads and tails have 0 heads? 1 head? 2 heads? 3 heads? 4 heads? 5 heads?

b. How many sequences of heads and tails are possible in all?

c. What row of Pascal's Triangle can be used in solving this problem?

OPEN-ENDED QUESTIONS

17. Of the students at a high school, 60% are bused to school. Of those who are bused, 80% favor a rule mandating the use of seat belts on the school bus. Of those who are not bused, 90% favor mandating this rule.

a. Draw a tree diagram to illustrate this problem.

b. What is the percent of the students who favor this rule?

c. If a randomly selected student favors the rule, what is the probability that the student rides the bus?

18. Suppose you were talking to a friend on the telephone. Write a list of instructions you would give your friend to duplicate the given diagram without being able to see it. Note any tools or materials you would ask your friend to use.

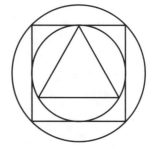

19. Use the iteration rule $x \rightarrow x^2 - 1$ to investigate what happens for two different initial values, 0 and −1.

   a. Show the first five terms based on each initial value.

   b. What can you conclude about the sequences formed by the iteration for each value?

   c. Name another initial value for which you would get a similar result.

20. A sorting algorithm can be used to arrange a list of n numbers in decreasing order. The algorithm makes successive passes through the list of numbers from left to right. In each pass, successive pairs of adjacent numbers are compared; if the number on the left is smaller than the one on the right, the two are exchanged; otherwise, they are left as is. Hence, after the first pass, the smallest number sorts all the way to the right.

Show how this sorting algorithm can be used to arrange the numbers 1, 7, 8, 2, 9, 6 in decreasing order. How many passes did it take until the numbers were in order?

21. The figure consists of 21 small congruent squares. What is the total number of different squares (of any size) that one can trace using the lines of the figure? Explain a process that ensures that all of the squares are counted in an efficient manner.

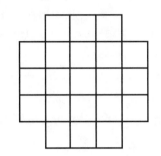

22. There are nine points A, B, C, D, E, F, G, H, and I in a given plane, no three on the same line. You want to figure out the number of triangles determined by the nine points.

   a. Explain why this can be considered a "combinations" problem.

   b. How many triangles are determined by the nine points?

   c. If one of these triangles is selected at random, what is the probability that it contains the point A as a vertex?

1. Two dice are rolled. What is the probability that either the sum is 3 or the sum is 8?

   A. $\dfrac{7}{36}$ B. $\dfrac{1}{6}$ C. $\dfrac{5}{36}$ D. $\dfrac{1}{12}$

2. Which of the following is TRUE about the data?

Score	Frequency
80	2
82	4
86	3
90	5

   A. The mean is greater than the median.
   B. The median is greater than the mean.
   C. The mean equals the median.
   D. There is no mode for the data.

3. Data that describes a situation in which any value between two given values can theoretically occur is called **continuous data**. Continuous data often results from measurements.

   If the data is not continuous, it is called **discrete**. Discrete data comes from counting situations.

   Which of the following situations illustrates discrete data?

   A. Temperatures recorded every half hour at a weather station
   B. Lengths of 1,000 bolts of fabric produced in a factory
   C. The heights of individuals
   D. The number of children in a family

4. This table shows the amounts of candy sold by the classes in Washington High School.

Candy Sale Results	
Freshmen	11,200
Sophomores	9,600
Juniors	11,700
Seniors	7,500

   Which graph is the POOREST representation of the data?

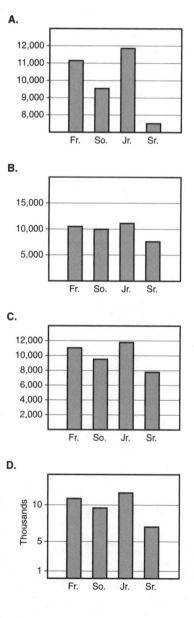

5. Which of the following situations represents events that are *independent*? (That is, the outcome of the first event has no effect on the outcome of the second event.)

   A. Two marbles are selected from a container without replacement.
   B. Two children born in a family are a boy, then a girl.
   C. A ticket is selected for second prize after the first-prize ticket has been removed.
   D. A king is selected from a deck of cards after two kings have already been dealt.

6. A theater did a survey of the ages of people who came to their cabaret. The table summarizes the results. Find the median age of the viewers.

   A. 13–30
   B. 31–48
   C. 49–66
   D. over 66

Ages	Numbers
12 and under	87
13–30	298
31–48	481
49–66	364
over 66	95

7. The rules for a board game call for a player to lose a turn if the player rolls three consecutive doubles on a pair of dice. What is the probability that a player will lose a turn in her first three rolls?

   A. $\dfrac{1}{6}$ B. $\dfrac{1}{18}$ C. $\dfrac{1}{36}$ D. $\dfrac{1}{216}$

8. A basketball player with a free throw shooting average of 60% is on the line for a one-and-one free throw (the player gets a second shot if the first shot is successful). What is the probability the player will score two points at the free-throw line?

   A. 0.6   B. 0.4   C. 0.36   D. 0.24

9. If y varies directly with x, then when x is doubled y will ___.

   A. not change   B. be halved
   C. increase by 2   D. be doubled

10. Use this data found in the telephone directory to answer the question that follows.

Sample Telephone Day Rates		
From Passaic to	First Minute	Each Add'l Minute
Freehold	0.33	0.11
Morristown	0.17	0.07
Newark	0.09	0.03
Toms River	0.37	0.11

    Which graph is a possible illustration of the charges for calls?

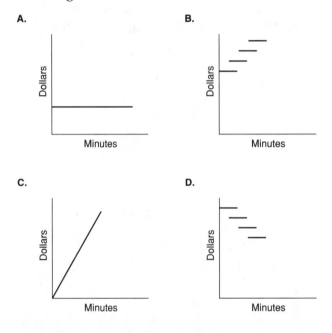

11. In how many different ways can you arrange all of the letters A, B, C, D, E, F, G if each arrangement must begin and end with a vowel and the middle letter must be G?

    A. 7!   B. 5!
    C. $_5P_5 \times 2$ D. $2 \times 4!$

12. A sequence is generated by the formula $T_k = 2^k - 1$ where T_k is the kth term. If k must be a whole number, which of the following numbers would NOT be a term of the sequence?

    A. 257   B. 63   C. 31   D. 1

13. A contest offers a prize of a trip to London, Paris, or Rome in either spring, summer, or fall.

    How many different choices are possible if a prize consists of one city and one season?

14. If a pair of dice is rolled, what is the probability of getting a sum of 8?

15. The mean of a set of 10 scores is 61. What is the sum of the 10 scores?

16. Eight scores have a mean of 30. The bottom two scores have a mean of 21. The top two scores have a mean of 50. What is the mean of the four middle scores?

17. The ratio of the central angles of a spinner is $1:2:5:7$. The sections (sectors) of the spinner are marked BOB, ANN, SAM, TAD (in the same order as $1:2:5:7$). If the spinner is spun, what is Probability(BOB)?

18. Starting at P and proceeding downward on a diagonal either left or right each time, how many different paths spell the word PASCAL?

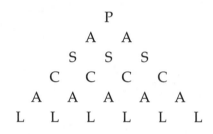

19. A test consists of 13 questions. Each student must choose 10 questions and omit 3 questions. How many different groups of questions could be chosen?

20. Brightline Company guarantees that its light bulbs will last for at least 1,000 hours. If a bulb fails before 1,000 hours of use, the customer can request a refund. The product research division of the company calculated the average life of a bulb to be approximately normally distributed with a mean of 1,020 hours and a standard deviation of 20 hours. What is the approximate percentage of light bulbs that will not last 1,000 hours?

21. Morse code is a system of communicating information in which ordered sets of dots and dashes represent the letters of the alphabet, numerals, etc. An "e" is represented by a single dot, while a dash followed by 2 dots represents a "d." How many distinct letters can be represented by arrangements of 1 to 5 symbols, each of which is a dot or a dash?

22. Rectangle $ABCD$ has dimensions as shown below. E is the midpoint of $\overline{DC}$, F is the midpoint of $\overline{EC}$, and G is the midpoint of $\overline{DE}$. If a dart is thrown at random into the rectangle, what is the probability that it lands inside the unshaded region?

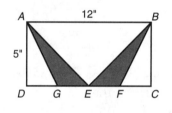

23. Give a set of data that has the following measures of central tendency: mode = 9, mean = 12, median = 12. Explain how you constructed the set.

24. The following data represent the heights in inches of students in a kindergarten class. Construct a line plot from the data. State the median, the mode, and the mean for the data.

$$48 \ 47 \ 44 \ 46 \ 48 \ 46 \ 42 \ 46 \ 51$$
$$46 \ 50 \ 43 \ 42 \ 45 \ 43 \ 47 \ 49$$

25. The Greek mathematician Euclid devised an algorithm for finding the greatest common factor of two numbers. The algorithm states:

- Divide the greater number by the lesser number.
- Divide the previous divisor by the remainder.
- Repeat the process until the remainder is 0.
- The greatest common factor is the divisor used in the last division.

Show how the Euclidean algorithm can be applied to find the greatest common factor for 38 and 98.

26. Construct a bar graph from the information in this table.

Nicole's Fall Fund-Raiser Sales	
Gift Bags	卌 卌 卌 卌 卌 卌 III
Rolls of Wrap	卌 卌 卌 III
Bags of Bows	卌 卌 III
Gift Tabs	卌 卌 I

27. A discount clothing store has the following policy. Each week that an item remains on the rack it is discounted by 10% of its current price.

   a. A suit is originally priced at $450. Generate a table to show the price of the suit for the first six weeks it is on the rack.

   b. Write a formula to generalize the sequence produced in part a.

   c. Determine the number of weeks it will take for the suit to be priced less than $100.

28. Given a set of eight elements {a, b, c, d, e, f, g, h}, {c, d, e} is a subset with three members and {c, d, e, f, a} is a subset with five members. Explain why the total number of subsets of three elements is exactly the same as the total number of subsets of five elements.

29. A gymnastic competition is being scheduled with the following events: floor exercises, horse, parallel bars, balance beam, and rings. If participants have signed up as follows for the events, design a practice schedule that uses the minimum number of time blocks possible and avoids all conflicts. Call the time blocks Block 1, Block 2, etc.

   Floor Exercises: Deanne, Michelle

   Horse: Deanne, Dora

   Parallel Bars: Deanne, Michelle, Hilga, Dora

   Balance Beam: Michelle

   Rings: Hilga, Dora

30. Jose and Ray were discussing major league baseball players. Jose pointed out that there were 186 players currently with batting averages from .250 to .299. Ray said at least four of the players must have the same average. Is Ray correct? If yes, explain why. If not, explain why not. (Note that batting averages are always rounded to the nearest thousandth.)

31. Two dice are rolled.

   a. Explain why the probability of obtaining a sum less than or equal to 5 is the same as the probability of obtaining a sum greater than or equal to 9.

   b. If the probability of obtaining a sum less than or equal to 6 is the same as the probability of obtaining a sum greater than or equal to k, find the value of k.

   c. If three dice are rolled, what is the probability that the sum obtained is less than or equal to 3?

   d. The answer to part c would be the same as the probability that the sum obtained is greater than or equal to what value?

32. Matrix A represents the enrollment at Washington High School. Matrix B represents the enrollment at Jefferson High School. The columns represent the number of students in grades 9–12 respectively and the rows the number of male and female students.

$$A = \begin{pmatrix} 130 & 128 & 143 & 121 \\ 120 & 131 & 137 & 135 \end{pmatrix}$$

$$B = \begin{pmatrix} 192 & 201 & 193 & 205 \\ 197 & 214 & 201 & 192 \end{pmatrix}$$

   a. What percent the total enrollment of each school is made up of 12th graders?

   b. What percent of each school's total enrollments is male?

33. A school offers baseball, soccer, and basketball to its 120 students. A survey showed that 35 students played baseball, 70 played soccer, 40 played basketball, 20 played both soccer and basketball, 15 played both soccer and baseball, 15 played both basketball and baseball, and 10 played all three sports.

   a. How many students played none of the three sports?

   b. What percent of the students played baseball as their only sport?

   c. How many students played both basketball and baseball, but not soccer?

34. Describe in writing the process used to generate the fractal shown. Be sure to indicate where the process repeats. Then draw the fractal as it would appear in stage 3.

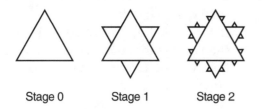

Stage 0   Stage 1   Stage 2

35. Construct a scatter plot using the following information. Is there a correlation? If so, is it positive or negative? What can you conclude about time spent doing homework and time spent watching television?

Time Spent Doing Homework vs. Viewing Television		
Student	Homework (min)	Television Viewing (min)
A	30	60
B	90	45
C	90	0
D	75	90
E	60	120
F	75	30
G	45	60
H	60	0
I	0	180
J	45	30

36. A restaurant offers five entree choices on its dinner menu: turkey, hamburger, chicken, pork chops, and fish. With each entree, the customer may choose one type of potato: french fried, mashed, or baked, and one of two desserts: ice cream or pudding.

a. Make a tree diagram to show the possible dinner choices.

b. How many different meals are available assuming the customer selects an entree, potato, and dessert?

c. Suppose the diner has the option of not taking a potato or a dessert. How does that change the number of different meals that are available? Show all work.

37. A bicycle race is set up so that a biker must visit each station on the course to have his card stamped. Stations can be visited in any order. The course is pictured below. The letters represent the stations and the numbers the distances in kilometers between stations.

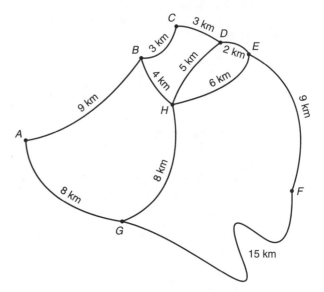

a. Find a route through the course that enables the biker to visit each station and pass through it exactly once.

b. Find the shortest route which includes each station at least once.

c. Explain how the conditions of parts a and b of this question are different.

38. Refer to the graph given.

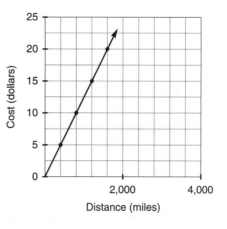

a. Does the graph illustrate a direct or inverse variation in the data?

b. Give two additional ordered pairs that would appear in the graph if it were extended.

c. Suggest a practical situation that might be represented by this graph.

39. Use the data in the table for questions a–c.

U.S. Population	
Year	Population (in millions)
1890	63
1900	76
1910	92
1920	106
1930	123
1940	132
1950	151
1960	179
1970	203
1980	227
1990	249
2000	281

a. Draw a line graph of the data given in the table.

b. *Interpolation* is the process of estimating a value between two known values. Using the graph, interpolate to find the U.S. population in 1975.

c. Examine the population changes between 1980–1990 and 1990–2000. Predict what the population might be in the year 2010 if this pattern continues. Explain your reasoning.

CUMULATIVE ASSESSMENT

For Clusters 1, 2, 3

1. How many three-digit numbers have all of the following characteristics?

   I. The number is a multiple of 72.
   II. The number is divisible by 5.
   III. The number is less than 500.

   A. 0   B. 1   C. 2   D. 5

2. The measures of two supplementary angles are in the ratio 9 : 1. What is the difference in degree measure between the two angles?

   A. 18   B. 72   C. 144   D. 162

3. Which of the following is NOT equal to the other numbers?

   A. 0.2   B. $\sqrt{\dfrac{1}{25}}$ C. $\dfrac{1}{2} + \dfrac{1}{3}$ D. $\dfrac{0.05}{0.25}$

4. Triangle ABC is isosceles with $\overline{AB} \cong \overline{AC}$.

   $\angle DAB \cong \angle BAC \cong \angle EAC$

   What is the measure of $\angle EAC$?

   A. 40   B. 55   C. 70   D. 80

5. A school club consists of only juniors and seniors. If the ratio of juniors to seniors in the club is 3 : 2, which of the following could NOT be the total number of club members?

   A. 16   B. 20   C. 25   D. 30

6. Using four of the five digits 1, 3, 4, 7, 8, how many four-digit numbers can be formed, with no repetition of digits, if the number must be odd?

   A. 625   B. 120   C. 72   D. 36

7. Which of the following does NOT exist?

    A. A rhombus with two angles each measuring 5°
    B. A quadrilateral with one angle measuring 80° and each additional angle measuring 10° more than the previous one
    C. A trapezoid with two right angles
    D. An obtuse isosceles triangle

8. Three dice are rolled. What is the probability of obtaining a sum that is less than or equal to 4?

    A. $\frac{1}{216}$ B. $\frac{1}{108}$ C. $\frac{1}{72}$ D. $\frac{1}{54}$

9. This list shows test scores for fifteen students:

    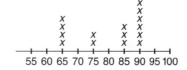

    Which of the following is true about the data?

    A. The mean equals the median.
    B. The median is greater than the mean.
    C. The median is less than the mean.
    D. There is no mode for the data.

10. During a recent month, the exchange rate of Canadian dollars to United States dollars was 1 to 0.81. If you paid $65 in Canadian dollars for a toaster-oven, what would you have paid in United States dollars? (Disregard tax.)

    A. $52.65
    B. $65.81
    C. $80.25
    D. $84.00

11. Which symbol has 90° rotational symmetry?

    A. T   B. □   C. 3   D. ♡

12. About what percent of the big square is shaded?

    A. 5%
    B. 15%
    C. 20%
    D. 25%

    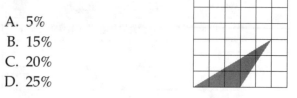

13. Daniel, David, and Darryl independently answer a question on a test. The probability that Daniel answers correctly is .9. The probability that David answers correctly is .6. The probability that Darryl answers correctly is .8. What is the probability that not one of the three answers the question correctly?

    A. .008   B. .432   C. .568   D. .72

14. There are four times as many boys as girls on the newspaper staff of Central High School. If there are 40 staff members in all, how many of them are girls?

    A. 8   B. 10   C. 30   D. 32

15. Point A is reflected over the y-axis and then the image is reflected over the x-axis, resulting in the point A'' with coordinates $(-4, -2)$. What was the y-coordinate of the original point A?

    A. -4 B. -2 C. 0   D. 2

16. Lin bought a sweater at 30% off the original price. The discount saved him $12.60. What was the original price of the sweater?

    A. $8.82   B. $21.42
    C. $29.40   D. $42.00

17. Which of the following would be a reasonable value for the percent of the figure that is shaded?

    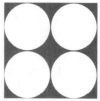

    A. 75%   B. 40%
    C. 20%   D. 10%

18. The population in Culver Heights increased from 1990 to 1993 as shown in the table. What was the average annual percent increase in population over the three-year period?

Years	Population
1990 to 1991	10,000 to 11,000
1991 to 1992	11,000 to 12,000
1992 to 1993	12,000 to 13,000

A. 8.33%   B. 9.14%   C. 10%   D. 27.42%

19. A square has vertices at $(-3, 0)$, $(0, 3)$, $(3, 0)$, and $(0, -3)$. How many of the following points are in the exterior of the square?

$(-1, 1)$ $(1.5, 1.5)$ $(2, 2)$ $(0, -4)$
$(-2, -2)$ $(-3, 1)$

A. 2   B. 3   C. 4   D. 5

20. Set G consists of the three-digit multiples of 3. Set H consists of the three-digit multiples of 4. Set L consists of the three-digit multiples of 6.

Which of the following statements is true about the three sets of numbers?

A. If a number is in Set G, it is also in Set L.
B. The smallest number contained in all three sets is 144.
C. If a number is in Set L, it is also in Set G.
D. No multiple of 9 is in Set H.

21. A club consists of eight boys and six girls. A committee of five is to be selected so that the committee consists of three boys (one of them must be Roger) and two girls (one of the girls must be Jennifer). How many different committees are possible?

A. 26   B. 48   C. 105   D. 210

22. There are 30 students in a class. The mean grade for that class on a test was computed as 80, but two students' grades were read incorrectly as 90 instead of 50. What will the average grade (rounded to the nearest tenth) be when it is recomputed using the correct scores?

23. How many different isosceles triangles are possible where the sides have integral lengths and the perimeter is 31 units?

24. The diagram shows a structure made with nineteen cubes. If each cube has an edge of 1 cm, what is the surface area of the structure (in square centimeters)?

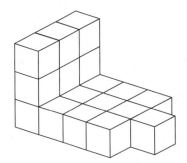

25. Four regular hexagons are similar. Corresponding sides of the four hexagons have lengths in the ratio $1 : 2 : 5 : 10$. If a side of the largest hexagon has a length of 30 centimeters, find the sum of the perimeters (in centimeters) of the other three hexagons.

26. Winter Spring bottled water comes in three sizes:

   6-pack of 0.5-liter bottles at $3.59 per 6-pack
   1-liter bottles at $0.99 each
   1.5-liter bottles at $1.59 each

   If you need 9 liters of bottled water, how much would you save by buying 1.5-liter bottles instead of 6-packs of 0.5-liter bottles?

27. There are seven toppings available for pizza at Joe's Pizzeria. You can order any one of 21 different pies that have exactly 2 toppings. What row and number in the row of Pascal's Triangle are represented by the 21?

28. A 12' ladder is placed against a building so that the ladder makes an angle of 50° with the ground. To the nearest tenth of a foot, at what height does the ladder touch the building?

29. The two spinners shown have eight and four congruent sections respectively. If you spin each spinner once, what is the probability of obtaining the largest possible sum?

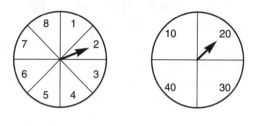

30. *ACEF* is a square.

    ABC is an isosceles right triangle.

    CDE is an equilateral triangle.

    Find the measure of ∠*BCD*.

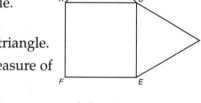

31. To find the next term of the given sequence, find the area of a square whose sides are twice as long as the sides of the previous square. What is the area of the sixth term?

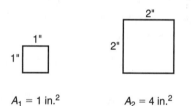

$A_1 = 1$ in.^{2} $A_2 = 4$ in.^{2}

32. A craft store has orders to ship wreaths to 4 stores: Westwood Garden Center, Creative Gifts, Hands-On Crafts, Gifts for All. The wreaths come in three sizes: small, medium, and large. The given matrix shows the number of wreaths shipped to each store. Columns represent the four stores; rows represent the three sizes small, medium, and large respectively. If the small wreath sells for $18, medium for $24, and large for $40, what is the total amount billed to each store?

$$\begin{pmatrix} 4 & 6 & 0 & 5 \\ 5 & 3 & 3 & 5 \\ 2 & 1 & 6 & 5 \end{pmatrix}$$

33. Use a collection of congruent equilateral triangles. Indicate the minimum number of these equilateral triangles which you can place together to form:

    a. a rhombus

    b. an isosceles trapezoid

    c. a regular hexagon

34. An isosceles triangle has vertices at $(0, 6)$, $(k, 0)$ and $(-k, 0)$. Find the value of k such that the slope of the congruent sides of the triangle would be +6 and −6.

35. These are tests scores in Mme. Dubin's French class:

    93, 92, 84, 81, 68, 81, 78, 77, 84, 63, 62, 90

    a. Construct a line plot for the data.
    b. State the median score for the data.
    c. What would happen to the median if one point were added to each of the test scores? Explain.

36. Find the area and perimeter of the hexagon. Show your complete procedure.

    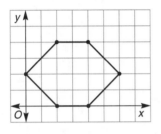

37. A package of gum has a price increase from $0.50 to $0.60. At the old price, a package contained 10 sticks of gum; now a package contains 8 sticks. Determine the percent increase in going from the old situation to the new. Explain your procedure and thinking.

38. In still water a swimmer's speed is 3 mph. If the swimmer swims perpendicular to a 5-mph current, find the actual speed and direction of the swimmer.

    Show a diagram to illustrate the situation.

    Explain how you determined the speed and the angle of the current.

39. Kathryn invests $2,000.00 for six years at 10% interest compounded annually. After the first three years, Elizabeth invests $3,000.00 for three years at 5% interest compounded annually. At the end of the six years, who would have more money? Explain.

40. Given the following four views for a three-dimensional figure, draw the figure on the isometric paper provided. Then give the volume and surface area for the figure drawn.

    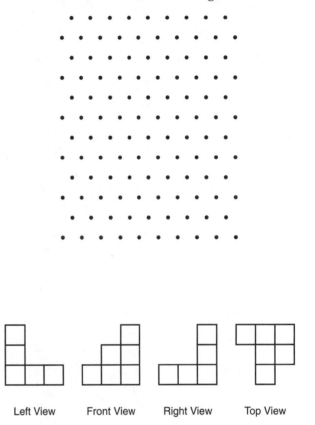

    Left View   Front View   Right View   Top View

Patterns, Functions, and Algebra

Macro A:

Recognize, create, and extend a variety of patterns and use inductive reasoning to understand and represent mathematical and other real-world phenomena.

4 A 1 Patterns

In a number of applications, problems can be solved by discovering a pattern and using the pattern to draw different conclusions. The pattern might be numerical or visual.

Computational Patterns

Many numerical situations involve patterns.
Examples:

a. repeating decimal

$$\frac{1}{11} = 0.0909$$

b. equivalent fractions

$$\frac{1}{2} = \frac{2}{4} = \frac{3}{6} = \frac{4}{8}$$

c. powers of ten

$10^1 = 10$
$10^2 = 100$
$10^3 = 1,000$
.
.
.
$10^9 = 1,000,000,000$

d. concept of percent

$$1\% = \frac{1}{100}$$

$$10\% = \frac{10}{100}$$

$$50\% = \frac{50}{100}$$

$$100\% = \frac{100}{100}$$

e. multiplication pattern

$9 \times 1 = 9$
$9 \times 2 = 18$
$9 \times 3 = 27$
$9 \times 4 = 36$
$9 \times 5 = 45$
$9 \times 6 = 54$
$9 \times 7 = 63$
$9 \times 8 = 72$
$9 \times 9 = 81$

MODEL PROBLEMS

1. What is the units digit in the number equivalent of 3^{24}?

Solution: Since it is not convenient to compute the value of 3^{24}, you need to see if a pattern exists by examining small powers of 3.

$3^1 = 3$
$3^2 = 9$
$3^3 = 27$
$3^4 = 81$

For the first four powers of 3, the units digits are different (namely, 3, 9, 7, 1).

$3^5 = 243$
$3^6 = 729$
$3^7 = . . 7$
$3^8 = . . 1$

Then the units digit begins to repeat. Assume that the pattern for the units digit continues as 3, 9, 7, 1. Note that this pattern is in groups of 4. You may conclude that every power of 3 that is a multiple of 4 will have a units digit of 1.

Answer: Since 3^{24} is a power of 3 that is a multiple of 4, the value of 3^{24} will have a units digit of 1.

2. In the decimal representation for $\frac{5}{33}$, what digit would be in the 30th decimal place?

Solution: The decimal representation for $\frac{5}{33}$ is 0.15151515. . . . Notice that in the repeating pattern, a 1 is in every odd position and a 5 is in every even position.

Answer: The digit in the 30th decimal place would be a 5.

Visual Patterns

Patterns often occur in diagrams and through visualization.

Example:

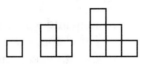

Visualizing this pattern shows that the next term is generated by adding a row of squares one greater in length than the bottom row of the previous term.

Visual patterns are often found in flooring, wallpaper, wrapping paper, store displays, and fabric.

To extend a visual pattern:

1. Explore the pattern concretely, building succeeding terms.
2. Convert the visual pattern to a numerical pattern.

MODEL PROBLEM

How many unit squares are needed to represent the fifth term of the following pattern?

Solution:

METHOD 1: concrete

Notice that the first term is a 1 × 1 square, the second term is a 2 × 2 square, and the third term is a 3 × 3 square. Then, build the fourth term (4 × 4) and the fifth term (5 × 5).

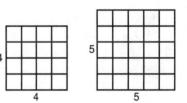

Answer: Counting the unit squares in the fifth term produces a result of 25 unit squares.

METHOD 2: converting to a numerical pattern

Analyzing the number of unit squares used to build the three given terms produces the numerical pattern 1, 4, 9. Recognizing these numbers as consecutive perfect squares, you realize that the fifth term would have to be the fifth square, or 25.

Answer: 25 unit squares

1. What is the units digit in 2^{40}?

   A. 2   B. 4   C. 6   D. 8

2. Which one of the following bases does NOT produce the same units digit when raised to any whole-number power?

   A. 10   B. 9   C. 6   D. 5

3. Which of the following would yield a repeating decimal pattern?

   A. $\frac{1}{6}$ B. $\frac{1}{4}$ C. $\frac{3}{16}$ D. $\frac{1}{25}$

4. What digit is in the 45th decimal place in the decimal value of $\frac{7}{11}$?

   A. 1   B. 3   C. 6   D. 7

5. Terrence decides he is going to start saving pennies in a large plastic jar he has found. On Monday, he puts 1 cent into the jar. On Tuesday, he doubles the amount to 2 cents. On each succeeding day, he doubles the number of pennies he put in the day before. How many days will it take Terrence to save at least $20?

   A. 11   B. 12   C. 15   D. 26

6. Which of the following decimals shows a pattern equivalent to the visual pattern below?

   A. 0.12891289 . . .   B. 0.313131 . . .
   C. 0.541541541 . . .   D. 0.7777 . . .

7. Analyze the pattern:

   PENCILPENCILPENCIL . . .

   If the pattern is continued, what latter will be in the 83rd position?

   A. P   B. E   C. I   D. L

8. Juan and Kim started a debating club. It was decided that once a month each member would debate every member of the club. It was also decided to add 1 new member to the club each month. Which of the following patterns could be used to determine the total number of debates in the fifth month the club was operating?

   A. 2, 6, 12, 20, 30   B. 1, 4, 9, 16, 25
   C. 1, 3, 6, 10, 15   D. 2, 3, 4, 5, 6

9. If the pattern below continues until all letters of the alphabet are shown, how many letters, including repetitions, will precede the last Z?

   ABBCCCDDDD

10. How many dots are needed to represent the first five terms, in total, for the given sequence?

    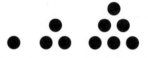

11. Given that: $\frac{1}{2} + \frac{1}{4} = \frac{3}{4}$

    $$\frac{1}{2} + \frac{1}{4} + \frac{1}{8} = \frac{7}{8}$$

    $$\frac{1}{2} + \frac{1}{4} + \frac{1}{8} + \frac{1}{16} = \frac{15}{16}$$

    Find: $\frac{1}{2} + \frac{1}{4} + \frac{1}{8} + \frac{1}{16} + \frac{1}{32}$

12. A local restaurant has small tables that seat 4 people, one on each side. When the restaurant must seat larger groups of people, tables are put together so that they share a common side. When 2 tables are put together, 6 people can be seated. If 5 tables are put together into a long row, how many people can be seated?

13. Jared painted a $4 \times 4 \times 4$ cube green on all 6 faces. When the paint dried, Jared cut the cube into 64 smaller cubes ($1 \times 1 \times 1$). If Jared looked at each small cube, how many would have green paint on exactly 2 faces? In completing this problem, discuss cases involving a smaller original cube in order to show a pattern to use to answer the question.

14. Mary notices that on a 2 × 2 checkerboard there are 5 squares of various sizes.

 This 2 × 2 board has four 1 × 1 squares and one 2 × 2 square.

Mary thinks that a 4 × 4 checkerboard would have twice as many squares. Do you agree or disagree with Mary's idea? Explain your reasoning.

15. For the given sequence, determine the total number of squares needed to represent the fifth term.

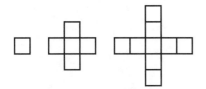

16. If the pattern is continued, how many dots would be in the 20th diagram?

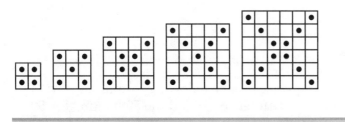

17. In successive stages of the pattern shown, each side of the equilateral triangle has a length equal to 110% of the length in the previous stage. To the nearest hundredth, what would be the perimeter of the triangle in the 6th stage?

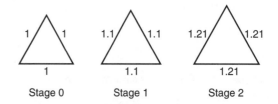

Stage 0   Stage 1   Stage 2

18. Suppose this pattern is continued. On the eighth figure, what percent of the figure is shaded? Explain your thought process.

---

4 A 2 Sequences and Series

A *sequence* is a list of numbers in a particular order which follows a pattern. A *series* is the sum of the terms of a sequence.

Arithmetic Sequences

An *arithmetic sequence* has a *common difference* between two consecutive terms.

Example: 5, 8, 11, 14, 17, . . .

                3   3   3   3   common difference = 3

The next term is 17 + 3 = 20.

1. Which of these are arithmetic sequences?

    I. 9, 15, 21, 27, 33, . . .

    II. 18, 10, 2, −6, −14, . . .

    III. 7, 11, 16, 22, 29, . . .

Solution: Check for a common difference.

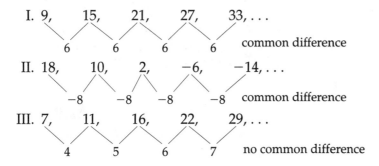

Answer: I and II are arithmetic sequences.

2. Find the 50th term of the arithmetic sequence:

$$3, 7, 11, 15, 19, 23, . . .$$

Solution: To find a particular term in an arithmetic sequence use the following formula: $a_n = a_1 + (n − 1)d$, **where n = term number and d = the common difference.** To find the 50th term, $n = 50$, $d = 7 − 3 = 4$, and $a_1 = 3$. By substituting into the formula you get:

$$a_n = a_1 + (n − 1)d$$
$$a_{50} = 3 + (50 − 1)4$$
$$a_{50} = 3 + 49 \cdot 4 = 199$$

Answer: The 50th term is 199.

Geometric Sequences

A *geometric sequence* has a *common ratio* between two consecutive terms.
Example: 2, 6, 18, 54, 162, . . .

$$\frac{6}{2} = 3, \frac{18}{6} = 3, \frac{54}{18} = 3, \frac{162}{54} = 3 \quad \text{common ratio} = 3$$

The next term is 162 × 3 = 486.

MODEL PROBLEMS

1. Which of these are geometric sequences?

    I. 16, 8, 4, 2, 1, . . .

    II. 10, 20, 80, 640, . . .

    III. 10, 50, 250, 1,250, . . .

Solution: Check for a common ratio.

    I. 16, 8, 4, 2, 1, . . .

$$\frac{8}{16} = \frac{1}{2}, \frac{4}{8} = \frac{1}{2}, \frac{2}{4} = \frac{1}{2} \quad \text{common ratio} = \frac{1}{2}$$

    II. 10, 20, 80, 640, . . .

$$\frac{20}{10} = 2, \frac{80}{20} = 4 \quad \text{no common ratio}$$

    III. 10, 50, 250, 1,250, . . .

$$\frac{50}{10} = 5, \frac{250}{50} = 5, \frac{1,250}{250} = 5 \quad \text{common ratio} = 5$$

Answer: I and III are geometric sequences.

2. Find the 10th term of the geometric sequence:

$$\frac{1}{2}, 1, 2, 4, 8, \ldots$$

Solution: To find a particular term in a geometric sequence you can use the following formula: $a_n = a_1 \cdot r^{n-1}$, **where r is the common ratio and n is the term number.**

For the given problem, $n = 10$, $r = 1 \div \frac{1}{2} = 2$, $a_1 = \frac{1}{2}$.

Using the formula and substituting the appropriate values gives:

$$a_{10} = \frac{1}{2} \cdot 2^{(10-1)} = \frac{1}{2} \cdot 2^9 = 256$$

Answer: The 10th term of the sequence is 256.

Note: 2^9 can be evaluated using the y^x key on a calculator.

Fibonacci Sequence

The *Fibonacci Sequence* is generated by adding the two previous terms to form the next term.

$$1, \quad 1, \quad 2, \quad 3, \quad 5, \quad 8, \ldots$$
$$\quad\quad (1+1) \quad (1+2) \quad (2+3) \quad (3+5)$$

MODEL PROBLEM

In the Fibonacci Sequence 1, 1, 2, 3, 5, 8, . . .

    a. What is the 10th term of the sequence?

    b. What is the sum of the first 10 terms?

Solution:

    a. To determine the 10th term, extend the sequence using the rule "add the two previous terms to form the next term."

Answer: 1, 1, 2, 3, 5, 8, 13, 21, 34, 55

    b. To find the sum, add the 10 given numbers.

$$1 + 1 + 2 + 3 + 5 + 8 + 13 + 21 + 34 + 55 = 143$$

Answer: The sum of the 10 terms is 143.

Arithmetic Series

The sum of the first n terms of an arithmetic sequence is given by the formula:

$$S_n = n\left(\frac{a_1 + a_n}{2}\right) \quad \text{where } a_1 = \text{first term}$$
$$a_n = n\text{th term}$$

MODEL PROBLEM

For the arithmetic series $5 + 7 + 9 + \ldots + 99 + 101$ compute the sum.

Solution: Use the formula $S_n = n\left(\frac{a_1 + a_n}{2}\right)$ where $a_1 = 5$ and $a_n = 101$.

To find n use the arithmetic sequence formula.

$$a_n = a_1 + (n - 1)d \qquad a_1 = 5, a_n = 101, d = 2$$
$$101 = 5 + (n - 1)2$$
$$96 = 2(n - 1)$$
$$48 = n - 1$$
$$49 = n$$

Therefore, $S_n = 49\left(\dfrac{5 + 101}{2}\right) = 49\left(\dfrac{106}{2}\right) = 49 \cdot 53 = 2{,}597$

Geometric Series

The sum of the first n terms of a geometric sequence is given by the formula:

$$S_n = \frac{a_1(r^n - 1)}{r - 1}$$

where a_1 = first term

n = term number

r = common ratio

 **MODEL PROBLEM**

For the geometric series $3 + 6 + 12 + \ldots$ compute the sum of the first 10 terms.

Solution: Using the formula

$$S_n = \frac{a_1(r^n - 1)}{r - 1} \qquad \text{where } a_1 = 3, n = 10, r = 2$$

$$S_n = \frac{3(2^{10} - 1)}{2 - 1} = \frac{3(1,024 - 1)}{1} = \frac{3(1,023)}{1} = 3,069$$

Infinite Geometric Series

When the absolute value of the ratio in a geometric sequence is greater than 1 the sequence *diverges* and as a result there is no limit or sum for an infinite number of terms. However, when the absolute value of the ratio is less than 1 the sequence *converges* and there is a limit or sum which can be obtained.

For example: (1) $5 + 15 + 45 + 135 + \ldots$ has no limit or sum for an infinite number of terms since $r = 3$.

$$(2) \ \frac{1}{2} + \frac{1}{4} + \frac{1}{8} + \frac{1}{16} + \ldots \text{ has a limit because } r = \frac{1}{2}.$$

The sum of the infinite series is 1.

The formula for an infinite geometric series where the absolute value of $r < 1$

is $S = \dfrac{a_1}{1 - r}$ where a_1 = first term and r = common ratio.

MODEL PROBLEM

Find the sum: $1 + \dfrac{1}{3} + \dfrac{1}{9} + \dfrac{1}{27} + \ldots$

Solution: $r = \dfrac{1}{3}, a_1 = 1$

$$S = \frac{a_1}{1 - r}$$

$$S = \frac{1}{1 - \dfrac{1}{3}} = \frac{1}{\dfrac{2}{3}} = \frac{3}{2}$$

Answer: $\dfrac{3}{2}$ is the sum or limit for the series.

PRACTICE

1. Which of the following is a geometric sequence?

   A. $6, 7\dfrac{1}{3}, 8\dfrac{2}{3}, 9, \ldots$

   B. $\dfrac{1}{2}, \dfrac{1}{3}, \dfrac{1}{4}, \dfrac{1}{5}, \ldots$

   C. $-10, -100, -1{,}000, \ldots$

   D. $2, 4, 2, 4, 2, 4, \ldots$

2. Which of the following would give you the 20th term of the arithmetic sequence 6, 13, 20, 27, . . . ?

   A. 20×6 B. $6 + 20 \times 7$

   C. 20×7 D. $6 + 19 \times 7$

3. Which of the following is NOT an arithmetic sequence?

   A. $2, 8, 32, 128, \ldots$ B. $\dfrac{1}{2}, \dfrac{3}{4}, 1, \dfrac{5}{4}, \ldots$

   C. $10, 10, 10, 10, \ldots$ D. $8, 4, 0, -4, \ldots$

4. Which of the following would NOT be a term of this geometric sequence?

   $$3, 6, 12, 24, \ldots$$

   A. 48   B. 64   C. 96   D. 192

5. Which is the next term in the given Fibonacci Sequence?

   $$1, 1, 2, 3, 5, 8, \ldots$$

   A. 11   B. 13   C. 16   D. 40

6. Which of these sequences is a Fibonacci sequence?

   A. $1, 4, 5, 9, 14, 23, \ldots$ B. $1, 4, 4, 16, 64, \ldots$
   C. $1, 4, 9, 16, 25, \ldots$ D. $1, 4, 8, 12, 16, \ldots$

7. The sum of the arithmetic series $-27 + -17 + -7 + \ldots + 43$ is

   A. 32   B. 64   C. 128   D. 280

8. The sum of the first 10 terms of the geometric series $1 + 2 + 4 + 8 + 16 + \ldots$ is

   A. 128   B. 255   C. 512   D. 1,023

9. The sum of the infinite series $1 + \dfrac{1}{4} + \dfrac{1}{16} + \ldots$ is

   A. $\dfrac{1}{4}$ B. $\dfrac{3}{4}$ C. $\dfrac{4}{3}$ D. 4

10. For which of the following is it possible to find the sum?

    A. $\dfrac{1}{2} + \dfrac{1}{3} + \dfrac{1}{4} + \dfrac{1}{5} + \dfrac{1}{6} + \ldots$

    B. $\dfrac{1}{2} + \dfrac{1}{2} + \dfrac{1}{2} + \dfrac{1}{2} + \dfrac{1}{2} + \ldots$

    C. $\dfrac{1}{2} - \dfrac{1}{4} + \dfrac{1}{8} - \dfrac{1}{16} + \ldots$

    D. $\dfrac{1}{2} + 1 + 2 + 4 + \ldots$

11. A special sequence is formed by taking twice the sum of the two previous terms to find the third term and all succeeding terms. If the first four terms are 1, 2, 6, 16, find the 8th term.

12. In an arithmetic sequence, the 5th term is 23 and the 7th term is 33. Find the common difference for the sequence.

13. The first four terms of an arithmetic sequence are 2, 8, 14, 20, and 122 is the 21st term. What is the value of the 20th term?

14. In this geometric sequence, what is the common ratio? $81, 27, 9, 3, \ldots$

15. If the 9th term of an arithmetic sequence is 100 and the 10th term is 111, find the value of the first term.

16. Create an arithmetic sequence of at least six terms for which the common difference is -3. Explain why the sequence you wrote is arithmetic. Also explain why there would be an infinite number of possible sequences fitting the given condition.

17. A tennis ball hit in the air 27 feet rebounds to two-thirds of its previous height after each bounce. Find the total vertical distance (up and down) the ball has traveled when it hits the ground the tenth time.

18. A small business had sales of $50,000 during its first year of operation. If the sales increase by $6,000 per year, what is its total sales in its eleventh year?

19. The number of bacteria in a culture triples every four hours. If 1,000 bacteria are present initially, how many bacteria will be present at the end of 24 hours?

20. A machine's value depreciates annually at a rate of 30% of the value it had at the beginning of that year. If its initial value is $10,000, find its value at the end of the eighth year.

4 A 3 Representation of Relationships and Patterns

The relationship "The perimeter of a square depends on the length of a side" can be expressed in a variety of ways.

a. Verbal statement: The perimeter of a square is four times the length of a side.

b. Table of values:

Side Length	Perimeter
1	4
2	8
3	12
4	16

c. Set of ordered pairs: {(1, 4), (2, 8), (3, 12), (4, 16)}

d. Equation: $P = 4s$, where s is the length of a side of the square and P is the perimeter.

e. Graph: Plot the table of values to obtain the graph.

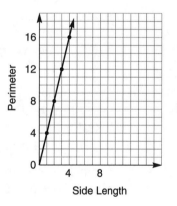

MODEL PROBLEM

A can of soda costs $0.75. The amount of money you spend on soda is related to the number of cans you purchase. Show the relationship as a table of values containing 5 sets of values and write an equation to summarize the relationship.

Solution: Table of values

Number of Cans	Cost
1	$0.75
2	$1.50
3	$2.25
4	$3.00
5	$3.75

Equation: To obtain the cost (C), multiply the number of cans by the cost of one can.

$$C = 0.75n, \text{ where } n \text{ is the number of cans.}$$

PRACTICE

1. This table indicates a linear relationship between x and y.

x	1	3	5	7	9
y	1	7	13	?	25

According to this pattern, which number is missing from the table?

A. 15   B. 19   C. 21   D. 23

2. A plumber charges $48 for each hour she works plus an additional service charge of $25. At this rate, how much would the plumber charge for a job that took 4.5 hours?

3. The cost of a long-distance telephone call can be computed based on the following formula:

$T = C + nr$, where T = total cost of the call in dollars

C = charge for the first three minutes in dollars

n = number of additional minutes the call lasts

r = rate per minute for each additional minute in dollars

What is the cost of a 15-minute long-distance call if a person is charged $1.75 for the first three minutes and $0.15 for each additional minute?

4. A local parking lot charges $1.75 for the first hour and $1.25 for each additional hour or part of an hour. Represent the relationship of parking charges to hours parked:

a. in a table of values for 1 to 6 hours.

b. in an equation in which t represents time parked in hours and C the total cost of parking.

c. as a graph with hours parked on the horizontal and total cost on the vertical.

1. What is the next term in this sequence?

$$2, 3\frac{1}{4}, 4\frac{1}{2}, 5\frac{3}{4}, \ldots$$

   A. $6\frac{1}{4}$ B. $6\frac{1}{2}$ C. $6\frac{3}{4}$ D. 7

2. What is the 30th term of this arithmetic sequence?

$$4, 9, 14, 19, 24, \ldots$$

   A. 124   B. 129   C. 149   D. 154

3. Which of these sequences is a geometric sequence?

   A. 2, 4, 6, 8, 10, ...
   B. 2, 4, 8, 16, 32, ...
   C. 2, 4, 8, 32, 256, ...
   D. 2, 4, 6, 10, 16, ...

4. Which of the following terms could NOT be a term of the sequence $\frac{1}{4}, \frac{1}{2}, 1, 2, \ldots$?

   A. 16   B. 32   C. 84   D. 128

5. Which of the following numerical patterns is equivalent to this visual pattern?

   A. 0.33333 ...   B. 123123123 ...
   C. 133133133 ...   D. 313131 ...

6. Suppose this pattern were continued:

A	BA	BBA	BBBA
	AB	BAB	BBAB
		ABB	BABB
			ABBB

   How many B's will be in the 20th diagram?

   A. 20   B. 60   C. 360   D. 380

7. What is the units digit in 3^{47}?

   A. 1   B. 3   C. 7   D. 9

8. What is the pattern of the units digits in the sequence $8^1, 8^2, 8^3, 8^4, \ldots, 8^n$?

   A. 8, 4, 6, 2   B. 8, 6, 4, 2
   C. 8, 2, 4, 6   D. 8, 4, 2, 6

9. In January, a certain item sells for $10.00. In February, the price increases 10%. In March, it decreases 10%. In April, it increases 10%, and so on. (It continues to alternate between the 10% increase and 10% decrease.) Which of the following graphs is suggested by the situation described above?

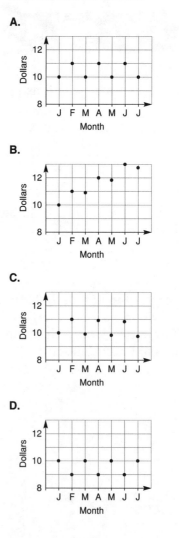

10. Examine the pattern:

     MONDAYMONDAYMONDAY . . .

     If this pattern is continued, what letter will be in the 121st position?

     A. M   B. N   C. D   D. Y

11. The first term of an arithmetic series is 2 and the common difference is 3. The sum of the series is 187. How many terms are in the series?

     A. 10   B. 11   C. 12   D. 17

12. In an arithmetic sequence, the 9th term is 27 and the 11th term is 33. Find the common difference.

13. 3, 9, 27, . . . are the first three terms of a geometric sequence. What is the 8th term?

14. If this pattern is continued, how many dots will be needed to represent the ninth term?

15. What is the next term of the sequence 5, 7, 12, 19, 31, . . . ?

16. What digit is in the 52nd decimal place in the decimal value for $\frac{3}{11}$?

17. A ball is dropped from a building 80 feet tall. If on each bounce the ball rebounds to 80% of the height of the previous bounce, how far does it travel by the time it hits the ground for the eighth time?

18. Find the sum of the following infinite geometric series.

$$\frac{3}{10} + \frac{3}{100} + \frac{3}{1,000} + \frac{3}{10,000} + \ldots$$

OPEN-ENDED QUESTIONS

19. By using a pattern, investigate this sum:

$$\frac{1}{1 \cdot 2} + \frac{1}{2 \cdot 3} + \frac{1}{3 \cdot 4} + \cdots + \frac{1}{49 \cdot 50}$$

     State the sum and show how your pattern allowed you to find the sum without doing the actual computation.

20.
     > *Problem:* Find the sum of the first 50 odd numbers.

     Martin decided to develop a pattern to help obtain the solution to the above problem. The first sum he looked at was $1 + 3 + 5 + 7 = 16$. Write a suggestion for Martin so that he could formulate a helpful approach to the original problem. Solve the original problem.

21. Suppose the pattern shown were continued.

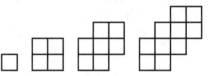

     a. Extend the pattern for two more terms.
     b. Discuss how the pattern is produced.
     c. How many squares would be in the 100th diagram?

22. A rectangle with an area of 24 square units may have dimensions 8 by 3. Consider other possible sets of dimensions for rectangles with an area of 24 square units.

     a. Draw a graph of length vs. width for all such rectangles.
     b. What does the graph tell you concerning what happens when the length gets extremely large?

23. The lengths of a sequence of rectangles have a common difference of 2, and the widths have a common difference of 1. The first rectangle has a length of 3 and a width of 2.

   a. What are the dimensions of the tenth rectangle in the sequence?

   b. What is the sum of the perimeters of the first ten rectangles?

   c. What is the sum of the areas of the first ten rectangles?

24. A college lecture hall has 15 rows of seats. The first row has 18 seats and the last row has 46 seats. The numbers of seats in each row form an arithmetic sequence.

   a. How many more seats are in row $(n + 1)$ than row n? Explain your approach.

   b. How many total seats are in the lecture hall?

Macro B:

Use various types of functions to represent mathematical or real-world situations.

4 B 1 Relations and Functions

Recall that the formula for the circumference of a circle is $C = \pi d$. The circumference *depends* on the length of the diameter. The length of the diameter is the **independent variable** and the circumference is the **dependent variable**. Another way to express the relationship is to say "circumference is a **function** of diameter." For different values of d, the function can be displayed by a table, set of ordered pairs, equation, or graph.

   a. **Table**

d	1	2	3	4
C	3.14	6.28	9.42	12.56

(d and C in inches)

   b. **Set of ordered pairs**

$$\{(1, 3.14), (2, 6.28), (3, 9.42), (4, 12.56), \ldots\}$$

   c. **Equation**

$$C = \pi d$$

d. Graph

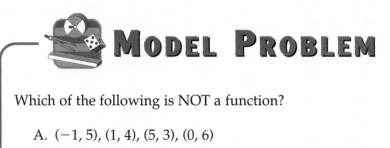

A set of ordered pairs is called a *relation.* The example above shows that circumference and diameter constitute a relation. One can observe that for any specified value for the diameter, there can be only one resulting value for the circumference. A relation with this property is called a *function.*

When a relation is listed as a set of ordered pairs, a function exists when for every x-value (first coordinate) there is only one y-value (second coordinate).

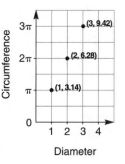

MODEL PROBLEM

Which of the following is NOT a function?

   A. $(-1, 5), (1, 4), (5, 3), (0, 6)$
   B. $(2, 4), (4, 8), (9, 18)$
   C. $(3, 0), (3, 1), (3, 2), (3, 3)$
   D. $(9, 0), (7, 0), (-5, 0), (13, 0)$

Solution: To be a function a given set of ordered pairs must be such that for every value of x there is only one value for y. In choice C, 3 is repeated for x with four different y-values. Hence, C is not a function.

In a function the values for the independent variable are considered as the input or domain; the values for the dependent variable are considered output or range. For the function $y = 2x$, if the domain is the set of whole numbers, the output or range would be the set of even whole numbers.

$$\nearrow \overset{y = 2x}{} \nwarrow$$

dependent   independent
variable,   variable,
output   input

Consider the following relations displayed as graphs:

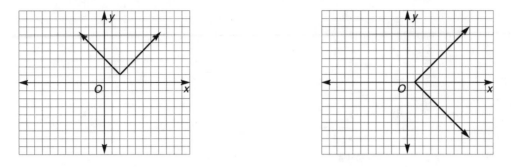

The one on the left is a function, while the one on the right is not. In the graph on the left, one can observe a unique value for y for each value of x considered. In contrast, the graph on the right has two different values for y for given values of x. This distinction can be visualized through a technique known as the vertical line test.

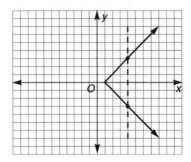

If the vertical line passes through a graph more than once, the graph is not the graph of a function.

MODEL PROBLEM

Explain why the graph of a circle is not a function.

Solution: Draw a graph of a circle. Using the vertical line test, a line would pass through the circle at two points showing two different y-values for the same x. Hence, it is not a function.

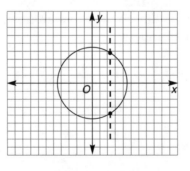

Consider the following nonlinear function.

Equation: $y = x^2 + 3$

Table of values: Set of ordered pairs: $\{(0, 3), (1, 4), (-1, 4), (2, 7), (-2, 7) \ldots\}$

x	y
0	3
1	4
−1	4
2	7
−2	7

Graph:

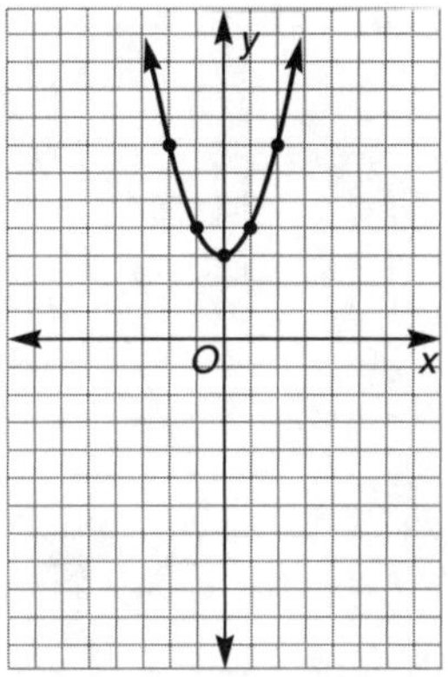

In this example, y is clearly a function of x. For any given value of x the value of y is found by adding 3 to the square of x. Since any value can be used for input, the domain of the function is the set of real numbers. Since the square of a real number must be nonnegative, the output values in this function must be 3 or greater. This means that the range is the set of real numbers greater than or equal to 3.

The following table summarizes some different types of functions.

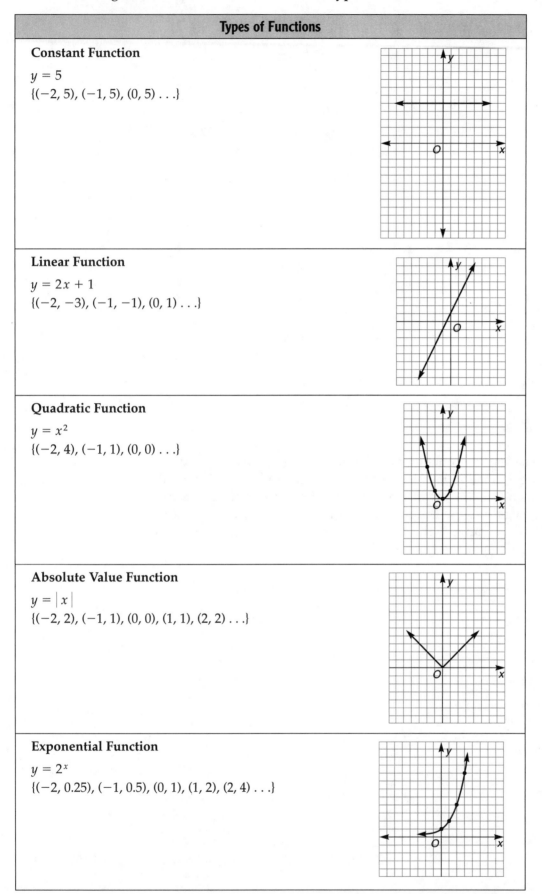

Types of Functions
Constant Function $y = 5$ $\{(-2, 5), (-1, 5), (0, 5) \ldots\}$
Linear Function $y = 2x + 1$ $\{(-2, -3), (-1, -1), (0, 1) \ldots\}$
Quadratic Function $y = x^2$ $\{(-2, 4), (-1, 1), (0, 0) \ldots\}$
Absolute Value Function $y = |x|$ $\{(-2, 2), (-1, 1), (0, 0), (1, 1), (2, 2) \ldots\}$
Exponential Function $y = 2^x$ $\{(-2, 0.25), (-1, 0.5), (0, 1), (1, 2), (2, 4) \ldots\}$

An alternative notation used for functions is referred to as $f(x)$ (read as "f of x" or "f at x").

$$\text{Given } y = x^2 + 3 \qquad f(x) = x^2 + 3$$

For this function, $f(4) = 4^2 + 3 = 19$ and $f(-2) = (-2)^2 + 3 = 7$.

Formulas can often be expressed using function notation. For example, the formula for the perimeter of a square can be expressed as $p(s) = 4s$; perimeter of a square is a function of side length.

Greatest-Integer Function

Consider a function in which:

$y = -2$ when $-2 \le x < -1$

$y = -1$ when $-1 \le x < 0$

$y = 0$ when $0 \le x < 1$

$y = 1$ when $1 \le x < 2$

$y = 2$ when $2 \le x < 3$

This function is called the *greatest-integer function* (notation $y = \lfloor x \rfloor$) since for any real number x in the domain, the function gives the greatest integer less than or equal to the domain value. For example:[]

$$\lfloor 4.2 \rfloor = 4; \lfloor 4.99 \rfloor = 4; \lfloor 5 \rfloor = 5; \lfloor 0.001 \rfloor = 0; \lfloor -4.1 \rfloor = -5; \lfloor \pi \rfloor = 3$$

The *least-integer function* is a similar function that gives the least integer greater than or equal to the domain value. For example:

$$\lceil 4.2 \rceil = 5; \lceil 4.99 \rceil = 5; \lceil 5 \rceil = 5; \lceil 0.001 \rceil = 1; \lceil -4.1 \rceil = -4; \lceil \pi \rceil = 4$$

The graphs of these functions are called step functions:

Greatest-Integer Function

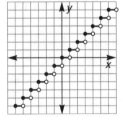

Least-Integer Function

First class postal rates are an example of a real-world situation that can be represented by a least-integer function.

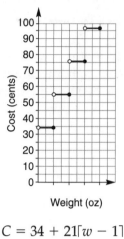

Weight (oz)

$$C = 34 + 21\lceil w - 1 \rceil$$

where C = postage charge in cents

w = weight of the envelope in ounces

Note: the domain would contain only values for w that are greater than 0.

MODEL PROBLEM

In a parking lot, the charges are $3.00 for the first hour (or any part of the hour) and $1.00 for every additional hour (or part of the hour).

   a. How much would the charge be for 4 hours and 20 minutes?

   b. Explain why the graph of parking charges as a function of time would be a step function.

   c. Graph the function from part b.

Solution:

   a. 4 hours and 20 minutes would be the same charge as 5 hours. With $3.00 for the first hour and 4 hours at $1.00 per hour, the final charge would be $7.00.

   b. The graph would be a least-integer function because you have an interval of values for time yielding the same total parking charge. For example, anything over 1 hour but not more than 2 hours would have a charge of $4.00; anything over 2 hours but not more than 3 hours would have a charge of $5.00, etc.

   c.

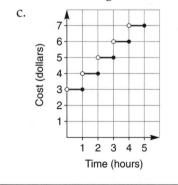

Time (hours)

1. Which of the following sets of ordered pairs does NOT represent a function?

    A. $\{(-2, 2), (2, 2), (-5, 5), (5, 5)\}$
    B. $\{(7, 5), (8, 5), (-8, 5), (-7, 5)\}$
    C. $\{(2, 3), (2, 4), (2, 5), (2, 6)\}$
    D. $\{(1, 1), (2, 8), (3, 27), (4, 64)\}$

2. If the volume of a cube is a function of the length of an edge, which of the following equations represents the situation?

    A. $V = 3e$ B. $V = e^3$
    C. $V = e + 3$ D. $V = \sqrt[3]{e}$

3. A function is described by the equation $R = 2t + 3$. What value for R is missing from the table?

t	1	2	3	...	10
R	5	7	9	...	?

    A. 11   B. 15   C. 23   D. 26

4. Which of the following equations represents the line containing the points given in the graph?

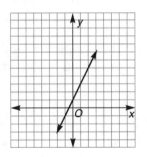

    A. $y = x + 1$ B. $y = x + 2$
    C. $y = 2(x + 1)$ D. $y = 2x + 1$

5. If $f(x) = 3^x - 2^x$, what is the value of $f(-2)$?

    A. $\dfrac{1}{5}$ B. $\dfrac{5}{36}$ C. $\dfrac{-5}{36}$ D. -2

6. Which of the following tables would be a reasonable representation for the relationship between the price (P) of an item and the sales tax (T) for that item?

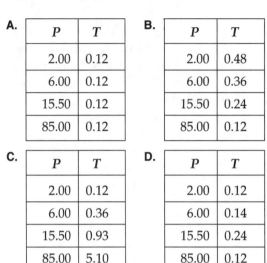

A.

P	T
2.00	0.12
6.00	0.12
15.50	0.12
85.00	0.12

B.

P	T
2.00	0.48
6.00	0.36
15.50	0.24
85.00	0.12

C.

P	T
2.00	0.12
6.00	0.36
15.50	0.93
85.00	5.10

D.

P	T
2.00	0.12
6.00	0.14
15.50	0.24
85.00	0.12

7. This graph illustrates a constant function:

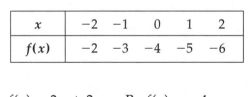

Which of the following is a situation that can be modeled by a constant function?

    A. The number of cars at a parkway toll-booth during the day
    B. The ratio of the circumferences of various circles to the lengths of their diameters
    C. Your heart rate during a 20-minute exercise period
    D. The value of a car over a 10-year period

8. The given table is generated from which of the following rules?

x	−2	−1	0	1	2
$f(x)$	−2	−3	−4	−5	−6

    A. $f(x) = 2x + 2$ B. $f(x) = -4 - x$
    C. $f(x) = x + 4$ D. $f(x) = -3x$

9. What is the range of the function $y = x^2 + 1$ when the domain is {0, 2, 4}?

A. {1, 3, 5} B. {1, 5, 9}
C. {1, 9, 25} D. {1, 5, 17}

10. If $f(x) = 2^x$, what is the value of $f(10) - f(6)$?

A. 4 B. 64 C. 512 D. 960

11. Carol purchases an appliance on an installment plan. She pays $50 a month until the appliance is paid off. Which of the following graphs matches the relationship between months and the unpaid balance?

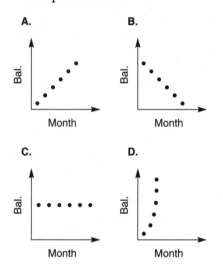

12. The functions $y = 3x$ and $y = 3^x$ represent very different relationships. If you take $x = 4$ from the domain of each, how many times larger is the range value for $y = 3^x$ than for $y = 3x$?

A. They are equal. B. 6.75

C. $\dfrac{4}{27}$ D. 5.33

13. The given graph shows the linear function $y = 2x + k$ ($k > 0$).

Based on the graph, which of the following must be true about the solution to the equation $2x + k = 0$ ($k > 0$)?

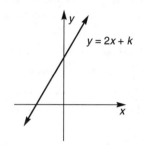

A. There is no solution.
B. The solution is approximately $x = 3$.
C. There is one negative real number solution.
D. There are two solutions, one positive and one negative.

14. If $f(x) = |x - 4|$, find the value of $f(8) - f(-8)$.

A. −8 B. −4 C. 0 D. 4

15. This graph illustrates a step function:

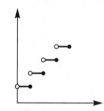

Which of the following applications could NOT be represented by the graph?

A. Postage rates per ounce
B. Charges at a parking lot per hour
C. Taxicab fare compared to distance
D. Temperature over the course of an afternoon

16. A periodic function is a function whose graph shows a continuously repeating pattern. For example:

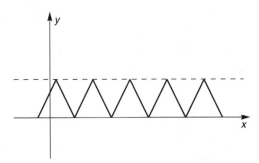

Which of the following is an example of a periodic function?

I.

II.

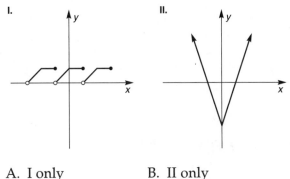

A. I only
B. II only
C. I and II
D. Neither

17. Karen and Samantha were looking at the table showing selected New Jersey towns and cities with their zip codes.

Town or City	Zip Code
Little Falls	07424
West Paterson	07424
Wayne	07470
West Orange	07052
Newark	07101
Newark	07102
Newark	07103

The two girls agreed that the relationship of town or city to zip code was not an example of a function. Karen said the Little Falls/West Paterson example was the reason. However, Samantha said that it was the Newark example that resulted in it not being a function. Who is correct? Explain your position.

18. The graph below displays a function: $y = f(x)$.
    a. What is the value of $f(1)$?
    b. What is the value of $f(6.73)$?
    c. What two values satisfy $f(x) = 4$?

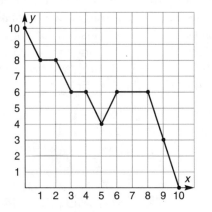

19. Consider the exponential functions $y = 4^x$ and $y = 5^x$.

    a. The graphs of these functions intersect at exactly one point. What are the coordinates of the point?
    b. In the first quadrant, which graph is closer to the y-axis? Explain or show an illustration.
    c. Explain what happens to the graphs as they cross the axis and enter the second quadrant.
    d. Explain why these graphs do not cross into quadrant III or IV.

4 B 2 Slope

Slope of a Line

Consider the linear function $y = 2x + 3$. By looking at a table of values, one can see that as the x-value increases by 1, the y-value always increases by 2. This means that there is a constant rate of change for the function. The rate of change is called the *slope*. This can also be shown through the graph of the line associated with the function.

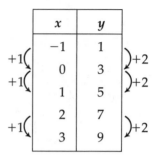

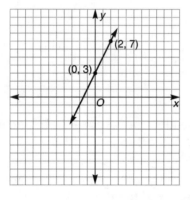

If the coordinates of two points on the line are known, the slope can be found using the formula included in Cluster 2.

$$\text{slope} = \frac{\text{rise}}{\text{run}} = \frac{\text{change in } y}{\text{change in } x} = \frac{y_2 - y_1}{x_2 - x_1} = \frac{7 - 3}{2 - 0} = \frac{4}{2} = 2$$

Lines with different types of slopes:

If a line is parallel to the x-axis, the line has no steepness. Its slope is zero.

If a line is parallel to the y-axis, the line has an undefined slope.

If a line rises from left to right, its slope is positive.

If a line falls from left to right, its slope is negative.

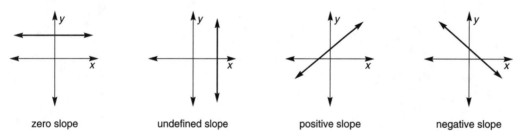

zero slope   undefined slope   positive slope   negative slope

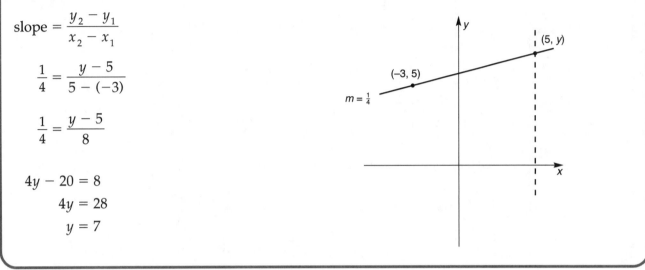

MODEL PROBLEM

A line passing through the points $(-3, 5)$ and $(5, y)$ has a slope of $\frac{1}{4}$. Find the value of y.

Solution:

$$\text{slope} = \frac{y_2 - y_1}{x_2 - x_1}$$

$$\frac{1}{4} = \frac{y - 5}{5 - (-3)}$$

$$\frac{1}{4} = \frac{y - 5}{8}$$

$$4y - 20 = 8$$
$$4y = 28$$
$$y = 7$$

Slope-Intercept Form of the Equation of a Line

For the family of parallel lines shown, the lines have the same slope. However, note that each line crosses the y-axis at a different point. This point is known as the y-intercept. For the linear function, $y = 2x + 3$, when x is equal to zero, the value of y becomes 3. Hence, the ordered pair $(0, 3)$ becomes the y-intercept for the line.

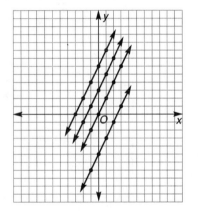

Slope-Intercept Form:	
$y = 2x + 3$	$y = mx + b$
↑ ↑	↑ ↑
slope y-intercept	slope y-intercept

Equation	Slope	y-intercept	Illustration
$y = -3x - 1$	$m = -3$	$b = -1$	
$y = \dfrac{3}{4}x$	$m = \dfrac{3}{4}$	$b = 0$	
$y = 5$	$m = 0$	$b = 5$	

MODEL PROBLEMS

1. Change the equation $3y - 5x = 15$ into slope-intercept form and graph the resulting line.

Solution: $3y - 5x = 15$

$$3y = 5x + 15$$

$$y = \frac{5}{3}x + 5$$

Since the equation is now in slope-intercept form, $m = \frac{5}{3}$ and $b = 5$.

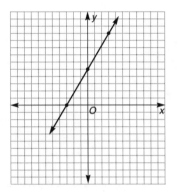

2. Find the equation of the line passing through the points $(-2, 5)$ and $(6, 1)$.

Solution: In order to use slope-intercept form, first find the slope.

$$m = \frac{y_2 - y_1}{x_2 - x_1} = \frac{5 - 1}{-2 - 6} = \frac{4}{-8} = -\frac{1}{2}$$

The equation would be $y = -\frac{1}{2}x + b$. It is now necessary to find the value of b. Knowing that either given point satisfies the equation, one can substitute in the coordinates of either point in order to find b.

$$y = mx + b$$

$$y = -\frac{1}{2}x + b$$

Using $(6, 1)$ $\quad 1 = \left(-\frac{1}{2}\right)6 + b$

$$1 = -3 + b$$

$4 = b$ and the final equation is

$$y = -\frac{1}{2}x + 4$$

3. A small company makes a new type of container. A mathematician employed by the company claims that the total cost (in dollars) of producing n containers is given by the formula

$$C = 2n + 600$$

Graph this cost function and explain the significance of the slope and the y-intercept.

Solution: The y-intercept, $(0, 600)$, shows that the cost is $600 before any containers are produced. The slope, 2, indicates that the cost of producing each new container is $2.

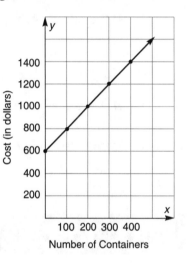

Nonlinear functions

x	$y = 3x + 1$
1	4
2	7
3	10
4	13
5	16

x	$y = x^2$
1	1
2	4
3	9
4	16
5	25

x	$y = 2^x$
1	2
2	4
3	8
4	16
5	32

In contrast with the linear function on the left ($y = 3x + 1$), the other two are examples of nonlinear functions. In these examples, you do not obtain a constant rate of change.

$$y = x^2$$

From (1, 1) to (2, 4) the rate of change is $\dfrac{4 - 1}{2 - 1} = \dfrac{3}{1} = 3$

From (2, 4) to (3, 9) the rate of change is $\dfrac{9 - 4}{3 - 2} = \dfrac{5}{1} = 5$

$$y = 2^x$$

From (1, 2) to (2, 4) the rate of change is $\dfrac{4 - 2}{2 - 1} = \dfrac{2}{1} = 2$

From (2, 4) to (3, 8) the rate of change is $\dfrac{8 - 4}{3 - 2} = \dfrac{4}{1} = 4$

PRACTICE

1. Which of the following is true about rates of change?

   A. Rates of change are always constant.
   B. A horizontal line has a rate of change of zero.
   C. Two perpendicular lines have the same rate of change.
   D. The line $y = 8x$ has the same rate of change as $y = -8x$.

2. Find the equation of the line containing the points $(-1, -3)$ and $(0, 5)$.

   A. $y = 8x$
   B. $y = -8x + 5$
   C. $y = 8x + 5$
   D. $y = \dfrac{1}{8}x + 5$

3. How many of the following lines have a slope of 2?

   $$y = x + 2 \qquad y = 2x \qquad 2y = x$$
   $$4y - 8x = 11 \qquad 8x - 4 = 7$$

   A. 1   B. 2   C. 3   D. 4

4. Write the equation, in slope-intercept form, for the line passing through (8, 0) perpendicular to the line $y = 2x$.

   A. $y = -\dfrac{1}{2}x + 8$
   B. $y = -\dfrac{1}{2}x + 4$
   C. $y = -2x + 4$
   D. $y = -2x + 8$

5. Isosceles triangle *ABC* has vertices at *A*(−6, 0), *B*(6, 0), *C*(0, 10). Point *M* is the midpoint of *BC*. What is the equation, in slope-intercept form, of the line containing segment *AM*?

6. Brittany has a potted kudzu vine that is 10 inches long. As long as she waters it, it grows two inches each day.

   a. Explain why this situation is an example of linear change.

   b. Write an equation, in slope-intercept form, to represent the situation.

   c. Draw the resulting graph.

   d. If Brittany keeps watering the vine, when will it be 30 inches long? Show where this answer is on the graph.

7. In a linear function there is a constant rate of change.

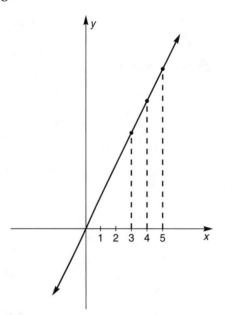

For example, in the graph shown, $f(5) - f(4) = f(4) - f(3)$. Show that this does not hold for each of the following nonlinear functions. Include a graph with your explanation.

   a. $y = x^2$

   b. $y = 2^x$

4 B 3 Transformations of Functions

Many functions have graphs that result from performing simple transformations of other functions.

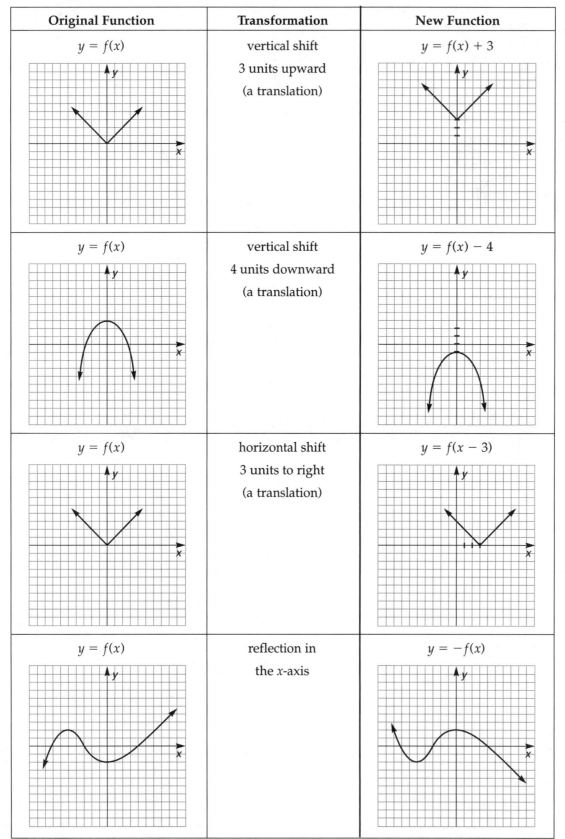

Original Function	Transformation	New Function
$y = f(x)$	vertical shift 3 units upward (a translation)	$y = f(x) + 3$
$y = f(x)$	vertical shift 4 units downward (a translation)	$y = f(x) - 4$
$y = f(x)$	horizontal shift 3 units to right (a translation)	$y = f(x - 3)$
$y = f(x)$	reflection in the x-axis	$y = -f(x)$

Original Function	Transformation	New Function
$y = f(x)$	reflection in the y-axis	$y = f(-x)$

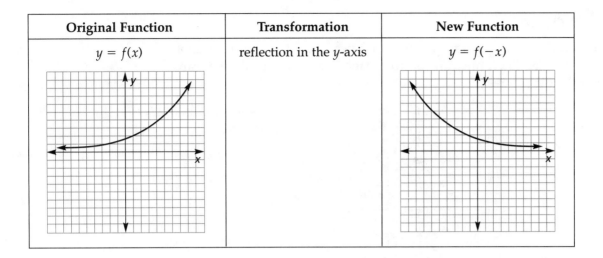

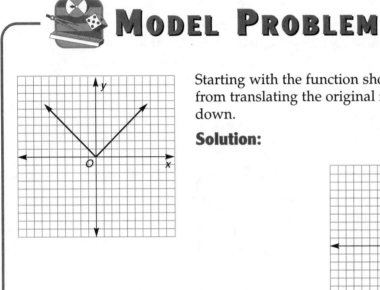

MODEL PROBLEM

Starting with the function shown at the left, draw the graph resulting from translating the original function 3 units to the right and 2 units down.

Solution:

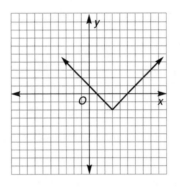

Family of Functions

Vertical and horizontal shifts generate a family of functions. For example, in looking at a graph of parallel lines, one can consider each line as the result of a translation on any of the other lines.

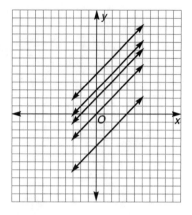

In this illustration, the line $y = x - 4$ results from translating (or shifting) $y = x + 2$ down 6 units; the line $y = x + 5$ results from translating the line $y = x + 2$ left 3 units.

The following illustrations show a family of absolute value functions and a family of quadratic functions.

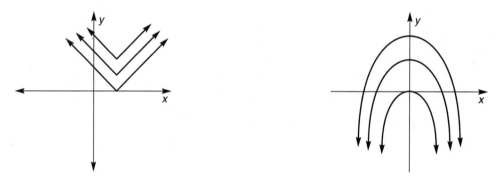

Dilations

The function $y = x^2$ is graphed as a standard parabola. If you change the coefficient of x^2 from 1 to some other number, the resulting parabola is a dilation of the original.

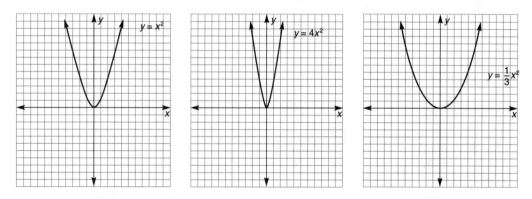

As you can see from the graphs, the parabola is wider than $y = x^2$ when the absolute value of the coefficient is less than 1, and narrower when the absolute value of the coefficient is greater than 1.

1. The graph of the function $f(x)$ is given below.

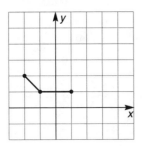

Which graph would represent $-f(x)$?

A.

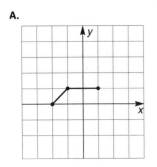

B.

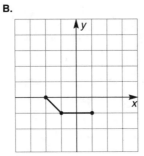

C.

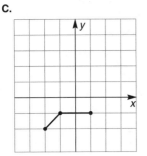

D.

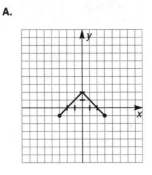

2. The graph of a function, $f(x)$, is given below.

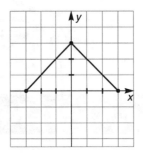

Which graph results from a translation 3 units to the left and 1 unit down?

A.

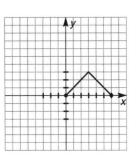

B.

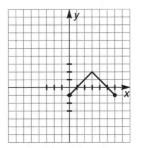

C.

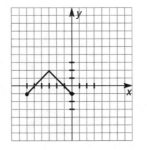

D.

3. Explain how each graph would differ from the graph of $f(x) = |x|$.

a. $g(x) = |x| + 7$
b. $g(x) = -|x| - 2$
c. $g(x) = |x + 3| + 3$

4. Name a point on the graph of $y_1 = -f(x) + 4$ if (5, 9) is a point on the graph of $y_2 = f(x)$.

ASSESSMENT MACRO B

1. Which of the following illustrates a constant function?

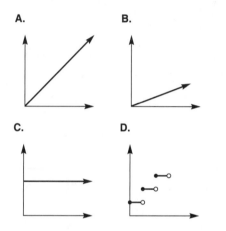

A.   B.

C.   D.

2. If you say that the volume of a cylinder is a function of the height and the length of a radius of the base, which of the following formulas represents the situation?

A. $V = \pi r^2$ B. $V = \pi r^3$
C. $V = \pi r^2 h$ D. $V = \pi h$

3. Which of the following diagrams suggests the existence of a function?

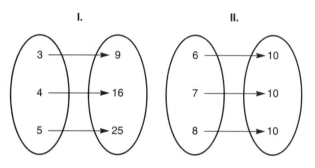

I.   II.

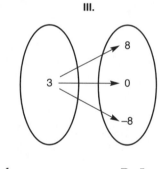

III.

A. I only   B. I and II
C. III only   D. I and III

4. Find the slope of the line containing the points $(-10, -6)$ and $(-13, -10)$.

   A. $\dfrac{4}{3}$ B. $\dfrac{3}{4}$ C. $-\dfrac{3}{4}$ D. $-\dfrac{4}{3}$

5. For the function $y = x^2$, the domain is the set of all real numbers. Which of the following would NOT have the set of all real numbers as a domain?

   A. $y = -4x + 2$ B. $y = x^3$

   C. $y = \dfrac{1}{x}$ D. $y = 2^x$

6. This graph shows the cost of electricity:

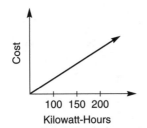

   Which of the following statements is NOT true concerning this graph?

   A. The graph illustrates a function.
   B. The graph shows that the cost of electricity levels off at some point.
   C. As the number of kilowatt-hours increases, the cost also increases.
   D. The cost increases at the same rate between 100–150 kilowatt-hours and 150–200 kilowatt-hours.

7. Use the given graphs to determine which statement is true.

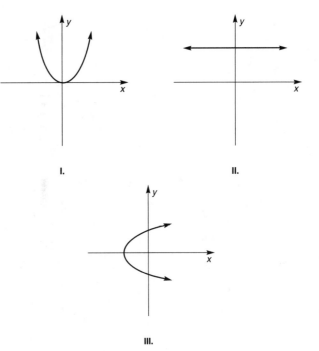

   A. Graphs I, II, and III represent functions.
   B. Graphs I and II represent functions.
   C. Only graph II is a function.
   D. Graphs II and III are functions.

8. Which of the following functions would have the set of all real numbers as its range?

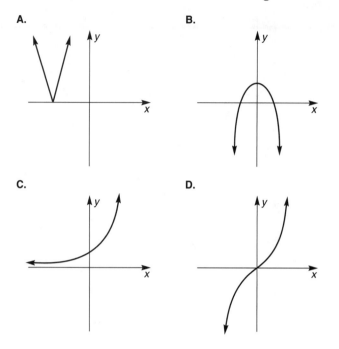

A.

B.

C.

D.

9. Which of the following graphs would NOT match the set of clues for a function $f(x)$?

I. The domain is $-2 \leq x \leq 6$

II. The range is $-4 \leq y \leq 4$

III. $f(-2) = f(0) = f(6)$

A.

B.

C.

D.

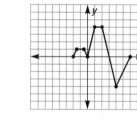

10. Consider a function in which $f(a) = f(b)$ for at least one pair of different values, a and b, from the domain. Which graph illustrates such a function?

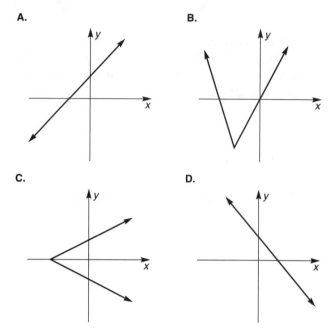

A.

B.

C.

D.

11. Which of the following is NOT true about the relation represented by the graph?

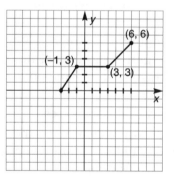

(6, 6)

(−1, 3)

(3, 3)

A. The relation is a function.

B. A portion of the graph represents a constant function.

C. The domain and range are the same.

D. $f(-1) = f(3)$

12. During a winter storm in northern Maine, the temperature dropped from 20°F at 5 p.m. to −10°F at 3 a.m. What was the average rate of change in the temperature per hour? (Note: You can use the formula for slope.)

   A. −3°F per hour

   B. −1°F per hour

   C. −7.5°F per hour

   D. −3.75°F per hour

13. What kind of line has no y-intercept?

   A. A line with a slope of 1

   B. A line with a slope of −1

   C. A horizontal line

   D. A vertical line (other than the y-axis)

14. A function is defined as follows:

$$f(x) = \begin{cases} 5x - 1 \text{ when } x \geq 5 \\ 1 - 5x \text{ when } x < 5 \end{cases}$$

Find the value of $f(6) + f(-2)$.

   A. 0   B. 20   C. 37   D. 40

15. Find the equation of a line containing the point $(3, 3)$ if the line is parallel to a line passing through the points $(-2, 0)$ and $(0, 8)$.

   A. $y = 4x$ B. $y = 4x - 9$

   C. $y = -4x - 15$ D. $y = 4x + 9$

16. From the graph find the following values of $f(x)$.

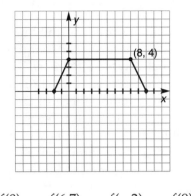

(8, 4)

Find: $f(0)$ $f(6.7)$ $f(-2)$ $f(9)$

17. The perimeter of an equilateral triangle depends on the length of a side. Represent the function as

   a. an equation

   b. a table of values

   c. a graph

18. Here is a function represented in words:

The cost of mailing a first class letter depends on the weight of the letter.

   a. What is the independent variable?

   b. What is the dependent variable?

   c. State two other ways to represent this function.

OPEN-ENDED QUESTIONS

19. Draw a graph representing a function which satisfies all the following clues:

   I. The domain is $-4 \leq x \leq 4$

   II. The range is $1 \leq y \leq 5$

   III. $f(-4) = f(-2) = f(0) = f(2) = f(4) = 1$

   IV. $f(-3) = f(-1) = f(1) = f(3) = 5$

20. The table at the right shows the number of degrees in the sum of the measures of the interior angles of a convex polygon with n sides.

n	s
3	180
4	360
5	540
6	720

   a. Write the formula to summarize the relationship shown.

   b. Explain why this is a function.

   c. Explain why this is a linear function as opposed to some other type of function such as quadratic or exponential.

21. On a grid, draw any function that has a domain of $-4 \le x \le 4$ and a range of $-6 \le y \le 6$ if you are given that $f(-3) = f(3) = 5$.

22. The usual formula for the area of a circle is $A = \pi r^2$, where r is the length of the radius. We can also write $A(r) = \pi r^2$ to indicate that area of a circle is a function of the radius. Since the circumference of a circle is also a function of the radius ($C = 2\pi r$), it should be possible to express the area A of a circle as a function of its circumference C. What would be this new formula? Show your algebraic work in arriving at your formula.

23. a. Name a point on the graph of $y_1 = -f(x) - 2$ if (3, 4) is a point on the graph of $y_2 = f(x)$.

   b. Show a sketch of a possible set of graphs for y_1 and y_2.

Macro C:

Use algebraic concepts and processes to concisely express, analyze, and model real-world situations.

4 C 1 Expressions and Open Sentences

A *variable* is a letter used to represent a number. The value of a variable can change. A *term* is a number, a variable, or the product or quotient of a number and a variable. A *variable expression* is made up of one or more terms.

Variable Expressions
$6a$
$x + 4$
$a^2 b$

Constant Terms
7
4π
$\sqrt{2}$

The value of an expression involving a variable depends upon the value used for the variable.

When evaluating an expression be sure to follow the established algebraic *order of operations*.

- Perform any operation(s) inside grouping symbols.
- Simplify any terms with exponents.
- Multiply and divide in order from left to right.
- Add and subtract in order from left to right.

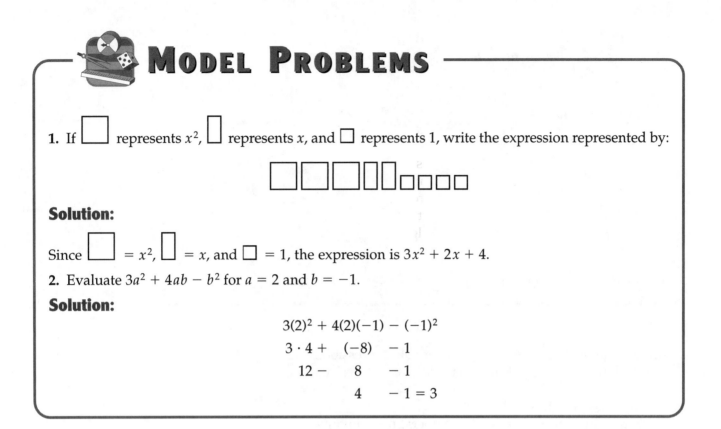

MODEL PROBLEMS

1. If ▢ represents x^2, ▯ represents x, and ▫ represents 1, write the expression represented by:

$$▢▢▢▯▯▫▫▫▫$$

Solution:

Since ▢ $= x^2$, ▯ $= x$, and ▫ $= 1$, the expression is $3x^2 + 2x + 4$.

2. Evaluate $3a^2 + 4ab - b^2$ for $a = 2$ and $b = -1$.

Solution:

$$3(2)^2 + 4(2)(-1) - (-1)^2$$
$$3 \cdot 4 + \quad (-8) \quad - 1$$
$$12 - \quad 8 \quad - 1$$
$$4 \quad - 1 = 3$$

In a term that contains a variable, the numerical factor is called the *coefficient*.

coefficient ⌐ ⌐ exponent
$$3x^2$$
⌐ base

If terms have exactly the same variables raised to the same powers, they are called *like terms*.

Like Terms
$5x^2$ and $\frac{1}{2}x^2$
$5a^2b$ and $6a^2b$

Not Like Terms
$3x^2$ and $3x^3$
$5ab$ and $6ac$

If an expression contains like terms, the terms can be combined to simplify the expression.

To combine like terms:

- Add (or subtract) the coefficients.
- Carry along the like base and exponent.

MODEL PROBLEM

Simplify $5x^2 + 8y + 2x^2 - 5y$.

Solution: Combine like terms.

$$\overset{\displaystyle 3y}{\overbrace{5x^2 + \underbrace{8y + 2x^2 - 5y}}}$$
$$7x^2$$

$$5x^2 + 8y + 2x^2 - 5y = 7x^2 + 3y$$

Verbal statements can be written as variable expressions.
To translate from a verbal statement to a variable expression:

- Identify the variable(s) to be used.
- Using the key words, determine the operation(s) involved.
- Form the expression, using symbols of grouping as needed.

MODEL PROBLEM

Write a variable expression for each of the verbal statements:

   a. The product of two consecutive integers
   b. 10 less than twice a number

Solution:

   a. $n(n + 1)$
   b. $2n - 10$

Variable expressions can be used to translate word problems into equations or inequalities, which are also called open sentences.

To translate a word sentence into an open sentence:

- Write a variable expression to represent each word phrase.
- Determine the appropriate relationship symbol to be used ($=$, $\neq$, $<$, $>$, $\leq$, $\geq$).

Word Phrase	Symbol
is equal to	$=$
is not equal to	$\neq$
is greater than	$>$
is less than	$<$
is at least	$\geq$
is greater than or equal to	$\geq$
is at most	$\leq$
is less than or equal to	$\leq$

 **MODEL PROBLEM**

Translate each verbal sentence into an open sentence.

a. What number doubled gives a result of 18?
b. Three times one more than a number gives a result of at least 26.

Solution:

a. $2x = 18$
b. $3(n + 1) \geq 26$

1. Evaluate a^2b^3 when $a = 2$ and $b = -1$.

   A. 4   B. -4 C. -32 D. -64

2. Evaluate $5 + x(x + 2)$ when $x = 8$.

   A. 71   B. 85   C. 122   D. 130

3. If $n + 7$ is an even number, the next larger even number is:

   A. $n + 5$ B. $n + 9$
   C. $10n + 7$ D. $2n + 14$

4. Which of the following cannot be simplified?

   A. $2a^2 + 5a^2$
   B. $3a^2 - 3a$
   C. $5a - 11a$
   D. $16a^3 - 6a^3$

5. Which expression must be added to $2x - 4$ to produce a sum of 0?

   A. 0   B. $x + 2$
   C. $2x + 4$ D. $-2x + 4$

6. The perimeter of the parallelogram is $6a + 8b$. Find the length of each of the other two sides.

   A. $2a + 3b$
   B. $2b + 3a$
   C. $4a + 6b$
   D. $3a + 4b$

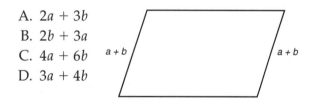

7. Write an open sentence to represent the statement.

   If 7 is subtracted from 4 times a certain number, the difference is 25.

   A. $7 - 4n = 25$ B. $4(n - 7) = 25$
   C. $4(7 - n) = 25$ D. $4n - 7 = 25$

8. Write an open sentence to represent the statement.

   5 less than twice a number is 3 more than the number.

   A. $2n - 5 = 3n$ B. $2n - 5 = n + 3$
   C. $5 - 2n = n + 3$ D. $5 - 2n = 3n$

9. Write an equation to show that segment y is 5 units longer than 3 times the length of segment x.

   A. $y = 15x$
   B. $y = 3x + 5$
   C. $x = 3y + 5$
   D. $y = 3x - 5$

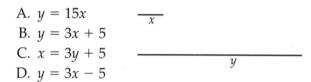

10. Find the value of A in the formula $A = \frac{1}{2}bh$ if $b = h = 5$.

11. A rectangle has dimensions $2x$ by $x + 3$. Write an expression for the perimeter of the rectangle. Combine any like terms.

12. Write the open sentence represented by the following situation. The congruent sides of an isosceles triangle have lengths that are each 5 inches greater than the length of the base. The perimeter is at most 31 inches.

13. Pat thinks that if $y = 5$, the expression $-y^2$ and the expression $(-y)^2$ will result in the same value. Write an explanation to agree or disagree.

14. Is the expression for twice the sum of a number and 10 the same as the expression for the sum of twice a number and 10? Explain.

15. Write the equation modeled by the following diagram.

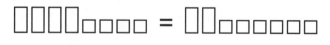

4 C 2 Linear Equations and Inequalities

An equation represents that two expressions are equal to each other.
   An equation is similar to a balanced scale.
   To determine the unknown weight in a balance:

- Remove (cancel) identical items from both sides of the scale.
- Determine a relationship among the remaining items.
- Substitute the value for the known quantity.
- Determine the weight of the unknown quantity.

MODEL PROBLEMS

Given the balances as shown, find the weight of one cube if each ball weighs 1 pound and the cubes are all the same weight.

1.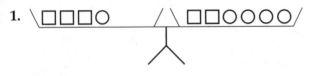

Solution:
- Remove two cubes and one ball from each side of the scale.
- One cube is balanced by three balls.
- Each ball weighs 1 pound.
- One cube weighs 3 pounds. **Answer**

2.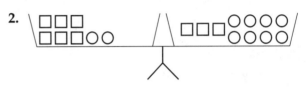

Solution:
- Remove three cubes and two balls from each side of the scale.
- Three cubes are balanced by six balls.
- Each ball weighs 1 pound.
- Three cubes weigh 6 pounds, and one cube weighs 2 pounds. **Answer**

The more traditional method of solving an equation involves use of mathematical properties.
   To solve an equation:

- Remove parentheses by multiplication. (Apply the Distributive Property.)
- Combine like terms in each member of the equation. Use addition or subtraction as indicated.
- Collect the terms containing the variable on one side and the number terms on the other side. Using the opposite operation of the one indicated (the inverse operation) will move a term from one side of the equation to the other.
- Rewrite the variable term with a coefficient of 1. Use the opposite operation of the division or multiplication indicated.

MODEL PROBLEMS

1. Solve for x: $6x = 2(x + 1) + 10$

Solution:

$$6x = 2(x + 1) + 10$$

$6x = 2x + 2 + 10$	Remove parentheses.
$6x = 2x + 12$	Combine like terms.
$6x - 2x = 2x - 2x + 12$	Collect the variable terms on one side.
$4x = 12$	
$\dfrac{4x}{4} = \dfrac{12}{4}$	Rewrite the variable term with a coefficient of 1. Divide.
$x = 3$	

2. Solve for y: $-5y + 7 = -2(y - 5)$

Solution:

$$-5y + 7 = -2(y - 5)$$

$-5y + 7 = -2y + 10$	Remove parentheses. No need to combine like terms. Collect the variable terms on one side
$-5y + 2y + 7 = -2y + 2y + 10$	
$-3y + 7 = 10$	
$-3y + 7 - 7 = 10 - 7$	and the number terms on the other side.
$-3y = 3$	
$\dfrac{-3y}{-3} = \dfrac{3}{-3}$	Rewrite the variable term with a coefficient of 1. Divide.
$y = -1$	

Solutions to some equations can be found by using a table or a graph.

Consider the equation $6(x + 1) = 15$. If you graph $6(x + 1) = y$ and locate the point on the graph where $y = 15$, the corresponding x-value of the ordered pair containing $y = 15$ would represent the solution to the equation.

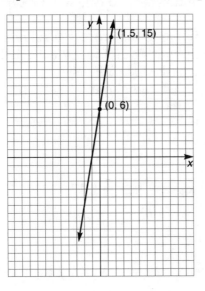

Another approach involves using a table of values. Look at the table given for $6(x + 1) = y$.

x	y
0	6
1	12
2	18

To solve $6(x + 1) = 15$, observe that 15 is midway between 12 and 18. Therefore the value of x that satisfies the equation must be midway between 1 and 2, or 1.5.

Use a table to find the solution for the linear equation $3x + 4 = 6$.

Solution: Consider $3x + 4 = 6$ as $3x + 4 = y$ and generate a table of values.

x	y
0	4
1	7
2	10

Notice that $y = 6$ falls between 4 and 7. In fact it is $\frac{2}{3}$ of the way between 4 and 7. Therefore the corresponding x value must be $\frac{2}{3}$ of the way between 0 and 1, or $\frac{2}{3}$.

Answer: $x = \frac{2}{3}$

Inequalities

An inequality consists of two or more terms or expressions connected by an inequality sign.

The solution to an inequality is given as a solution set and can be represented on a number line.

The process of solving an inequality is very similar to the process of solving an equation. The major difference is if you are multiplying or dividing the inequality by a *negative number*, you must reverse the order of the inequality sign.

Note: A closed circle indicates the value is included in the solution set. An open circle indicates the value is excluded from the solution set.

 **MODEL PROBLEMS**

1. Graph the inequality on the number line: $-2 < x \le 4$

Solution: The inequality is read "x is between -2 and 4 with -2 excluded and 4 included." On the number line the graph would be:

$$\text{-3 -2 -1 0 1 2 3 4 5 6}$$

2. Solve for x: $-4x + 4 \le -16$

Solution:

$$-4x + 4 \le -16$$

$$-4x + 4 - 4 \le -16 - 4 \quad \text{Add } -4.$$

$$-4x \le -20$$

$$\frac{-4x}{-4} \ge \frac{-20}{-4} \quad \begin{array}{l}\text{Divide by } -4; \text{ reverse} \\ \text{inequality sign.}\end{array}$$

$$x \ge 5$$

$$\text{0 1 2 3 4 5 6 7}$$

3. Write an inequality to describe the following situation and solve: Seven less than twice a number is greater than -3. Find the number.

Solution:

$$2x - 7 > -3$$

$$2x > 4$$

$$x > 2$$

$$\text{0 1 2 3 4}$$

1. Within the set of integers, which of the following represents the solution of the inequality?

$$3x + 1 < 8$$

A. $\{\ldots, -3, -2, -1, 0, 1, 2\}$
B. $\{\ldots, -3, -2, -1, 0, 1, 2, 3\}$
C. $\{\ldots, -3, -2, -1, 0, 1, 2, 3, 4, 5, 6, 7\}$
D. $\left\{\ldots, -3, -2, -1, 0, 1, 2, 2\frac{1}{3}\right\}$

2. Which of the following transformations is NOT correct?

A. $3x + 1 < 8 \quad \rightarrow 3x < 7$
B. $5x - 4 > 0 \quad \rightarrow 5x > 4$
C. $3(x + 1) < -5 \rightarrow 3x < -8$
D. $3x - 7 < 0 \quad \rightarrow 3x > 7$

3. Which equation has NO integral solution?

A. $3x = 9$ B. $16x = 32$
C. $3x = 2$ D. $17x = 51$

4. Solve for c: $\dfrac{c}{6} + 14 = 38$

A. 4   B. 144   C. 214   D. 312

5. Which number line shows the graph of $-3 \le x < 4$?

A.
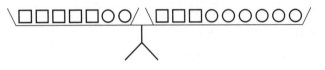

B.

C.

D.

6. Solve for x: $-5x + 3 \ge 28$

7. Write an inequality to describe the following situation and solve:

Nine more than half a number is at most -8.

8. Solve for x: $2(x + 1) - 4 = x + 3$

9. How do you know that the solution to the equation $3x = 251$ is NOT an integral value?

10. Given the balance shown, find the weight of each identical cube if each ball weighs 1 pound.

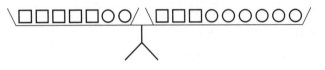

11. Solve for r.

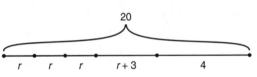

12. The temperature at High Point is 28°C and is dropping at the rate of 1.5° per hour. The temperature at Belmare is about 18°C and rising to 2° per hour.

a. Write an expression representing the temperature at each place after x hours.

b. Write an equation to represent that both cities are at the same temperature.

c. Solve the equation to find out how many hours (to the nearest tenth) it will take for the two cities to be at the same temperature.

1. What is the weight of one cube if each pyramid weighs 3 pounds and the cubes are all the same weight?

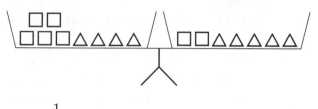

   A. $\frac{1}{3}$ pound   B. 1 pound

   C. 3 pounds   D. 9 pounds

2. Evaluate $\frac{a}{b} + b$ for $a = 16$ and $b = -2$.

   A. 6   B. -6 C. -10 D. -16

3. The inequality $-3x > 12$ is equivalent to which of the following?

   A. $x < -4$ B. $x > -4$
   C. $x < 4$ D. $x > 4$

4. Solve this inequality: $3(x - 1) - 7 < x - 3$

   A. $x < 0.5$ B. $x < 2.5$
   C. $x < 3.5$ D. $x < 6.5$

5. Which of these expressions have been combined correctly?

   I. $3x^2 + 5x + 9x^2 - 4x = 12x^2 + 1$
   II. $5ab + 3c^2 - 2ab + 8c^2 = 3ab + 11c^2$
   III. $8p^3 + 8p^2 + 8p + 8 = 8p^3 + 8p^2 + 8p + 8$

   A. I and II only
   B. I and III only
   C. II and III only
   D. I, II, and III

6. If x and y are being used as variables and a, b, c, d as coefficients, simplify:

$$ax^2 + by^2 + cx^2 - dy^2$$

   A. $(a^2 + c^2) \cdot x + (b^2 - d^2) \cdot y$
   B. $(a + c) \cdot x^2 + b - d$
   C. $(a + c)x^2 + (d - b)y^2$
   D. $(a + c)x^2 + (b - d)y^2$

7. A price p is increased 10%. Which of the following is NOT a representation for the new price?

   A. $p + 0.1p$ B. $110\% \cdot p$
   C. $1.1p$ D. $0.1p$

8. If the area of a trapezoid $= \frac{1}{2}h(b_1 + b_2)$, which of the following expressions represents the area of the trapezoid shown?

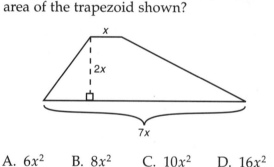

   A. $6x^2$ B. $8x^2$ C. $10x^2$ D. $16x^2$

9. Within the set of integers, which of the following represents the solution of the inequality?

$$4x + 1 < -9$$

   A. $\{-1, 0, 1, 2, 3, \ldots\}$
   B. $\{-2, -1, 0, 1, 2, 3, \ldots\}$
   C. $\{\ldots, -5, -4, -3\}$
   D. $\{\ldots, -5, -4, -3, -2\}$

10. Which of the following transformations is NOT correct?

 A. $5x - 4 < 0 \quad \rightarrow \quad 5x < 4$
 B. $-5x - 4 < 0 \quad \rightarrow \quad 5x > -4$
 C. $12x + 4 > 3x \quad \rightarrow 9x + 4 > 0$
 D. $\qquad 3x < -21 \rightarrow \qquad x > -7$

11. Which of the following sentences does the equation $5n - 3 = n + 11$ correctly represent?

 A. 3 less than 5 times a number is 11.
 B. 5 times 3 less than a number is 11 more than the number.
 C. 3 more than 5 times a number is 11 more than the number.
 D. 3 less than 5 times a number is 11 more than the number.

12. Which of the following represents the situation described?

 Joyce had $950 in her savings account. She withdrew the same amount each month for 5 months. After depositing $100 in her account, the balance was $908. How much money did she withdraw each month?

 A. $950 - 5x = 908 + 100$
 B. $950 + 5x - 100 = 908$
 C. $950 - 5x + 100 = 908$
 D. $950 - 5x - 100 = 908$

13. Write an equation to describe the situation. A car is rented for $15 a day plus $0.20 a mile. Martin paid $59.40 for a one-day rental.

 A. $0.20x = \$59.40$
 B. $0.20x - 15 = \$59.40$
 C. $0.20x + 15 = \$59.40$
 D. $0.20x + 15 + \$59.40$

14. Which inequality matches the situation? Take a number, add 3, multiply by 3, and subtract twice the original number. The result is greater than 5.

 A. $3x + 3 > 5 - 2x$
 B. $3x + 3 - 2x > 5$
 C. $3(x + 3) - 2x > 5$
 D. $9x - 2x > 5$

15. Select the inequality that describes the situation. Luis has $22. He works for 5 days, receiving the same pay for each day. Then he will have no more than $100.

 A. $5x + 22 \geq 100$ B. $5(x + 22) \leq 100$
 C. $22 - 5x \leq 100$ D. $5x + 22 \leq 100$

16. Which of these sequences of steps transforms the equation $3(x + 4) = 18$ into the equation $x = 2$?

 A. Distribute the 3, subtract 4 from both sides, divide both sides by 3.
 B. Distribute the 3, subtract 12 from both sides, divide both sides by 3.
 C. Distribute the 3, subtract 12 from both sides, divide both sides by $\frac{1}{3}$.
 D. Distribute the 3, divide both sides by 3, subtract 12.

17. For these equations, determine which ones have the same solution:

 I. $4x = 32$ II. $\frac{1}{4}x = \frac{1}{32}$ III. $40x = 320$

 A. I and II only B. I and III only
 C. II and III only D. I, II, and III

18. In which pair of equations are the two equations NOT equivalent?

 A. $\quad \dfrac{x}{5} = 3$
 $\quad 5 \cdot \dfrac{x}{5} = 3 \cdot 5$

 B. $\quad k + 14 = 8$
 $\quad k + 14 - 14 = 8 - 14$

 C. $\quad 6x = 21$
 $\quad \dfrac{1}{6} \cdot 6x = \dfrac{1}{6} \cdot 21$

 D. $\quad 3k - 4 = 11$
 $\quad 3k - 4 + 4 = 11 - 4$

19. A parking garage charges $2.00 for the first hour and $1.25 for each additional hour of parking. The parking fees are given by the formula:

$$F = 2.00 + 1.25(h - 1)$$

where h is the number of hours and F is the total fee. What value completes the table showing parking fees?

h	1	2	4	...	10
F	2.00	3.25	5.75	...	?

20. Solve for a.

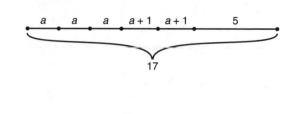

OPEN-ENDED QUESTIONS

21. If the sum of four consecutive even integers is less than 250, what is the greatest possible value for one of these even integers? Explain your procedure.

22. This table shows a linear relationship between x and y.

x	y
1	3
2	5
3	7
4	9

Based on the indicated relationship:

a. Provide three additional pairs of values in the table.
b. Graph the relationship on a coordinate grid.
c. Express the relationship between x and y as an equation.

23. For the following number puzzle, explain why the answer will always be 3.

> Start with a number. Multiply it by 4. Add 6, divide by 2, and subtract twice your original number.

24. A train leaves the town of Monroe and heads for the town of Jackson 200 miles away. The train travels at the speed of 40 mph.

a. If t represents the number of hours since the train left Monroe, write an expression to represent how far the train must still travel to reach Jackson.
b. If the train has been traveling for more than three hours, how far is the train from Jackson?
c. For what range of time will the train be between 30 and 100 miles from Jackson?

1. Which of the following is NOT a geometric sequence?

   A. 1, 1, 1, 1, 1, . . .
   B. 10, 100, 1,000, 10,000, . . .
   C. 6, 4, 2, 0, −2, . . .
   D. 6, 3, 1.5, 0.75, . . .

2. Which of the following diagrams does NOT represent a function?

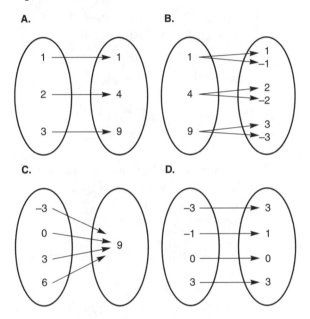

3. What digit is in the 20th decimal place in the decimal value of $\dfrac{35}{101}$?

   A. 3   B. 4   C. 5   D. 6

4. What is the units digit in 12^{15}?

   A. 2   B. 4   C. 6   D. 8

5. Given the pattern TEXASTEXASTEXAS . . . , what letter is in the 99th position?

   A. A   B. T   C. X   D. S

6. Which graph corresponds to $x − y = 5$?

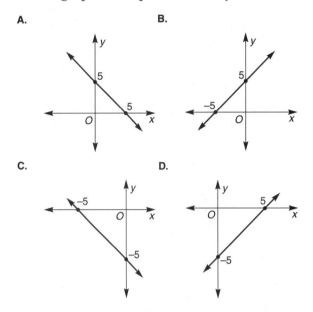

7. The table illustrates the function $y = −2x − 2$. What value do you get for y when $x = −6$?

x	y
0	−2
1	−4
2	−6

   A. 14   B. 10   C. −10   D. −14

8. Which of the following equations expresses the area of a square as a function of the perimeter?

   A. $A = \dfrac{p^2}{16}$ B. $A = 4p$
   C. $A = p^2$ D. $A = \dfrac{1}{4}p^2$

9. A sequence is generated by the rule $3n^2 − 4$, where n represents the number of the term in the sequence. What is the difference in the values of the 25th and 26th terms in the sequence?

   A. 6   B. 153   C. 159   D. 459

10. Which of the following is a translation for "6 less than 3 times a number"?

A. $6 < 3n$ B. $3n > 6$

C. $3n - 6$ D. $3(n - 6)$

11. A function uses the following rules:

a. Input any number greater than or equal to zero, and the function yields the same value that was input.

b. Input any negative number, and the function yields the opposite of that number.

Which of the following graphs matches the description of the function?

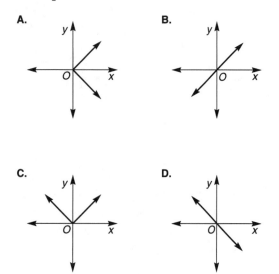

A.   B.

C.   D.

12. In which of the inequalities would you need to reverse the inequality symbol when solving?

A. $-5x > -35$ B. $6y \leq 20$

C. $x + 16 \geq -14$ D. $\frac{1}{5}x \leq 6$

13. If the horizontal axis is used for time and the vertical axis is used for price, which graph shows the sharpest increase in price over a period of time?

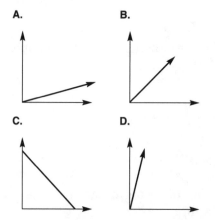

A.   B.

C.   D.

14. What is the difference between the 15th terms of Sequence A and Sequence B?

Sequence A: 2, 4, 8, 16, . . .
Sequence B: −2, 4, −8, 16, . . .

A. 0   B. 16,384

C. 32,768   D. 65,536

15. The number of mold cells on a piece of bread doubles every 12 minutes. If there are 35 mold cells on the bread now, about how many cells will there be 2 hours from now?

A. 420   B. 840   C. 2,458   D. 35,840

16. Suppose you start with $39.65 in your bank. Each day you put in $1.35 more than you put in on the previous day. That is, on day 1 you put in $1.35, on day 2 you put in $1.35 + $1.35 or $2.70, on day 3, $4.05, and so on. How much money will you have in the bank on the 12th day?

A. $55.85   B. $128.75

C. $144.95   D. $492

17. At We-Carry, shipping charges are $4.25 for the first 3 pounds and 75¢ for each additional pound. At that rate, how much did a package weigh if the charges were $11?

A. 6 pounds B. 9 pounds
C. 12 pounds D. 15 pounds

18. Which of the following lines has a negative slope?

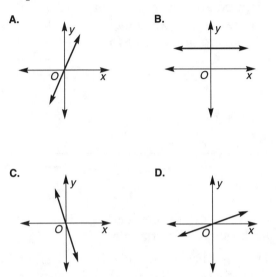

19. Which of the following points is NOT on the graph of $3x + y = 15$?

A. $(5, 0)$ B. $(-5, 0)$ C. $(3, 6)$ D. $(6, -3)$

20. Which of the following equations represents the line containing the points given in the graph?

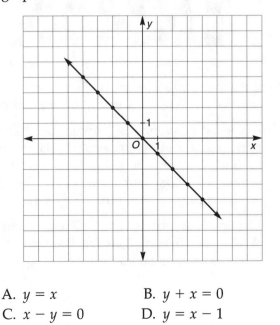

A. $y = x$ B. $y + x = 0$
C. $x - y = 0$ D. $y = x - 1$

21. Heather spends the equivalent of d days, h hours, and m minutes on a task. Into what expression does this translate for the total number of MINUTES on the task?

A. $d + h + m$
B. $24 \cdot 60d + 60h + m$
C. $7d + 24h + 60m$
D. $24d + 60h + m$

22. Which transformation is NOT correct?

A. $6x > 18 \rightarrow x > 3$
B. $-7x + 4 < 0 \rightarrow -7x < -4$
C. $-5x < 20 \rightarrow x < -4$
D. $\frac{x}{4} > 10 \rightarrow x > 40$

23. Solve for x: $4(x + 2) - 2(x - 3) = 20$

A. $x = 10.5$ B. $x = 9$
C. $x = 7.5$ D. $x = 3$

24. Evaluate $3 - 5c^3$ when $c = 2$.

A. -27 B. -37 C. -120 D. -997

25. A function is defined for the domain of all real numbers as follows: when $x < 0$, $f(x) = 6$
when $x = 0$, $f(x) = 0$
when $x > 0$, $f(x) = -6$

Which of the following would be the graph of the function described?

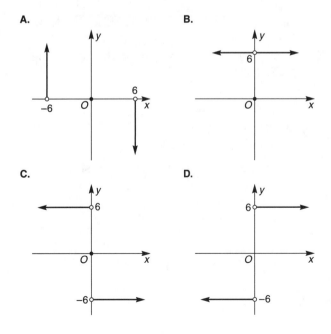

26. Which of the following equations is TRUE for all values that could replace x?

A. $3(x - 2) = 3x - 6$
B. $15 - x = x - 15$
C. $\dfrac{x}{6} = \dfrac{6}{x}$
D. $7(x - 5) = 7x - 5$

27. Note the following pattern:

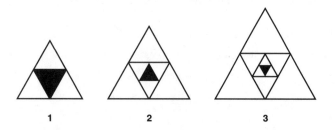

1 2 3

If the pattern is extended, what percent of the 5th diagram would be shaded?

A. Less than 1% B. 4%
C. 40% D. 400%

28. Find the sum of the infinite geometric series

$$1 + \frac{1}{3} + \frac{1}{9} + \frac{1}{27} + \cdots$$

A. $\dfrac{1}{3}$ B. $\dfrac{2}{3}$ C. $\dfrac{3}{2}$ D. 3

29. For the arithmetic series $1 + 4 + 7 + 10 + \ldots + 97 + 100$ the sum is:

A. 150 B. 606 C. 1,700 D. 1,717

30. If $y = f(x) = x^3$, which of the following is NOT true?

A. $f(x)$ is a function.
B. $\left| f(-4) \right| = \left| f(4) \right|$
C. $f(x)$ is a periodic function.
D. $f(x)$ does not have a constant slope.

31. Which of the following does NOT result from a translation of $y = x^2$?

A. $y = 7x^2$
B. $y = x^2 + 4$
C. $y = (x - 2)^2$
D. $y = (x + 3)^2$

32. Evaluate $a^b + b^a$ when $a = 5$ and $b = 2$.

33. Pictured are nine congruent squares. If the total area is 144 square units, solve for x.

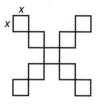

34. Solve for r.

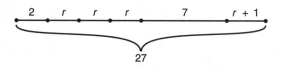

35. A display of Frisbees has been hung on a wall in the shape of a triangle.

There is 1 Frisbee in the top row, 2 Frisbees in the second row, 3 in the third, and so on, with each row containing one more Frisbee than the row above.

The display contains 12 rows.

How many Frisbees are used in the entire display?

36. Consider the following pattern:

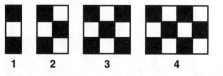

1 2 3 4

If the pattern is continued, how many small squares would be shaded in the 9th diagram?

37. A special sequence is formed by taking 5 more than the sum of the two previous terms to find the third term and all succeeding terms. If the first four terms of the sequence are 1, 2, 8, 15, . . . , find the 10th term.

38. The first four terms of an arithmetic sequence are 3, 7, 11, 15, and 123 is the 31st term. What is the value of the 30th term?

39. a. Plot the ordered pairs (8, 0), (7, 1), (6, 2), (5, 3).

    b. Sketch the graph suggested by the ordered pairs.

    c. Describe the pattern in words.

    d. What equation describes the pattern?

40. Starlite Pizzeria has regular expenses of $500 per week. In addition, their cost is $3 on average for each pizza made. They charge $8 for a pizza (this is the average price regardless of topping).

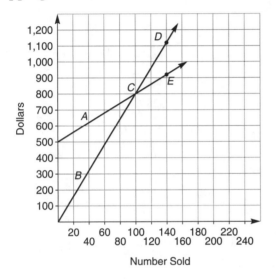

Using the given graph:

a. Identify the line that represents expenses and the line that represents revenue (income).

b. Explain the significance of point *C*.

c. What is the significance of the value of *D* less the value of *E*?

41. Miguel has read five novels this summer. His goal is to read two more by the end of each month.

a. Write an equation in slope-intercept form to represent the situation.

b. Draw the graph that illustrates the relationship.

c. If Miguel continues this process, how many novels will he have read at the end of two years? Show your work.

42. Use a pattern to find this product:

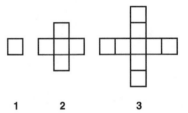

State the product and show how your pattern allowed you to find the product without doing the actual computation.

43. Consider the pattern shown.

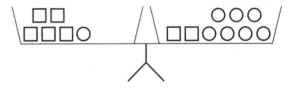

a. If the pattern is extended, how many small squares would there be in the 20th picture?

b. Explain why the number of small squares would always be 1 more than a multiple of 4.

44. The boxes are of equal weight. Each ball weighs 1 kg. The scales are in balance. Find the weight of one box. Explain your process.

45. Jack and Bob are twins. Jack is trying to save money at a weekly rate to have the same amount of money as Bob. Bob has $310 saved but has needed to withdraw $20 per week to help meet his expenses. Jack has $100 to start and adds $10 per week to the amount.

a. Write an expression that represents the amount of money Jack will have after *x* weeks.

b. Write an expression that represents the amount of money Bob will have after *x* weeks.

c. At this rate how many weeks will it take until Jack and Bob have the same amount of money?

Part 1: Multiple-Choice Questions

1. The number of Central High School students who gave to the United Fund this year was 342. This figure is 110% of what it was the previous year. This means that

   A. 10 more Central High School students gave to the United Fund.
   B. The number of Central High School students giving to the United Fund decreased from last year to this year.
   C. Central High School raised more money for the United Fund this year than it did last year.
   D. The number of Central High School students giving to the United Fund increased from last year to this year.

2. Which point on the number line below could represent the product of the numbers represented by W and X?

   $$U \quad V\,W \quad X \quad Y \quad Z$$
   $$0 \qquad\qquad 1$$

   A. U B. V
   C. Y D. Z

3. If triangular region ABC below is rotated 360° about side $\overline{BC}$, which of the following three-dimensional solids is formed?

   A. Pyramid   B. Ball
   C. Cylinder   D. Cone

4. Which of the following points lies on the graph of $3x - y = 6$?

   A. $(-1, -3)$
   B. $(0, 6)$
   C. $(1, -3)$
   D. $(1, 3)$

5. Start with the set of whole numbers between 10 and 40, including 10 and 40.

10	11	12	13	14	15	16	17	18	19
20	21	22	23	24	25	26	27	28	29
30	31	32	33	34	35	36	37	38	39	40

   Remove all prime numbers.
   Remove all perfect squares.
   Remove all factors of 72.
   Remove all multiples of 9.
   Remove all numbers in the following sequence 1, 1, 2, 3, 4, 5, 8, . . .

   How many numbers remain?

   A. 11   B. 12   C. 13   D. 14

6. Which of the following sets of coordinates could represent the vertices of a quadrilateral containing two right angles and no pairs of parallel sides?

   A. $(-4, 0), (0, 4), (4, 0), (0, -4)$
   B. $(0, 0), (0, 2), (4, 4), (6, 0)$
   C. $(0, 0), (0, 3), (7, 7), (7, 0)$
   D. $(-4, 0), (0, 4), (3, 0), (0, -4)$

7.

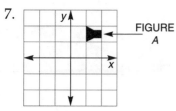

FIGURE A

Which of the following represents the result of reflecting figure A in the y-axis and then reflecting that image in the x-axis?

A.

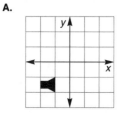

B.

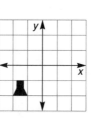

C.

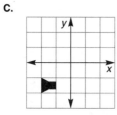

D.

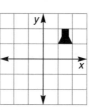

8. The baselines of a baseball diamond form a square with side lengths of 90 feet.

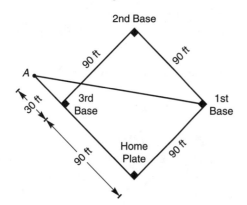

A player catches a ball at point A which is on the foul line 30 feet beyond 3rd base. How far from 1st base is the player when he catches the ball?

A. 120 ft
B. 150 ft
C. 180 ft
D. 210 ft

9. The table below indicates a relationship between a and b.

a	b
0	−2
1	1
2	4
.	.
.	.
5	13
.	.
.	.
8	22

Which of the equations below expresses the relationship between a and b that is indicated in the table?

A. $b = a^2$
B. $b = 2a + 3$
C. $b = 3a - 2$
D. $b = a + 3$

10. Each month, a high school does a feature newspaper article on one of its students who is picked at random. The numbers of male and female students in each grade in that high school are shown in the table below.

NUMBER OF STUDENTS							
Grade 9		Grade 10		Grade 11		Grade 12	
M	F	M	F	M	F	M	F
28	22	31	20	25	26	25	23

Based on this table, what is the probability the student chosen will be a female student in grade 9?

A. .11
B. .22
C. .24
D. .44

11. For a sale, a shopkeeper lowers the original price of an item by 20 percent. After the sale, the shopkeeper raises the price of that item by 20 percent of its sale price. The price of the item then is

A. More than the original price
B. Less than the original price
C. The same as the original price
D. There is not enough information to compare the two prices.

12. Which of the following graphs most likely shows an automobile's resale value plotted against its age?

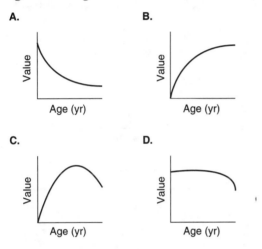

13. Which of the following sets of lengths does NOT represent a triangle?

A. 1, 1, 1   B. 6, 8, 10
C. 2, 3, 5   D. 9, 12, 15

14. The angles of a triangle are in the ratio of 1 : 2 : 7. What kind of triangle results?

A. Isosceles   B. Right
C. Acute   D. Obtuse

15. A right triangle has legs of 7 inches and 24 inches. Find the cosine of the smaller of the two acute angles of the triangle.

A. $\dfrac{7}{25}$ B. $\dfrac{24}{25}$ C. $\dfrac{7}{24}$ D. $\dfrac{25}{24}$

16. A dart is thrown at the circular region below. If the dart is equally likely to hit any point inside the circle, what is the probability that it hits the region outside of the inscribed square?

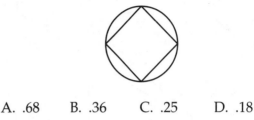

A. .68   B. .36   C. .25   D. .18

17. Which of these statements is TRUE?

A. All squares are similar.
B. All triangles are similar.
C. All rectangles are similar.
D. All parallelograms are similar.

18. Suppose that each time a ball bounces, it goes up $\dfrac{1}{2}$ the distance it fell. If that ball is dropped from a height of x feet, which of these expressions represents the total distance it has traveled when it hits the floor for the fifth time?

A. $x + \dfrac{1}{2} + \dfrac{1}{4} + \dfrac{1}{8} + \dfrac{1}{16}$

B. $x + \dfrac{1}{2} + \dfrac{1}{2} + \dfrac{1}{4} + \dfrac{1}{4} + \dfrac{1}{8} + \dfrac{1}{8} + \dfrac{1}{16} + \dfrac{1}{16}$

C. $x + \dfrac{x}{2} + \dfrac{x}{2} + \dfrac{x}{4} + \dfrac{x}{4} + \dfrac{x}{8} + \dfrac{x}{8} + \dfrac{x}{16} + \dfrac{x}{16}$

D. $(x)\left(\dfrac{1}{2}\right)\left(\dfrac{1}{4}\right)\left(\dfrac{1}{8}\right)\left(\dfrac{1}{16}\right)$

19. 1,376 students attending Cary High School all voted for president of the Student Council. With approximately one-fifth of the votes counted, the leading candidate had 185 votes. Assuming that candidate obtained the same proportion of the total number of votes, the total number of votes she received would be between

A. 250 and 300
B. 450 and 500
C. 600 and 700
D. 900 and 950

20. Based on the graph below, which car takes the least amount of time to go from 0 to 60 mph and about how much less time does it take?

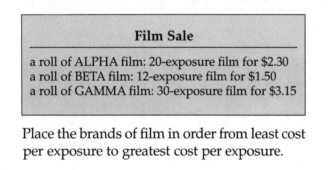

A. Car A by about 5 seconds

B. Car B by about 5 seconds

C. Car A by about $2\frac{1}{2}$ seconds

D. Car B by about $2\frac{1}{2}$ seconds

21. Sal's Drugstore is having a sale of photographic film.

Film Sale

a roll of ALPHA film: 20-exposure film for $2.30
a roll of BETA film: 12-exposure film for $1.50
a roll of GAMMA film: 30-exposure film for $3.15

Place the brands of film in order from least cost per exposure to greatest cost per exposure.

A. Alpha, Beta, Gamma
B. Beta, Alpha, Gamma
C. Gamma, Alpha, Beta
D. Gamma, Beta, Alpha

22. The cost of first-class postage recently changed from 33¢ to 34¢. This change translates to what percent increase?

A. 1%   B. 2%   C. 2.9%   D. 3%

23. The whole numbers from 1 to 36 are each written on a small slip of paper and placed in a box. If one slip of paper is selected at random from the box, what is the probability that the number selected is a factor of 36 and also a multiple of 8?

A. $\frac{13}{36}$ B. $\frac{1}{36}$ C. $\frac{1}{4}$ D. 0

24. If $f(x) = 2^x + 3^x + 6^x$, what is $f(1) - f(-1)$?

A. 0   B. 10   C. 11   D. 22

25. Suppose you construct a series of trapezoid trains using the following isosceles trapezoid block:

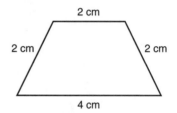

A 2-trapezoid train looks like:

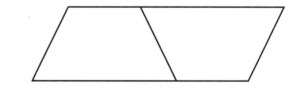

A 3-trapezoid train looks like:

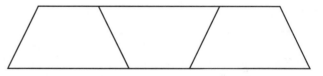

Which of the following statements is NOT going to be true?

A. An 8-trapezoid train would be a parallelogram.
B. A 9-trapezoid train would be an isosceles trapezoid.
C. The perimeter of a 9-trapezoid train would be 64 cm.
D. The perimeter of a trapezoid train would always equal an even number of centimeters.

26. If $2^x = 4^y = k$ where $1,000 < k < 2,000$ and x and y are integers, what is the value of $x - y$?

 A. -5 B. 0 C. 5 D. 10

27. While interviewing students at Washington High School, Paul asked 20 students (picked at random) what their favorite fall sport is. Maria asked 50 different students (picked at random) the same question. George combined Paul's data and Maria's data. All three graphed their results:

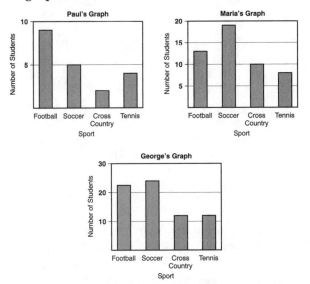

Which of these graphs could be used to give the most reliable estimate of the percentage of the Washington High School student population whose favorite fall sport is soccer?

A. Paul's
B. Maria's
C. George's
D. There is no reason to use one graph rather than another.

28. Which of these pieces of cardboard cannot be folded along the dotted lines to make a closed box?

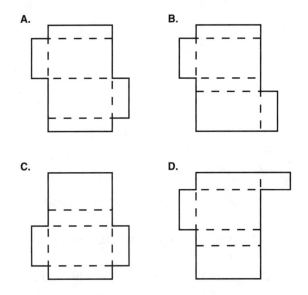

29. What is the weight of one of the cubes if each pyramid weighs 2 pounds?

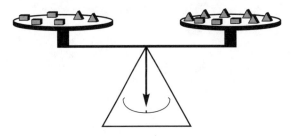

 A. $\frac{1}{4}$ pound
 B. 4 pounds
 C. 6 pounds
 D. 8 pounds

30. At what point does the graph of $3x - 2y = 6$ cross the x-axis?

 A. $(0, -3)$ B. $(-3, 0)$
 C. $(0, 2)$ D. $(2, 0)$

31. The graph shows a relationship between distance and time. Which statement is FALSE?

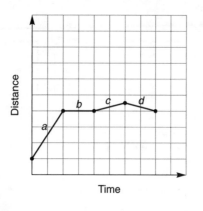

A. Segment *a* shows a sharp increase in distance.

B. Segment *b* shows distance remaining constant.

C. Segment *c* shows a gradual increase in distance.

D. Segment *d* shows a sharp decrease in distance.

32. Which graph below shows points that satisfy the equation $y = -\frac{2}{3}x + 2$?

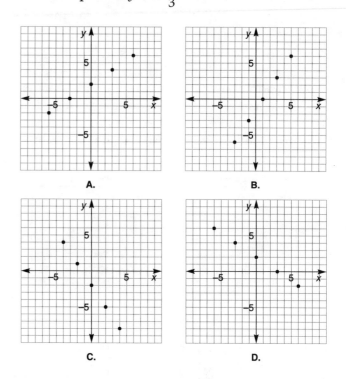

33. There are three extracurricular activity groups in a school—band, glee club, and science club. There are some students in each of those groups. Every student belongs to at least one of them, but some belong to more than one. Which of the following diagrams would best represent this situation?

A. ⭕⭕⭕   B. (overlapping two circles)

C. (three overlapping circles)   D. (circle within a circle)

DIRECTIONS: Respond in detail to each open-ended question. Show your process and provide an explanation as directed in the question. Your score for each question will be based on accuracy and the completeness of your process or explanation.

34. The math exam scores for the 21 students in Mr. Walker's homeroom were:

    65 90 82 78 84 92 88 86 70 68 75
    88 90 85 61 81 79 82 84 83 90

    a. The mean or average of the above scores is 81. What is the median score? What is the mode?

    b. Use a copy of the grid below to make a bar graph showing the frequency or number of scores in each of the score ranges 60–64, 65–69, 70–74, etc.

    c. Which is the best general indicator of this class's performance on the exam—the mean, median, or mode? Explain your answer.

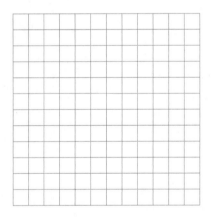

35. Use a ruler to determine the lengths of the sides of the figure below. Sketch the figure and label the corresponding sides of your sketch with the measurements you find. Use these measurements to find the perimeter and the area of the figure below. Show all work clearly.

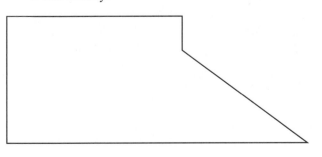

36. You are forming 3-digit numbers from the six digits listed below. Repetition of digits is not allowed.

3 4 5 6 7 8

    a. How many 3-digit numbers can be formed?

    b. How many 3-digit numbers would exist if you were allowed to repeat digits? Explain your process.

    c. If repetition of digits is not allowed, how many of the 3-digit numbers would be multiples of 5 that are greater than 500?

37. a. A rectangular solid has dimensions $4 \times 6 \times 5$. If a cylinder is going to have equal volume, what would one set of values be for the height of the cylinder and the radius of the cylinder?

    b. Is it possible for a cube to have the same volume if the lengths of the edges of the cube must be whole numbers? If yes, indicate the length of an edge. If no, between what two whole numbers is the exact answer?

38. Two major league baseball players, Ken and Sammy, are each currently batting .300. Ken has this batting average after 100 official at bats. Sammy has the batting average after 200 official at bats.

    a. If Ken and Sammy each go into a batting slump in which they go "0 for 20" (no hits in their next 20 official at bats), show what impact this slump would have on each player's batting average.

    b. Suppose Ken still has a .300 batting average near the end of the baseball season, after 550 official at bats. If he then goes into a season-ending slump in which he goes "0 for 20" in his last 20 official at bats, would the impact on his batting average be the same as the impact in part a? Explain and show your process.

39. The graph displays a function: $y = f(x)$.

a. What is the value of $f(-2)$?

b. Explain how you would convince someone that this does represent a function.

c. Find two values a and b for which $f(a) = f(b)$.

d. Draw the graph of $y = f(x) - 3$.

40. Three points are collinear if they are on the same line.

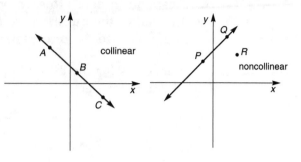

a. Explain how you would use slope to determine if three points were collinear.

b. Find the value for k such that $(4, 2)$, $(0, 8)$, and $(-2, k)$ are collinear. Show your approach.

Part 1: Multiple-Choice Questions

1. Three students started at the same flagpole in the middle of a large, flat, grassy area and chose three different directions in which to walk. Each walked for 10 yards in a straight line away from that pole. Suppose many more students did this, each walking in a direction different from the directions chosen by all the others. If you think of the final positions of the students as being points, which of the following figures would contain all of those points?

   A. Circle
   B. Square
   C. Rhombus
   D. Triangle

2. If $3y - 5 = 2 + 14y$, then $y =$

   A. $-\dfrac{7}{11}$ B. $-\dfrac{3}{17}$

   C. $\dfrac{3}{17}$ D. $\dfrac{7}{11}$

3. On some days, a history teacher has the students in a particular class work in groups of 4, on other days in groups of 6 or 8. However, when all students are present, there is always one student left over after the groups are formed. Which of the following could be the number of students in that class?

   A. 37   B. 33
   C. 29   D. 25

4. The general partners in a small company, Miranda, Cohen, and Brown, share its profits in the ratio of $3 : 2 : 5$, respectively. If that company's profits amount to $24,300 this year, what is Mr. Miranda's share?

   A. $2,430   B. $7,290
   C. $8,100   D. $14,580

5. Performing which set of transformations on the white figure below will NOT result in the white figure covering the black figure completely?

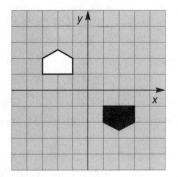

   A. Reflection in the y-axis followed by reflection in the x-axis
   B. Translation 4 units to the right followed by reflection in the x-axis
   C. Reflection in the y-axis followed by translation 4 units down
   D. Rotation of 180° about the origin

6. You are to form four-digit numbers using the digits below. If $a =$ the number of four-digit numbers if repetition is allowed and $b =$ the number if repetition of digits is not allowed, what is the value of $a - b$?

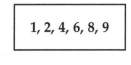

   1, 2, 4, 6, 8, 9

   A. 232   B. 696   C. 936   D. 1,040

7. Four friends are planning to eat at a restaurant where complete dinners cost between $12.00 and $17.00 per person. They want to leave the waiter a tip amounting to 15% of their total bill. Which of the following is the closest to what the four friends will need to leave for their combined TOTAL tip?

   A. $2.00   B. $4.00   C. $9.00   D. $15.00

8. Fifteen students' scores on their last math test are represented in the bar graph below.

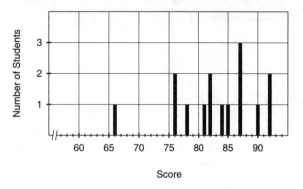

What are the mean, median, and mode for the set of scores represented in the graph above?

A. Mean = 83, median = 84, mode = 87
B. Mean = 84, median = 83, mode = 87
C. Mean = 83, median = 87, mode = 84
D. Mean = 84, median = 87, mode = 83

9. Consider the number 36; some pairs of matching positive integer factors of 36 are (2, 18), (3, 12), (4, 9), (6, 6), . . . (12, 3), (18, 2). Suppose someone graphs all possible pairs of matching positive integer factors of a given positive integer. Which of the following most likely represents such a graph?

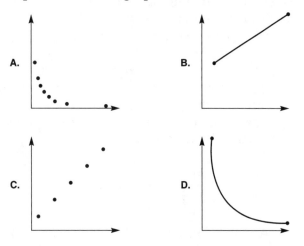

10. Which point on the number line below could represent the product of U and X?

A. Point T
B. Point V
C. Point W
D. Point Y

11. A diagram of a rectangle with dimensions 6 inches by 8 inches is placed in a copy machine which is set to enlarge all dimensions by 10 percent. Will the resulting figure fit on an $8\frac{1}{2} \times 11''$ sheet of paper?

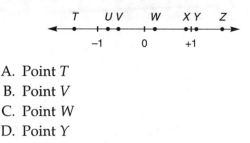

A. Yes, it will fit with room to spare.
B. Yes, it will just fit with no room to spare.
C. No, one dimension will fit, but not the other.
D. No, both dimensions will be too large.

12. For 45 cents, a snack-foot vending machine dispenses a small bag of chips which weighs one and one-eighth ounces. At this rate, the cost of one pound of these chips would be between

A. $2.30 and $2.75
B. $4.30 and $4.75
C. $6.30 and $6.75
D. $8.30 and $8.75

13. The graph of function $f(x)$ is given below.

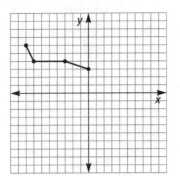

Which graph would represent $f(x) - 2$?

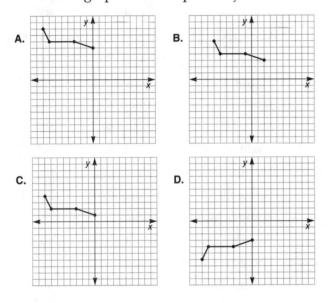

14. A right triangle has two sides of length 2 cm and 5 cm. Which of the following could be the length of the third side?

I. 3 cm   II. $\sqrt{21}$ cm   III. $\sqrt{29}$ cm

A. I only   B. III only
C. I and III   D. II and III

15. For the given right triangle the ratio $\dfrac{9}{41}$ defines

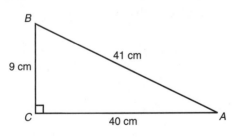

A. sin A B. cos A C. tan A D. sin B

16. Triangle MNP is an isosceles triangle with a vertex angle of 40°. If $\overline{AB} \parallel \overline{DC} \parallel \overline{NP}$, what is the measure of $\angle ABC$?

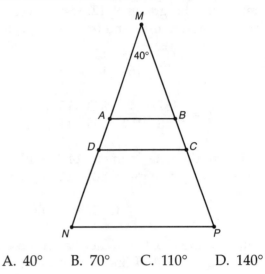

A. 40°   B. 70°   C. 110°   D. 140°

17. The tenth term of the geometric sequence $\dfrac{1}{3}$, $1, 3, 9, 27, \ldots$ is

A. 2,187   B. 6,561   C. 19,683   D. 59,049

18. Which one of the following points is included in the region defined by $-2 \leq x < 8$ and $4 < y < 12$?

A. $(-2, 7)$ B. $(-2, 4)$
C. $(-2, -2)$ D. $(8, 12)$

19. Suppose that 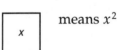 means $x + 3$

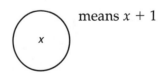 means x^2

means $x + 1$

What would be the value of

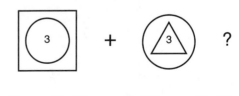

A. 13.   B. 15   C. 23   D. 26

20. Matrix *A* represents the enrollment of Memorial High School. Matrix *B* represents the enrollment of North High School. The columns represent the grades 9–12, respectively. The rows represent male and female, respectively.

$$A = \begin{pmatrix} 143 & 163 & 158 & 162 \\ 152 & 160 & 165 & 168 \end{pmatrix}$$

$$B = \begin{pmatrix} 167 & 143 & 173 & 151 \\ 158 & 152 & 168 & 147 \end{pmatrix}$$

What is the total number of twelfth-grade girls at the two high schools combined?

A. 290   B. 313   C. 315   D. 333

21. Suppose the U.S. Post Office has proposed increasing the cost of first-class postage to 35¢ for the first ounce or fraction thereof and 25¢ for each additional ounce or fraction thereof. Which of the graphs below best represents the cost of mailing a first-class item depending on the weight of that item in ounces?

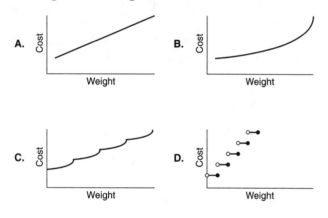

22. The students who took the written driver's test at a particular testing center one day were from three different high schools. Their test scores are given below.

Name	School	Score
Adams, J.	Gunnison	62
Baker, P.	Taylor	76
Chin, H.	Gunnison	87
Drabowski, C.	Braddock	79
Elmore, J.	Taylor	64
Ferris, W.	Braddock	83
Garver, G.	Gunnison	81
Greer, P.	Braddock	84
Harris, R.	Gunnison	92
Jacoby, P.	Taylor	92
Kelly, M.	Braddock	88
Lassiter, L.	Braddock	94
Martin, S.	Gunnison	82
Petrocelli, R.	Gunnison	74
Ramirez, R.	Taylor	84
Saunders, M.	Taylor	80
Thompson, L.	Braddock	89
Wilson, P.	Gunnison	90

All these students participated in the driver's education program offered in their own high school. Based on the students' test scores, which school's driver's education program appears to prepare its students best for the written driver's test?

A. Braddock
B. Gunnison
C. Taylor
D. Two schools appear to prepare their students equally well.

23. John has a 10-question quiz on Friday. His father agrees to give him on Saturday his regular $5 allowance plus 75 cents for each question he answered correctly on Friday's quiz. However, he will not give John any more than twice his weekly allowance. Which inequality below accurately represents the situation described above?

A. $0.75n \leq 10$
B. $5 - 0.75n \leq 10$
C. $0.75n + 5 \leq 10$
D. $(0.75 + 5)n \leq 10$

24. A plane passing through a solid gives you a cross section of the solid. For example, the cross section of a solid pyramid shown below is a triangular region. (See shaded figure.)

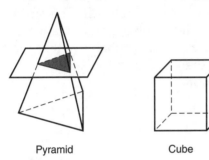

Pyramid   Cube

Which of the following plane figures cannot be a cross section of a solid cube?

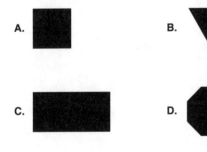

A.   B.

C.   D.

25.

Each of the students in a class rolled a number cube one hundred times and graphed how many times each number came up. (Each face of the cube is labeled with just one of the digits 1, 2, 3, 4, 5, 6.) Which graph below most likely represents the one the students made of the results of their whole class?

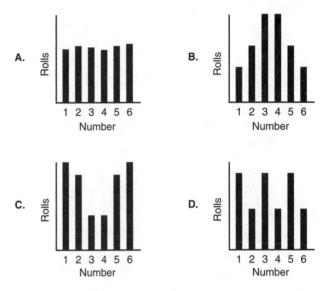

26. You are playing a game in which you move a chip on a number line. Where you move the chip is determined by the cards you draw from a pack. Each card has an integer printed on it. Your chip is now at the position shown below.

On each turn, you move your chip to the location with the coordinate equal to the sum of the coordinate of your current location and the number on the card you draw. Suppose you draw cards with the following sequence of numbers: $-2, 6, -7, -12, -4$. What is the coordinate of the location of your chip after you complete this sequence of moves?

A. 12   B. 11
C. -12 D. -19

27. The Burger Baron Restaurant is open from 6 a.m. until midnight and serves all meals. Every half hour during an 8-hour period last Tuesday, Ronald counted the number of customers in that restaurant. He graphed his data but forgot to label the time-of-day axis.

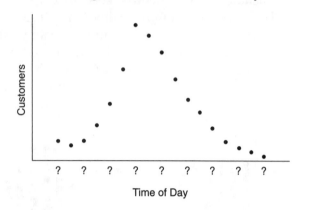

Time of Day

Which of the following time-of-day axes is most likely labeled the way it should have been in Ronald's graph?

A.

3 p.m.	4	5	6	7	8	9	10	11

B.

10 a.m.	11	12 p.m.	1	2	3	4	5	6

C.

12 p.m.	1	2	3	4	5	6	7	8

D.

6 a.m.	7	8	9	10	11	12 p.m.	1	2

28. Keisha works for a florist making bouquets. On a given day the florist has daisies, carnations, roses, lilies, and poppies in stock. How many combinations of flowers can she have for bouquets if she wants to include at least three different types of flowers?

A. 10   B. 15   C. 16   D. 60

29. The first three stages in the construction of a Sierpinski Triangle are shown. The initial triangle is an equilateral triangle with sides 1 unit long. The cut-out triangles are formed by connecting the midpoints of the sides of the shaded triangles.

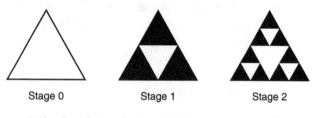

Stage 0   Stage 1   Stage 2

Which of the following formulas represents the number of shaded triangles in the nth stage of the fractal?

A. $3n$ B. 3^n C. 3^{n+1} D. 3^{n-1}

30. A card is drawn at random from a standard deck of 52 playing cards. The card is put back in the deck, and a card is again drawn at random. Find the probability that the first card is a diamond and the second card is also a diamond.

A. $\frac{1}{2}$ B. $\frac{1}{4}$ C. $\frac{3}{13}$ D. $\frac{1}{16}$

31. Which of the following figures does NOT have both line symmetry and rotational symmetry?

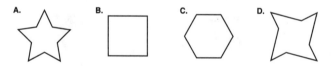

A.   B.   C.   D.

32. A solid box-shaped structure is made of layers of unit cubes stacked one above the other. A 2 × 3 × 3 block of unit cubes has been removed from this structure. Assume that no cubes other than the ones 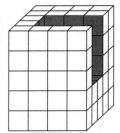 in the region indicated by shading have been removed. How many unit cubes are contained in the structure pictured above?

A. 73
B. 82
C. 94
D. 100

33. Jane threw a dart that landed in the 3-point area of the target pictured below. Bill threw a dart that landed in its 1-point area.

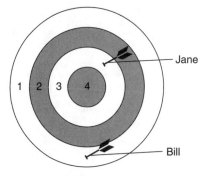

Each of them has just one more dart to throw. It is now Jane's turn. In what area(s) of the target could Jane throw her dart so that she is sure to win, that is, so that Bill's total points cannot tie or exceed her total points?

A. In the 4-point area only
B. In the 4-point or in the 3-point area only
C. In the 4-point, in the 3-point, or in the 2-point area
D. Jane cannot be sure she will win until after she and Bill both throw their darts.

OPEN-ENDED QUESTIONS

DIRECTIONS: Respond in detail to each open-ended question. Show your process and provide an explanation as directed in the question. Your score for each question will be based on accuracy and the completeness of your process or explanation.

34. The annual salaries of all the employees of a small company are listed below.

   President: $110,000

   Vice President: $60,000

   Senior Professionals: $50,000; $48,000; $48,000; $44,000

   Junior Professionals: $36,000; $36,000; $36,000; $32,000

   Clerical Staff: $22,000; $18,000; $14,000

What are the mean, the median, and the mode of the salaries of the employees of this company? How is each of these statistics affected if one excludes the president's salary? What do your findings tell you about the statistic that should probably be used in discussions of the salary of a typical professional baseball player? Explain.

35. A boat starts at point A, travels 9 miles west, and then turns and travels 12 miles north to reach point B on the shore.

a. Using grid paper, make a scale drawing using vectors to show the boat's movement starting from point A.

b. Draw a vector that would show the direct path from point A to point B.

c. What would be the approximate number of miles the boat could have traveled along this path?

d. Approximately how many degrees from south would the path be? Explain how you arrived at your answer.

36. The table gives the average weight for men of different heights. The data is for men of medium frame, ages 30–39 years.

MEN	
Height (in.)	Weight (lb)
64	145
66	153
68	161
70	170
72	179
74	188
76	199

a. Make a scatter plot of the given data. Put height on the horizontal axis and weight on the vertical axis.

b. Draw a line of best fit and determine an equation that can be used to describe the data.

c. Predict the average weight of a man 84 inches tall.

37. Every Wednesday at the Pizza Express, the manager gives away free slices of pizza and soda. Every eighth customer gets a free slice of pizza and every twelfth customer gets a free soda. The Pizza Express served 87 customers last Wednesday.

a. How many free sodas were given away last Wednesday?

b. How many free slices of pizza were given away?

c. Did any customer receive both a free slice of pizza and a free soda? If so, how many customers?

d. If soda sells for 99¢ and a slice of pizza sells for $1.25, how much did the Pizza Express lose in income by giving away these items? Justify your answer.

38. A standard $8\frac{1}{2}'' \times 11''$ sheet of paper is rolled along its short side to form a cylinder as shown.

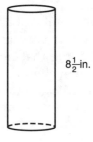

8½-in.

A second sheet of standard $8\frac{1}{2}'' \times 11''$ paper is rolled along its long side to form a second cylinder.

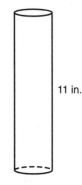

11 in.

There is no overlap.

a. Will the taller cylinder have the same surface area, greater surface area, or less surface area than the shorter cylinder? Explain your answer.

b. Will the taller cylinder have the same volume, greater volume, or less volume than the shorter cylinder? Explain your answer.

c. If a sheet of $11'' \times 17''$ paper was used to make a cylinder $17''$ tall, how would its volume and surface area compare to the volume and surface area of the $8\frac{1}{2}''$ tall cylinder? Explain your answer.

39. A ball was dropped from a height of 16'. Each time the ball bounced, it reached a maximum height of approximately half that of its previous height.

a. Complete the table to show the height reached after the ball bounced each of five times.

Bounce	Height After Bounce
Original height	16'
1	
2	
3	
4	
5	

b. Draw a graph to represent the relationship between the number of the bounce and the height reached by the ball.

c. What is the total vertical distance the ball traveled after bounce 5? Include the original height of 16' in your total.

d. What do you think the total would have been if the ball had bounced 25 times? Explain your reasoning.

40. Isosceles trapezoid *ABCD* has three vertices at *A*(2, 0), *B*(0, 4), and *C*(10, 4).

a. Find the coordinates of vertex *D*.

b. Find the area of the isosceles trapezoid. Explain your process.

c. Using slope-intercept form, write the equation for the line containing side *CD* of the trapezoid.

Part 1: Multiple-Choice Questions

1. The graph of $y = 3x$ is shown below. Which statement below is true about the graph of $y = 3x + 2$?

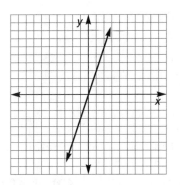

A. It is perpendicular to the graph of $y = 3x$.
B. It is a translation (slide) of the graph of $y = 3x$ two units up.
C. It intersects the graph of $y = 3x$ at the origin.
D. It is a translation (slide) of the graph of $y = 3x$ two units to the right.

2. Weatherpersons predict tomorrow's weather based on what has happened in the past on the days following days just like today. During the past 50 years, there have been 380 December days that have been just like today, and of those, 200 have been followed by a clear day. Which of the following is the approximate probability of a clear day tomorrow that would be given by a weatherperson using the prediction rule described in this problem?

A. 13 percent
B. 34 percent
C. 53 percent
D. 66 percent

3. Which of these inequalities would be most helpful in solving the problem stated below?

> Bart spent an evening playing video games and drinking sodas. Each video game cost 25 cents to play, and sodas cost 60 cents each. Bart had $8 to spend only on video games and sodas. If he had only 3 sodas and played as many video games as he could, how many video games did he play?

A. $0.25x + 1.80 \leq 8$
B. $x + 1.80 \leq 8$
C. $0.60x + 0.75 \leq 8$
D. $3x + 0.25 \leq 8$

4. Which statements are equivalent to one another?

I. Every year, Americans spend $2 million on exercise equipment and $10 million on potato chips.
II. Every year, Americans spend 5 times as much on potato chips as they do on exercise equipment.
III. Every year, Americans spend 20% as much on exercise equipment as they do on potato chips.

A. I and II only
B. I and III only
C. II and III only
D. I, II, and III

5. The squares pictured below are all congruent to the one shown at the right. Each of the squares has part of its interior shaded. Which of the squares appears to have the same fraction of its interior shaded as the given one has?

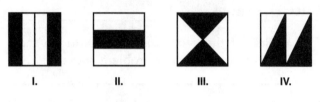

I.   II.   III.   IV.

   A. All of them
   B. I and II only
   C. I, III, and IV only
   D. None of them

6. Twin primes are primes that are two consecutive odd integers, such as 3, 5; 11, 13; 17, 19. How many twin primes (pairs) are there between 10 and 100?

   A. 5   B. 6   C. 7   D. 8

7. If the product of 7 integers is positive, then, at most, how many of the integers could be negative?

   A. 2   B. 4   C. 6   D. 7

8. Six slips of paper with the letters A through F written on them are placed into a shoe box. The six slips are drawn one by one from the box. What is the probability that the first three to be drawn are A, D, F in any order?

   A. $\frac{1}{20}$ B. $\frac{1}{6}$ C. $\frac{1}{3}$ D. $\frac{1}{2}$

9. Given: Circle A represents even numbers.
           Circle B represents perfect squares.
           Circle C represents powers of 10.

Which of the following would be included in the shaded region?

   A. {100, 200, 300}
   B. {64, 100, 144}
   C. {10, 100, 1,000}
   D. {100, 10,000, 1,000,000}

10. A particular plant starts as a single stem. At the beginning of the second year, it grows two branches and therefore has three tips growing. Each year, every branch does the same thing, that is, it grows two branches and continues to grow itself. How many tips are there on that plant in the 6th year if no tip or branch has died?

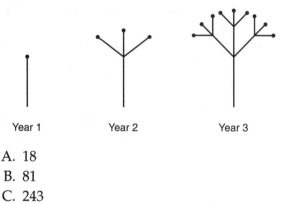

Year 1   Year 2   Year 3

   A. 18
   B. 81
   C. 243
   D. 729

11. A printing company makes bumper stickers that cost $0.75 per copy plus a $5.00 set-up fee. If you spend $80 to purchase a supply of bumper stickers, how many do you get?

A. 50   B. 75   C. 100   D. 150

12. The Mustangs and the Bruins play in a basketball tournament. The team that first wins three games wins the tournament. Assuming ties are not possible, find the number of possible ways in which the tournament can occur.

A. 6   B. 9   C. 20   D. 24

13. Which of the following would NOT be an illustration of a tessellation?

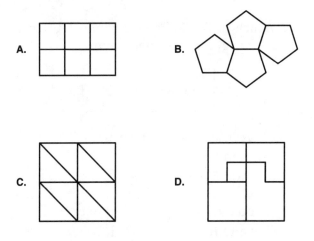

14. During a baseball season, 70 percent of the major league outfielders had at least 20 home runs. Knowing this, which of the following must be greater than or equal to 20?

I. The mean number of home runs
II. The mode of the number of home runs
III. The median number of home runs

A. I only   B. II only
C. III only   D. I and II

15. Malcolm graphed all possible combinations of the numbers of correct and incorrect responses students could obtain on a 20-question true-false test. Which graph below MOST LIKELY resembles Malcolm's graph?

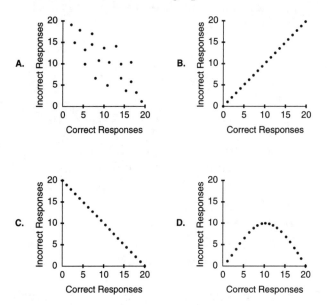

16. The graph of $x + y = 8$ crosses the x-axis at point A. The graph of $2x - y = 8$ crosses the line $y = 6$ at point B. What is the distance from point A to point B?

A. 6   B. $\sqrt{37}$ C. 7   D. $\sqrt{53}$

17. The given figure consists of 9 congruent squares. Which of the following is a square you could remove and not change the perimeter of the entire figure?

		1		
	2	3	4	
5	6	7	8	9

A. Square 1   B. Square 2
C. Square 7   D. Square 9

18. How many degrees are in the angle between the hands of a clock at 9:30?

    A. 90°   B. 95°   C. 105°   D. 120°

19. A special operation is defined by the rule (for real numbers):

$$a * b = \frac{a + b}{2}$$

For example, $6 * 10 = \frac{1}{2}(6 + 10) = \frac{1}{2}(16) = 8$.

Which of the following is NOT a valid property concerning this special operation?

    A. $a * a = a$
    B. $a * b = b * a$
    C. $a * (-a) = 0$
    D. $a * (b + c) = (a * b) + (a * c)$

20. A linear function is displayed in the given table. When graphed, where would the line cross the x-axis?

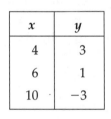

x	y
4	3
6	1
10	−3

    A. $(0, 7)$ B. $(7, -1)$ C. $(7, 0)$ D. $(8, 0)$

21. Three vertices of an isosceles trapezoid are at $(-4, 0)$, $(4, 0)$, and $(-1, 6)$. The bases of the figure are horizontal. Find the number of square units in the area of the isosceles trapezoid.

    A. 27   B. 30   C. 54   D. 60

22. Which of the following equations has two real solutions?

    A. $2^x = 32$ B. $x^2 + 16 = 0$
    C. $\frac{1}{x} = \frac{7}{11}$ D. $|x - 6| = 9$

23. Parallelogram $ABCD$ is not a rectangle. Which of these statements is NOT always true?

    A. The diagonals are equal in length.
    B. The diagonals bisect each other.
    C. There is no line of symmetry.
    D. All are true.

24. The whole numbers from 1 to 40 are each written on a small slip of paper and placed in a box. One slip of paper is selected at random from the box. What is the probability that the number selected is prime if you are given that it is a factor of 36?

    A. 0   B. $\frac{1}{20}$ C. $\frac{1}{18}$ D. $\frac{2}{9}$

25. Which of the following would NOT change the mean for these five scores?

20	30	40	50	60

    I. Add two scores: a 10 and a 70.
    II. Add three more scores of 40.
    III. Add 5 to each score.

    A. I only   B. II only
    C. I and II   D. I, II, and III

26. The Straight as an Arrow Company paints lines on the streets of different towns. The company charges $100 plus $0.25 per foot. Which of the following is a reasonable graph for length vs. total charge?

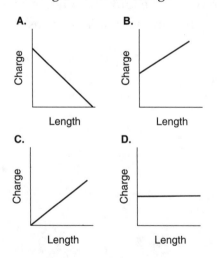

27. What is the value of $a + b + c$ if $(12)(18)(750) = (2^a)(3^b)(5^c)$?

A. 9   B. 10   C. 11   D. 12

28. The numbers -3, -4, and 6 are each used once and substituted at random for a, b, and c in the equation $ax + b = c$. What is the probability that x turns out to be negative?

A. 0   B. $\frac{1}{3}$ C. $\frac{1}{2}$ D. 1

29. What is the simplified expression for the shaded area of the given rectangle?

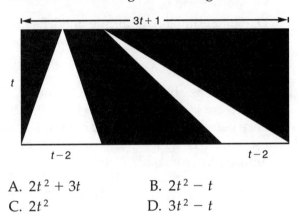

A. $2t^2 + 3t$
B. $2t^2 - t$
C. $2t^2$
D. $3t^2 - t$

30.

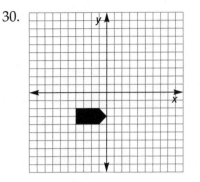

If the figure on the grid above were translated 3 units to the right and then reflected in the x-axis, which picture below would show the result?

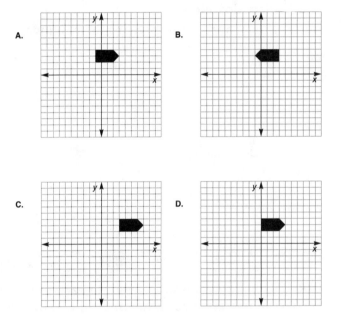

31. The graph at the right corresponds to Mrs. Johnson's auto trip from one town to another.

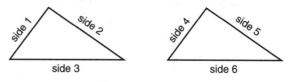

What was most likely happening between 2:00 and 2:30 p.m.?

A. Mrs. Johnson was in heavy traffic.
B. Mrs. Johnson had stopped for lunch.
C. Mrs. Johnson was looking for a parking place downtown.
D. Mrs. Johnson was traveling on a highway.

32. The congruent triangular regions pictured below could be glued together along entire matching sides to form different quadrilateral regions, depending on which pairs of sides are glued together. Which two sides should be glued together to form the region with the smallest perimeter?

A. Sides 1 and 4
B. Sides 2 and 5
C. Sides 3 and 6
D. The perimeters of all the quadrilateral regions formed in that way would be the same.

33. Four friends share an amount of money. The shares are in the ratio 1 : 2 : 3 : 6. If the difference between the largest share and the smallest share is $200, what was the original amount to be shared?

A. $400   B. $480   C. $1,200   D. $4,800

OPEN-ENDED QUESTIONS

DIRECTIONS: Respond in detail to each open-ended question. Show your process and provide an explanation as directed in the question. Your score for each question will be based on accuracy and the completeness of your process or explanation.

34. For a sale, a shopkeeper lowered the original price of an item by 30 percent. After the sale, the shopkeeper told his clerk, Mike, to raise the price of that item by 30 percent of its sale price. So Mike marked the item with its original price. Was Mike right or wrong in doing that? Present a convincing argument to support your answer; you may wish to include a simple, specific example as part of your argument.

35. An experienced automobile test driver tested two different cars. The time (in seconds) it took her to go from 0 to 60 miles per hour was determined five times for each car. The results of these tests are shown below.

Car	Times to Go From 0 to 60 mph				
A	8.8	9.0	9.1	8.7	8.8
B	8.6	9.0	8.8	8.7	16.2

Which of these two cars seems to be the faster one in going from 0 to 60 mph? Be sure to justify your conclusion about which car is faster.

36. A cylindrical jar with height 8 inches and diameter 6 inches is filled to 75% of its capacity with juice. The juice is then poured into another cylindrical container with a 10-inch diameter and height of 4 inches.

a. To what percent of its capacity is the second container filled with juice? Show your procedure.

b. A third cylindrical container is such that the entire amount of juice only takes up 27% of the capacity of the container. As a result, what would one pair of possible dimensions be for the diameter and height of this third container? Show your approach.

37. Figure ABCD is a square.

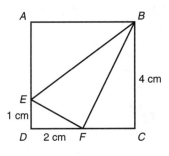

a. To the nearest tenth of a centimeter, find the perimeter of triangle EFB.

b. Vanessa was able to show that triangle EFB was a right triangle. Explain a method to show this.

c. As a result, Vanessa found the area of triangle EFB by using the formula for the area of a triangle. Her friend, Matt, was able to find the area of triangle EFB by using the area of other figures. What did Matt do? How many square centimeters are in the area of triangle EFB?

38. On the grid, draw the graphs of $f(x) = 2^x$ and $g(x) = 3^x$.

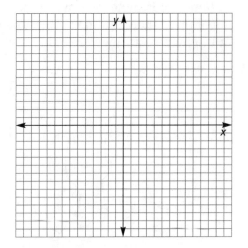

a. For what value of x would $g(x) - f(x) = 0$?

b. Describe what happens to the value of $g(x) - f(x)$ as x gets larger and larger, assuming $x > 0$.

c. How does your answer to part b show up on the graph in part a?

d. When $x < 0$, is $g(x) - f(x)$ positive or negative? Explain your response.

39. Maps are colored so that no two countries (or regions) containing a common border may be the same color (note: a common border consists of more than a single point). The following is a map requiring 2 colors:

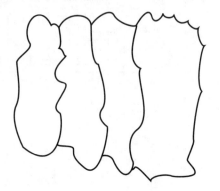

a. Explain why the following would not require 3 colors.

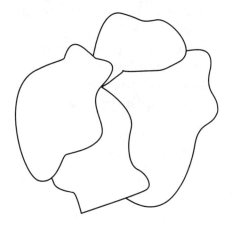

b. Draw a map that would require 3 colors.
c. Draw a map that would require 4 colors.

40. An auditorium has 40 rows of seats. There are 10 seats in the first row, 12 seats in the second row, and so on, with two more seats in each row than in the previous row.

a. How many seats are in the auditorium? Explain how you arrived at your answer.

b. Two students, Tom and Brandon, were looking at the seating arrangement in the auditorium. Tom came to the conclusion that 50% of the seats must be in the first 20 rows, since there are 40 rows in the auditorium. Brandon had a feeling that this couldn't possibly be so. Who is correct? Explain your thinking.

c. If 50% is not correct, give the correct percent for the fraction of the seats in the first 20 rows and show how you arrived at that value.

INDEX

nonlinear, 206
periodic, 201
quadratic, 196
step, 197–198
transformations of, 208–209

G

Gallon, 82
Geometric figures, properties of, 27–30
Geometric iteration, 155
Geometric relationships, 33–34
Geometric sequences, 182
Geometric series, 185
 infinite, 185
Geometric terms, 23–25
Geometry, coordinate, 58–60
Gram, 82, 84
Graphing calculator, factorial key on, 112
Graphs, 188, 193
 bar, 130
 circle, 130
 interpreting data in, 137–138
 line, 131
Greatest common factor (GCF), 9
 algorithm for finding, 168
Greatest-integer function, 197–198

H

Heptagon, 27
Hexagon, 27
Histogram, 131
Horizontal run, 59

I

Identity property, 7
Inch, estimating, 84
Independent events, 108, 167
Independent variable, 192
Inductive reasoning, 36–37
 patterns in, 177–179
Inequalities, 224
Infinite geometric series, 185
Integers, 1
Interpolation, 137, 171
Intersection of lines, 33
Inverse property, 7
Inverse variation, 119
Irrational numbers, 1
Isosceles trapezoid, 29
Isosceles triangle, 28
Iteration, 154
 fractals and, 156
 geometric, 155
Iteration diagram, 158

K

Kilogram, 82, 84
Kilometer, 82
Königsberg bridges, 151–152

L

Least common multiple (LCM), 9
Least-integer function, 197–198
Length
 customary system of, 82
 estimating, 84
 metric system of, 82
Like terms, 217
 combining, 217, 221
Limit of infinite geometric series, 185
Linear equations, 221
Linear function, 196
Line graph, 131
Line of best fit, 116
Line plot, 131
Lines, 23, 33
 intersection of, 33
 parallel, 33
 perpendicular, 33
 slope-intercept form of the equation of a, 203–204
 slope of, 58, 59, 60, 202
 trend, 116
Line segments, 23
 directed, 63
Line symmetry, 49
Liquid (capacity)
 customary system of, 82
 metric system of, 82
Liter, 82
Locus, 34–35

M

Mass. See Weight (mass)
Matrices, 132–133
 addition of, 132
 multiplication of, 133
 subtraction of, 132
Mean, 127
Measurements
 accuracy of, 84
 converting units and, 83
 estimating, 84
Measurement systems, 82–84
 converting units, 83
 customary, 82–84
 metric, 82–84
Measures
 of central tendency, 127
 statistical, 127
Median, 127
Meter, 82
 estimating, 84
Metric system, 82
Midpoint, 24, 58
 coordinates of, 58
Mile, 82
Mode, 127
Morse code, 168